C

Springer Series in Language and Communication 7

Editor: W.J.M. Levelt

Springer Series in Language and Communication
Editor: W.J.M. Levelt

Charles E. Osgood

Lectures on
Language Performance

With 31 Figures

Springer-Verlag New York Heidelberg Berlin

Dr. Charles E. Osgood

College of Communications
Institute of Communications Research
University of Illinois at Urbana-Champaign
Urbana, Illinois 61801
USA

Series Editor:

Professor Dr. Willem J.M. Levelt

Max-Planck-Institut für Psycholinguistik
Nijmegen, The Netherlands

Library of Congress Cataloging in Publication Data
Osgood, Charles Egerton.
    Lectures on language performance.
    (Springer series in language and communication ; v. 7)
    Bibliography: p.
    Includes index.
    1. Psycholinguistics—Addresses, essays, lectures.
2. Competence and performance (Linguistics)—Addresses,
essays, lectures. I. Title. II. Series.
P37.O74   401′.9   79-27248

Printed in the United States of America.

9 8 7 6 5 4 3 2 1

ISBN 0-387-09901-8 Springer-Verlag New York Heidelberg Berlin
ISBN 3-540-09901-8 Springer-Verlag Berlin Heidelberg New York

Preface

Titling this book *Lectures on Language Performance* was not done to be cleverly "eye-catching"—the title is quite literally appropriate. With minor adaptations for a general reading audience, the eight chapters in this volume are the actual lectures I gave as the Linguistic Society of America Professor for its Summer Institute held at the University of Illinois in 1978.

The eight lectures are an "anticipation" of my *magnum opus*—I guess when one has passed into his sixties he can be forgiven for saying this!— a much larger volume (or volumes) to be titled *Toward an Abstract Performance Grammar*. The book in your hands is an anticipation of this work in at least three senses: for one thing, it doesn't pretend to cover the burgeoning literature relevant to the comparatively new field of psycholinguistics (my study at home is literally overflowing with reference materials, all coded for various sections of the planned volume(s)); for another, both the style and the content of these Lectures were tailored to a very broad social science audience—including students and teachers in anthropology, linguistics, philosophy and psychology (as well as in various applied fields like second language learning and bilingualism); and for yet another thing, many sections of the planned *magnum opus* are hardly even touched on here—for example, these lectures do *not* "anticipate" major sections to be devoted to Efficiency vs. Complexity in Speaker/Listener Interactions, to the Pragmatics of Language Use in Situational Contexts, or to the Relations of this Abstract Performance Grammar to Other Linguistic and Psychological Models.

These *Lectures on Language Performance* do anticipate what I consider to be the "core" of my developing general theory, however: Lecture I, "What Is a Language?", offers criteria for anything being "a language" and then, specifically, being a humanoid language. Lecture II, titled (appropriately reversing that of Roger Brown's first book) "Things and Words", provides a capsule life history of behaviorism, leading into my own complex multi-level/semantically-componential model, which stresses the intimate parallelism between cognizing in perceptual and linguistic channels. Lecture III, "Paradigm Clash in Psycholinguistics"—using a frankly marital theme—traces the engagement, marriage, divorce and budding reconciliation between linguistics and cognitive psychology. These first three Lectures are essentially orientational.

Lecture IV, "Structure and Meaning in Cognizing", moves directly into the structural and functional principles of the Abstract Performance Grammar (APG for short)—postulating four basic mechanisms for cognitive processing (a LEXICON, an OPERATOR, a BUFFER and a (long-term) MEMORY) and three basic functional notions governing the acquisition and utilization of meanings (a global *sign-learning* paradigm, a finer bipolar *feature-learning* paradigm, and *frequency/intensity/recency* principles) governing the differential accessabilities of semantic features. Lecture V, "Naturalness in Cognizing and Sentencing"—starting from the axiomatic notion that the basic cognitive structures which interpret and initiate sentences are established in *prelinguistic* perceptual experience—states and elaborates the "naturalness" functional principles governing the ordering of constituents of simplex sentences, the ordering of words within constituents, and the ordering of clauses within complex, conjoined sentences.

Lecture VI, "Pollyanna and Congruence Dynamics: From Yang and Yin to AND or BUT", brings into the APG picture certain *primitive affective dynamics* of human thinking and sentencing—which, given the rationalist bias, have hardly been touched in linguistics. Lecture VII, "Salience Dynamics and Unnaturalness in Sentence Production", moves my APG fully into a domain of central concern to linguists and, increasingly, to psycholinguists as well—*the processing of unnaturally ordered transformations;* postulation of three *salience variables* affecting speakers (inherent semantic vividness, extrinsic motivation-of-speaker, and topicality) leads to functional notions governing how *speakers,* starting necessarily with naturally ordered cognitions, produce unnaturally ordered transforms that satisfy their motivations. And finally Lecture VIII, "Processing of Unnaturally Ordered Sentences in Comprehending", states and illustrates the functional notions governing how *listeners* detect unnaturalness in sentences received and, utilizing interactions between OPERATOR and BUFFER, "restore" the naturalness from which speakers "depart".

It is true that, in developing and trying to communicate a general performance theory of the most complex aspects of mankind's most complex cognitive capacity—the comprehension and production of sentences—things inevitably get complicateder and complicateder. Nevertheless, I hope the reader will persevere and find the effort profitable. I wish the reader "bon voyage"! I also wish to express my sincere "thanks", both to S. N. Sridhar, my linguist research assistant over the past few years—for his invaluable critical contribution to the development of this APG—and to Nioma Brown, my secretary over these same years—for her loyalty, and competence, in both preparing all the lectures and handouts during the summer of 1978 (how she kept up with a lecture-a-week is beyond me!) and typing the final manuscript for this *Lectures on Language Performance* volume.

October 1979   CHARLES E. OSGOOD

Contents

LECTURE I

What Is a Language?

Orientation

What is a language? You may well be wondering why I ask this question when everyone *knows* what a language is—it's what you're expressing and I'm comprehending, you say. Let's change the question's form a bit: how would one identify something as *a language* if he encountered what *might* be one in an obviously nonhuman species—for example, flowing kaleidoscopic color patterns on the bulbous bodies of octopuslike creatures who land in a space ship right in one's own backyard? And, for that matter, is the natural signing of deaf-mutes a language? the game of chess? and what about the "language" of music or art? Or suppose that pale, eyeless midgets were discovered in extended caverns far below the present floors of the Mammoth Cave—emitting very high-frequency pipings from their rounded mouths and apparently listening with their enormous, rotatable ears. How might one decide whether or not these cave midgets have an identifiably *humanoid language?*

Only if one can say what defines a language (in general) and defines a human language (in particular) can he go on to offer possible answers to some other, very important, questions: Do certain nonhuman animals "have" a language? What is common to prelinguistic cognizing and linguistic sentencing? When does a developing child "have" a language? How may languages have developed in the human species? Answers to all these questions, of course, would have relevance to the basic issue of universals and uniquenesses in human communication.

Defining Characteristics of Language Generally

If anything is to be called "a language", it must satisfy certain criterial conditions. With our Octopian visitors (from the planetary system of the nearest star, Arcturus, as was later discovered) particularly in mind, I will elaborate a bit on these criteria for something being "a language" in general.

(1) A NONRANDOM RECURRENCY CRITERION: *production of identifiably different and nonrandomly recurrent physical forms in some communication channel.* A few years ago there was quite a flurry of excitement over apparently nonrandom, recurrent signals being received over interstellar radio receivers—was it something unusual in sun-spot activity or, possibly, communication attempts from some distant form of intelligent life? (As I recall, the decision was in favor of sun-spots!) As far as ordinary communication is concerned, humans have opted for the vocal-auditory channel (for reasons that will be considered a bit later), but there are many other possible channels that we *are* aware of, because we also have these sensory modalities (light-visual, pressure, tactile, and chemical-odor, at which dogs seem particularly adept), and many others that we are *not* aware of (e.g., radiant wavelengths above or below the visible-to-humans range)—and what about ESP? The only critical thing is that such signals be combined in nonrandom ways to produce energy *forms* that are identifiably different (using special equipment if necessary) and are themselves nonrandom in distribution in time and/or space. Note that there is no requirement that the forms be discretely digital (as is generally the case for human languages); they could be continuously analogic in nature.

Back in our own backyard, having recovered from the shock, and being convinced that our octopuslike visitors intend us no harm, we note that as one Octopian pirouettes slowly, with its whole bulbous body flowing with multicolored visual forms, the other stands "silently" neutral grey—only to begin displaying and turning when the first has become "silent". We begin to think that this *may* be some form of communication—not merely displays of emotional states as in the "blushing" of the chameleon.

(2) A RECIPROCALITY CRITERION: *these forms being producible by the same organisms that receive them.* It is difficult to imagine a human society in which, say, women were the only ones who could produce language (but not comprehend it, even from other women) and men could only comprehend language (but not produce it). For one thing, knowing what we do about the intimate interactions between comprehending and expressing in the development of language in children, one would be hard put to account for the development of such a system. But what about communication *between* species? Yucca plants and Yucca moths certainly interact for their common survival, but one would hardly call this communication; the "language of flowers" is only a euphemism—we humans can't smell back! But what about mule drivers and their mules? There is no question but that there is communication here, even though the mule can only "kick" back when ornery, but obviously

the same organisms are not both producing and receiving the *same* forms—indicating clearly that communication is not the same as language. Noting that some of the flowing visual forms produced by Octopian A are reproduced in apparent "response" by Octopian B, always along with some uninterpretable contextual variations—and observing this systematically later with color movie films—we became convinced that this may, indeed, be some kind of language.

(3) A PRAGMATIC CRITERION: *use of these forms resulting in nonrandom dependencies between the forms and the behaviors of the organisms that employ them.* This criterion applies most testably to the recipients of messages (behaving in appropriately differential fashion to signals received) but also to the initiators of messages [displaying a nonrandom tendency to communicate about entities and events that are proximal in other channels—see (4) below]. This is really the criterion that there *is* communication going on. Except for obviously representational art and music—and for purely affective reactions—this criterion would seem to rule out anything other than euphemistic use of phrases like "the language of art" or "the language of music". There is no doubt that bright dogs (like my poodle, Pierre!) develop a large repertoire of appropriate behaviors dependent upon the verbal commands of their masters (e.g., fetching his bone rather than his ball when requested "go getcha *bone*").

Note, however, that there is no implication here that pragmatic dependencies must be acquired through experience (learning), although this is clearly the case for human languages. What about our Octopi friends? Satisfaction of this criterion would be indicated by, for example, a certain color pattern in Octopian A being conditionally dependent upon the presence in front of their space ship of some complicated scanning device and, when accompanied by various contextual color patterns, by behaviors with respect to this device (shifting its orientation, taking it back into the ship) on the part of Octopian B.

(4) A SEMANTIC CRITERION: *use of these forms following nonrandom rules of reference to events in other channels.* This criterion implies that for anything to be a language it must function so as to *symbolize* (represent for the organism) the not-necessarily-*here* and not-necessarily-*now*. This criterion is clearly *not* met by the game of chess (where the pieces, despite their names and their moves, bear no symbolizing relation to anything other than themselves) *or* by the "game" of mathematics (where the symbols are deliberately abstract and bear no necessary relations to anything in the real world, but by virtue of this property are potentially relatable to any set of real-world entities). Even in humans, semantic relations are not necessarily arbitrary: there is *onomatopoeia* (the name of a thing or event being based on its characteristic sound, e.g., *cuckoo, cough, hiss, slap,* and *wheeze* in English) and there is

phonetic symbolism (in my classes I like to ask the male students which blind date they would prefer, Miss *Pim*, Miss *Bowloaf*, or Miss *Lavelle*, and then to describe her probable appearance).

Forms in a language can also be *iconic*—witness much of the natural signing of the deaf as well as the gestural accompaniments by ordinary speakers (e.g., in describing my "blind dates" above)—and *this*, we come to infer, might well be the case, at least in part, for our Octopians: we noted that, on the first appearance of Pierre the poodle in our yard, there was a silvery blob followed by a rising line on Octopian A (possibly a question?—"What on earth [sic!] is that?") answered by a nondescript wobbly fuzz figuring near the bottom of Octopian B's bulbous body (possibly meaning, "I haven't the foggiest idea!").

(5) A SYNTACTIC CRITERION: *use of these forms following nonrandom rules of combination with other forms in the same channel.* As will be seen, all human languages are organized *temporally on a "left-to-right" basis*—that is, from prior-to-subsequent forms at all levels—as a necessary consequence of their utilization of the vocal-auditory channel. But these by no means must be defining characteristics of language-in-general, and one wonders to what extent space could be substituted for time in the organization of messages by organisms using other channels. Presumably there would be some limit—for example, we might discover (although the "how" of this is not as obvious as with the preceding criteria) that the Octopians "flash" the equivalents of whole paragraphs on their N "panels" as they rotate in the process of communicating, the within-paragraph information being spatially represented—"sentences" thus being an unessential carving up of the information flow (I might note that whole paragraphs, consisting of a single sentence, multiply conjoined and embedded, are not exactly a rarity in, particularly, scholarly writing!).

And yet *some* structuring, representing what is "natural" in sentencing based on prelinguistic cognizing experience—for Octopian "squidsters" just as for human youngsters—might be expected for all organismic languages. For humans, the two basic types of simple cognition appear to be Action and Stative Relations (and both in "SVO" order), the former highlighting the typically +Animate Actor as subject as against the typically ‾Animate (or at least relatively passive) Recipient as object and the latter highlighting the +Salient Figure as subject against the ‾Salient Ground as Object—thus *Pierre chased the ball* and *the ball was on the grass* as simple Action and Stative cognitions, respectively. After having mastered some of the pragmatics and semantics of Octopian, we might study our video-tapes with such Naturalness Principles in mind.

(6) A COMBINATORIAL PRODUCTIVITY CRITERION: *the users of the forms being capable of producing indefinitely long and potentially infinite numbers of novel combinations which satisfy (1)–(5) above.* At any

particular time, synchronically, this novelty in human language lies in the combining and not in what is combined; thus, my statements about the Octopians' linguistic behaviors, although entirely novel as wholes (I presume), utilized thoroughly familiar lexemes [criterion (4)] and constructions [criterion (5)] in contemporary American English. Of course over time, diachronically, human languages do display adaptive changes by both expanding the lexicon (4) and by changing the rules (5). Presumably, any organismic language would display such adaptivity— either via evolution over very long periods (for languages with innately based semantics and syntax) or via learning over relatively short periods, dependent upon changing environmental conditions (for languages with individually acquired semantics and syntax, as happens with human cultures and languages in contact).

Testing for the presence of this Combinatorial Productivity Criterion in another language—particularly a very strange one like Octopian— would undoubtedly be most difficult. Although nearly all of the communicative exchanges among the Octopians, and between them and ourselves, would seem novel in whole or in part *to us,* that would be no proof that they were not elaborately stereotyped patterns, analogous to most human telephone conversations. Only after we had mastered *their* language to the point where *we* could compose Octopian statements of indubitable novelty for them (and see if they comprehended them) and ask questions requiring indubitably novel answers (and see if they could produce them), could we determine if they had this crucial capability. And—horrors of horrors!—we might discover that they did *not,* that they were entirely "programed" like computers, and in fact were *robots* sent out by the real Arcturians, whatever they might be like. However, one thing this little experiment by Arcturians would have demonstrated is this: if two species each have a language by these criteria, then either directly or mediately, via appropriate equipment, they should be able to communicate to some extent with each other; the extent and direction would depend on the amount and balance of intelligence, that organism with the lower channel capacity determining the limit on communication (the dog in effect setting limits for the master).

Do Any Other, Nonhuman, Animals Have a Language?

One can trace a continuum of levels of interorganismic communication: from *proximal interactions* (contacting, mating, mothering, fighting and . . . consuming!), through *distal* SIGNAL *sending and receiving* [unintentional odors (as the bitch in heat), mating calls, baboon warning and food-supply noises], through *distal* SIGN *sending and receiving* (intentional expression of affect, like growls, tail-waggings, postural and facial

expressions designed to influence the behavior of the receiver), to
SYMBOL *creating and interpreting* ("play" in dogs and other higher
animals, referential gesturings by chimps and humans). For any given
species, we can ask, *does its intraspecies communication satisfy the six
criteria for something to be a language?* Take *the clam*—which, if
anything, seems to have specialized *away* from communication in its
evolution: Since, as far as I know, there is no evidence for clam-to-clam
nonrandom recurrency of signals in any channel [criterion (1)]—and,
given the limited motility and reactive capacity ("neck"-retracting, shell-
clamping, and . . . ?), it seems likely that communication would be
limited to chemical broadcasts at most (unless the clam has been fooling
us and specializing in the development of ESP!). If criterion (1) is not
satisfied, of course, then none of the others can be met. The answer to
whether *this* species has a language is, in a clam-shell, NO! So let's move
along up the evolutionary tree.

   The Bee. Briefly (necessarily), the bee communicates three species-
significant things: *showing its pass-badge* (a scent-pouch which is opened
on entering the hive and, if the scent is wrong—execution); *location of
a nectar supply* (the well-known "dance", whose angle with respect to
the sun indicates direction, whose number of turns per unit time indicates
distance, and whose number of abdomen-wags indicates quality of the
supply); *location of a new "home"* [a kind of "election" in which, when
local supplies have dwindled, that returning bee which gets the crowd at
home to follow his dance (usually the one that has found the richest
load, has had to fly the shortest distance back, and hence is the most
energetic)] ends up with the whole hive flying off to his new location.
Since the dance forms are obviously nonrandom, since any worker bee
functions equivalently as sender or receiver, since behaviors of both are
nonrandomly dependent upon the messages, and since the forms have
nonrandom rules of reference (to the not-here and not-now nectar
locations), criteria (1)–(4) appear to be clearly met. As far as (5), the
syntactic criterion, is concerned, since the messages involve three types
of forms (direction-, distance-, and quality-indicating) which must be
combined in certain nonrandom ways, this would seem to be met. But
what about (6), the combinatorial productivity criterion? For any given
bee "speaker" or bee "listener", a given combination of direction-,
distance-, and quality-indicators must often be novel, yet communication
is successful. So I conclude that, within very narrow limits of what can
be communicated, "the language of the bee" is not a euphemism—and,
most remarkably, it is entirely innate ("wired in").

   The Ape. I use this term to refer to nonhuman, but close-to-human
primates—rather than *the chimp*—because others have been shown to
have similar capabilities (e.g., recently the gorilla). I will also concentrate
on the Gardners' Washoe rather than the Premacks' Sarah. The labora-

tory research with Sarah demonstrates the astonishingly complex cognitive capacity of a chimpanzee but whether this represents comprehension and production of *sentences* or "simply" complex, differentially reinforced, reactions remains obscure (usually only a single set of alternative responses was required on any given problem).

Prior to the Gardners' work with Washoe, several psychologists (e.g., the Kelloggs' Gua and the Hayes' Viki) had also brought up an infant chimpanzee in their home as they would a child of their own, but the only attempts at "language" seemed to be to teach the ape to talk *human*—and they failed miserably (Viki ended up with about four imperfectly produced simple words like "papa" and "cup"). Given the lack of hemispheric dominance in nonhuman primates, critical for voluntary control over the medially located speech apparatus, this failure was not at all surprising. The decision to bring a chimp up in a human environment, *but with constant exposure to the natural sign-language of the deaf-mute,* was long overdue, and one of the most exciting developments in decades resulted.

So now let's check Washoe's communicative performance against our criteria for something being "a language". Criterion (1) (nonrandom recurrency of forms) is obviously met by the differential use (by age 4) of some 80 gestural signs. Criterion (2) (reciprocality, both sending and receiving) is obviously met—first with humans "at the other end" but more recently with other chimps. Criterion (3) (pragmatics) is satisfied by such evidence as her making the "tooth-brush" sign "in a peremptory fashion when its appearance at the end of a meal was delayed", by her signing "open" at the door of a room she was leaving, and so forth ad infinitum. There is also no question about satisfying criterion (4) (semantics): her learning to sign "dog", mainly to those in picture books, but then signing it spontaneously to the sound of an unseen dog barking outside; her signing "key" not only to keys being presently used to open locks but also to "not-here" keys needed to unlock locks! And there is also no question but that criterion (6) (combinatorial productivity) is satisfied: the Gardners report that as soon as Washoe had a vocabulary of a dozen or so signs [including verbs like "open" and "go", nouns like "key" and "flower", and pronouns "you" and "me", and adverbials (?) like "please", "more", and "hurry"] she spontaneously began combining them in sequences like "open flower" (open gate to flower garden), "go sweet" (to be taken to raspberry bush), and "you me out" (you take me outdoors).

But what about criterion (5) (syntax)? This has been the focus of most questioning of Washoe's "having a language", and in early critiques both Bronowski and Bellugi (1970, p. 672) and McNeill (1970, p. 55) stress the fact that Washoe's "utterances" display no constraints on "word" order, her signings seemingly having free ordering (e.g., "up please" or "please up", "open key" or "key open"). However, in an equally early commentary, Roger Brown (1970, pp. 224–30) makes several very significant points:

(a) that Washoe's linguistic performances should be compared with those of a 3–4-year-old *deaf-mute child* rather than with normal children of this age;

(b) that just as normal children already control several prosodic patterns when they begin to produce combinations (e.g., the falling pitch of declaratives, the rising pitch of interrogatives), so do the deaf *and quite spontaneously Washoe* hold for a perceptibly longer period the last sign of a sequence to indicate a question;

(c) that just as in human language development, Washoe displayed a gradual increase over time in the sign-length of her "utterances"—two common before three and three common before four—and Brown asks reasonably (p. 225), "Why should this be so if the sign combinations are not constructions?"

Perhaps most signifcantly, Brown observes (p. 229) that " . . . there is little or no communication pressure on either children or Washoe to use the right word order for the meanings they intend" when language is being used in contexts that are *perceptually unambiguous* to both producer and receiver—which is the case in much of early child language and in just about all of Washoe's signings (and it should be noted that, although Washoe's companions "corrected" the signings of particular lexical items, they apparently did not "correct" for sign orderings, as do most adult companions of young human children).

Defining Characteristics of Human Languages

Human languages must, of course, satisfy all of the criteria for *anything* to be called a language—thus having nonrandom recurrent signals in some channel, producible by the same organisms that receive them, which display nonrandom pragmatic, semantic, and syntactic dependencies that are combinatorially productive—but there are further, delimiting, criteria that must be met if something is to be called a natural *human* language. These additional defining characteristics can be categorized (at least superficially) as either *structural* or *functional*.

Structural Characteristics of Human Languages

For something that is a language to be called a *human* language, it must have the following *structural* characteristics: it must (7) involve use of the vocal-auditory channel, and thus (8) nondirectional transmission but directional reception and (9) evanescence in time of the forms in the channel, these characteristics requiring (10) integration over time of the information derived from the physical forms, but also (11) providing prompt feedback to the sender of his own messages. All of these structural characteristics are direct, combined functions of the *physical nature of sound* and the *biological nature of the human organism.*

Therefore I need not belabor them further—except to note the following: that, as to (7), the vocalic response system is both relatively "lightweight" energywise (as compared, e.g., to locomotion) and minimally interfering with other on-going activities like tool-making and hunting; that, as to (8), selective reception is simply a function of the fact that we have a head between our ears, this inter-aural distance yielding phase differences for sound waves originating in all directions except along the medial line; that, as to (9), evanescence of signals in time has the advantage of minimizing "cluttering up" of the channel, but the disadvantage of putting a heavy load on the memory—the major reason for the development of writing systems; that, as for (10), although there is some simultaneous patterning of sounds—for example, the way a rising intonation pattern signals a question and a falling one a statement—it is as nothing compared to the simultaneous patterning of sights (as fully utilized by our Octopian friends); and that, as for (11), it is the availability of prompt auditory feedback that allows children to model their own productions on what they hear from adults—and allows adults to edit *their* own productions ("Well, I did it all in one *swell foop* . . . /ah/ . . . in one *fell swoop*"!).

The signing of deaf-mutes would be ruled out, as far as being a *natural* human language, by use of the vocal-auditory channel, but of course it would still satisfy the requirements for being *a language.* And what about our Cave Midgets—in their domain far beneath the floors of the Mammoth Cave? While we were trying to determine if our visitors from Arcturus had something that could be called "a language", other intrepid human explorers (linguists) were doing the same with the pale little Cave Midgets. Tape recordings of their high-frequency pipings left no doubt but that nonrandom recurrent sound forms were being reciprocally produced and received; the nonrandom dependencies of their use of artifacts in mushroom-and-worm cultivating activities upon these distinctive piping forms clearly satisfied the pragmatic and semantic criteria.

Testing for syntactic structuring and combinatorial productivity took a bit of doing, particularly since our linguists were struggling with very sore throats brought on by continuous whisperings—the big-eared Cave Midgets fly into panic at any loud, low-frequency sound. However, after many sleepless days analyzing visual displays of ultrasonic piping patterns, one linguistic genius demonstrated "noun/verb" selection rules, and, a bit later, another had a brainstorm (not surprisingly, after consuming a worm-and-mushroom pizza) and created a computer-based Cave-

Midgetese synthesizer, at least for very simple utterances—and combinatorial productivity was firmly established. So there was no question but that these Cave Midgets had a language—and, given the piping sounds that went whistling around the cavern passageways plus the big ears that rotated to receive them, it seemed obvious that this language met the *structural* requirements for being human type—but what about the *functional* requirements?

Functional Characteristics of Human Languages

For something to be called a human language, it must also have the following *functional* characteristics, and since the Cave Midgets are a somewhat humanoid species of this Earth, we would be most interested in seeing how *their* language stacks up against them.

(12) ARBITRARINESS OF FORM-MEANING RELATIONS: *in human languages the rules relating forms in the communication channel to events in other channels* [cf (4)] *are typically arbitrary rather than iconic.* We must say "typically" because (as noted earlier) human languages do display both onomatopoeia and phonetic symbolism; however, for the most part form/meaning relations are arbitrary (witness *Pferd* in German, *cheval* in French and *horse* in English).

(13) DISCRETENESS OF FORM-SHIFTS SIGNALING DIFFERENCES IN MEANING: *in human languages, the changes in form that convey changes in meaning are discretely rather than continuously variable.* This characteristic holds at the phonemic level (the abrupt shifts in distinctive features of sound which distinguish, for example, *fail, gale, male, sail,* and *tail*), the morphemic level (the productive pluralizing morphemes for nouns in English are always *either* [-s], [-z] or [-iz], conditionally dependent on the voicing or sibilance of the preceding sound, as in *cats, dogs,* and *horses,* respectively), and on up to higher level syntactic units. Such discreteness has certainly simplified the discriptive task for linguistic science.

(14) THE HIERARCHICAL ORGANIZATION CRITERION: *in human languages, the stream of forms in the channel is analyzable into levels of units-within-units.* Complex sentences are analyzable into clauses (or "sentoids"), clauses are analyzable into immediate constituents (concatenations of NPs "hanging on" a VP), constituents into word forms (heads, modifiers and modulators), words into morphemes (stems and affixes), morphemes into phonemes, and phonemes into distinctive phonetic features. Implicit in this statement is the constraint that no higher-level unit can be embedded in a lower-level unit—and this raises some interesting questions about what is the proper linguistic analysis of, for example, sentences with relative clauses (*John liked the girl who arrived*

late at the party, where the *Wh*-clause is itself a sentential elaboration of an NP), what I call "commentative" sentences (like *it is a fact that John has been married before*) or monstrous center-embedded sentences (like *the boy the girl Pierre likes likes likes spaghetti!*).

(15) THE COMPONENTIAL ORGANIZATION CRITERION: *in human languages, large numbers of units at each higher level in the hierarchy are exhaustively analyzable as near-simultaneous combinations of relatively small numbers of units at each next lower level.* Potentially infinite numbers of sentences are analyzable into some hundreds of thousands of word units which are themselves analyzable into some thousands of morphemes, these being analyzable into some 40 or so phonemes which can be analyzed into an even smaller number of distinctive phonetic features for any given human language. And this componential analysis is exhaustive at all levels—no left-over pieces! This system represents a remarkably efficient way to satisfy the criterion of *combinatorial productivity*—which anything must meet if it is to be called "a language". But this is not the only *conceivable* way to achieve efficiency. Although these hierarchical and componential characteristics are in no obvious way dependent upon the *peripheral sensory or motor structures* of primates, they may well reflect ways in which the *central nervous systems* of higher organisms have evolved—and hence may be just as innately determined as those reflecting the constraints imposed by using the vocal-auditory channel.

(16) THE TRANSFERRAL-VIA-LEARNING CRITERION: *human languages are transferred to other members of the species, both generationally over time and geographically over space, via experience* (learning) *rather than via inheritance* (maturation). There is no evidence whatsoever that the offspring of speakers of some particular human language find it easier to acquire *that* language than any other; in other words, children come into the world cognitively equipped to speak any human-type language—a Japanese infant can learn to speak English or Papago just as easily as Japanese.

How did our intrepid linguists determine whether or not Cave-Midgetese met *these* criteria for being humanoid in type? First, using their visual displays for ultrasonic patterns, they were able to show that brief but distinguishable piping forms entered into diverse, longer piping-form patterns and these in turn similarly into still longer, more diverse piping sequences. The differences in these longer sequences displayed predictable behavioral (pragmatic) and referential (semantic) contingencies, as could be tested with the now much improved computerized Cave-Midgetese synthesizer. Thus there was strong evidence for both hierarchical and componential organization [criteria (14) and (15)]. The same equipment was used to demonstrate that the components of the wordlike piping forms (analogous to our phonemes) had essentially arbitrary, random relations to the *meanings* of the "words" but nonrandom relations to their piping *contexts* (analogous to our phones), thus fitting criterion (12). However, although differences in meaning were often signaled by discrete shifts in piping forms, thus fitting criterion (13), there was also much phonetic symbolism (for example, shifting the length and frequency of one vowel piping from low to high was found to modulate the meaning of otherwise constant forms from "doing something very slooooowst" to "doing the same thing very *slŏst*"!). So "the language of Cave Midgets" was, indeed, a human-type language — developed by an early branch of primates that, in the search for bigger and juicier worms and mushrooms, happened to end up in caverns deep in the earth. Table I.1 provides a summary listing of the defining characteristics for language-in-general and for humanoid languages.

Nondefining Characteristics of Human Languages

All of the defining characteristics considered so far are, ipso facto, universals. There are many other characteristics of human languages — some of them apparently absolute but many of them only statistical universals — which, I would argue, are not *defining* characteristics. That is, if one encountered something that was a *language* by criteria (1)–(6) and, further, was a human-type language by criteria (7)–(16), then, if it failed to display any one or more of these characteristics, it would *still* be considered a human language — albeit a rather strange one.

Characteristics Reflecting Intellectual and Cultural Traits

Let us now consider characteristics that reflect *certain intellectual and cultural traits common to humans:*

If a language was encountered whose speakers didn't PROPOSITION-ALIZE (that is, never produced sentences like *a robin is a bird, bears hibernate in the winter,* or *the moon is made of green cheese*), then they could have no science; our Cave Midgets might be a case in point, and interestingly there appears to be a complete lack of such "sentences" in Washoe's signings. But would we wish to claim that the *language* of a scienceless society was therefore not humanoid? If we found a language whose speakers didn't PREVARICATE (who would never intentionally lie, saying things like *We didn't come because we were ill* when they actually were not, be deceptive by saying things like *I was not involved in planning the Watergate Caper,* or produce meaningless sentences like *colorless green ideas sleep furiously*), then they could have neither fiction nor poetry, couldn't tell harmless "little white lies", and couldn't

Table I.1 Universals of Language?

If anything is to be called "a language", it must involve:

1. RECURRENT EVENTS: identifiably different and nonrandomly recurrent physical forms in some communication channel;
2. RECIPROCALITY: these forms being producible by the same organisms that receive them;
3. PRAGMATICS: resulting in nonrandom dependencies between the forms and the behaviors of the organisms that use them.
4. SEMANTICS: following nonrandom rules of reference to events in other channels;
5. SYNTAX: following nonrandom rules of combination with other forms in the same channel;
6. COMBINATORIAL PRODUCTIVITY: capable of producing potentially infinite numbers of novel combinations which satisfy #1–#5 above.

If something satisfying the defining characteristics above is to be called "a human language", it must further involve the following STRUCTURAL *characteristics:*

7. VOCAL-AUDITORY CHANNEL: use of vocality for production and audition for reception;
8. BROADCAST TRANSMISSION/DIRECTIONAL RECEPTION: nondirectional speaking (without artificial means) but directional hearing;
9. EVANESCENCE IN TIME: the signals in the channel fading rapidly in intensity;
10. INTEGRATION OVER TIME: interdependent forms being distributed in time on a "left-to-right" basis;
11. PROMPT FEEDBACK: the speaker normally being capable of hearing his own messages;

and the following FUNCTIONAL *characteristics:*

12. ARBITRARINESS OF SEMANTICS: the rules relating the forms of language to events in other channels (cf #4 above) being *typically* arbitrary rather than iconic;
13. DISCRETENESS OF SIGNALS: the signals in the code being *typically* discrete rather than continuously variable;
14. HIERARCHICAL ORGANIZATION: the forms of the language being exhaustively analyzable into levels of units-within-units;
15. COMPONENTIAL ORGANIZATION: large numbers of units at each higher level being exhaustively analyzable as simultaneous combinations of small numbers of units at each lower level;
16. TRANSFERRAL VIA LEARNING: extension of the language within the species, both generationally and geographically, being via experience rather than via the germ plasm.

Something which can be called "a human language" by all of the above defining criteria will remain such regardless of whether it has the following characteristics:

(A) Based on Intellectual and Cultural Traits Common to Humans
PROPOSITIONALIZING: all known human languages can be used to create propositional sentences which, in principle, are testable as to their truth or falsity.

Table I.1 (*continued*)

PREVARICATION: in all known human languages, messages can be
intentionally false, deceptive, or meaningless.

REFLEXIVENESS: in all known human languages, messages can be used to
talk about other messages and/or their components.

LEARNABILITY: any natural human language can be acquired by any
normal human being.

TRANSLATABILITY: any natural human language can be translated into any
other human language.

(B) Based on Language Performance Principles and Their Interactions

SELECTION AND COMBINATION RULES: across all languages and levels of
units, rules of selection and combination of alternative forms are
statistical rather than absolute universals [cf (14) and (15)].

A PROGRESSIVE DIFFERENTIATION PRINCIPLE: across all languages and
levels of units, a principle of progressive differentiation of meaning-
signaling forms operates, but the extent of differentiation varies
statistically.

A LEAST EFFORT PRINCIPLE: across all languages and levels of units, a
principle of least effort operates statistically, such that the higher the
frequency-of-usage level (a) the shorter the length of forms, (b) the
smaller the number of forms, and (c) the larger the number of different
meanings (senses) of the forms used.

AFFECTIVE POLARITY: across all languages and levels of units, it is
statistically universal that affectively Positive forms are distinguished
from affectively Negative forms (a) by marking (either overt or covert) of
the Negative members of pairs and (b) by priority of the Positive
members of pairs in both development (in the species and the individual)
and form-sequencing in language production.

THE POLLYANNA PRINCIPLE: across all languages and levels of units, it is
statistically universal that affectively Positive forms and constructions
are more diversified, more frequently used, and more easily processed
cognitively than affectively Negative forms.

---

play games with their language (like saying of a certain woman, "she'll
make someone a nice husband")—but would such lackluster communication rule out the *language* as being humanoid?

If the speakers of a language displayed no REFLEXIVENESS (never
would tell you what a word means, never would paraphrase, and never
would produce performative sentences like *I christen thee "the Jimmie
Carter"* for some aircraft carrier of the future), then they could have no
dictionaries, no philosophy, no linguistics . . . and no puns—but they
could still be said to have a human-type *language,* I think.

If the speakers of some language were unable to LEARN or TRANSLATE
some other humanoid language—either because they didn't have the
biological equipment (we couldn't learn to speak Cave-Midgetese, although we could translate it) or because they were not sufficiently

intelligent (we might not be able to translate or learn the language of some *Super-humanoids* from outer space because of its lexical and syntactic complexity)—surely we would have to agree that Cave-Midgetese (although untalkable by us), and humbly admit that Superhumanoidese (although not learnable or translatable by us), are *human-type languages,* if they satisfy all of the defining criteria.

Characteristics Reflecting Performance Principles

Now let's look at some nondefining characteristics that are *based on language performance principles and their interaction:*

SELECTION AND COMBINATION RULES: *across all languages and levels of units, rules of selection and combination of alternative forms are statistical rather than absolute universals.* At the phonological level, each language selects from those differences in sound which the human vocalic system makes possible a small subset of differences that will make a difference in meaning (i.e., are phonemic); certain differences (voiced/nonvoiced) are much more probable statistically than others (lip-flattening/lip-rounding) across languages. At the syntactic level, each language selects as its grammar a limited subset of "rewrite rules"; again, certain types of rules are statistically more probable than others (e.g., rewriting the Noun Phrase as Noun-followed-by-Adjectives is about twice as likely across languages as the reverse ordering—and for good psycholinguistic reasons). This differential rule selection and combination at all levels is one reason why any *particular* human language must be learned.

A PROGRESSIVE DIFFERENTIATION PRINCIPLE: *across all languages and levels of units, a principle of progressive differentiation of meaning-signaling forms operates, but the extent of differentiation varies statistically.* In phonology, for example, only if a high/low vowel distinction is phonemic will a lips flattened/rounded distinction also be phonemic— never the reverse order of differentiation. At the semantic level, Berlin and Kay (1969) offer evidence for progressive differentiation of color terms cross-linguistically—from only having terms for the most primitive bright vs dark distinction, to differentiation of the bright into red vs nonred, further in the red region into red vs yellow, and later in the blue region into blue vs green.

A LEAST EFFORT PRINCIPLE: *across all languages and levels of units, a principle of least effort operates statistically, such that the higher the frequency-of-usage level* (a) *the shorter the length of forms,* (b) *the smaller the number of forms, and* (c) *the larger the number of different meanings* (senses) *of the forms used.* This principle comes from G. Kingsley Zipf (1949), and he offers the entirely delightful analogy of a

composition) space at one end and his various tools (here, lexical forms) spread out along it; obviously, it would be most efficient to have the tools most often used closest at hand along the bench, and these tools themselves lightweight, few in number and multipurpose in function. Zipf reported functions for the lexicons of several languages which very neatly support these hypotheses, and there seems to be no reason to doubt that the same would appear for languages generally.

AFFECTIVE POLARITY: *across all languages and levels of units, it is statistically universal that affectively Positive forms are distinguished from affectively Negative forms* (a) *by marking of the Negative members of pairs and* (b) *by priority of the Positive members of pairs in both development and form-sequencing in messages.* Greenberg (1966) provides massive evidence at all levels: thus in phonology marked Nasal vowels are never more frequent in a language than unmarked Nonnasal vowels; thus in syntax it appears to be universal that Affirmation in unmarked (X *is* Y) and Negation is marked (X *is not* Y). As far as priority of Positive members in the development of language in the *species* is concerned, the mere fact that it is characteristically Positives that are marked to produce Negatives (*happy/unhappy* but not *sad/unsad*) clearly implies that the Positives must already exist to be marked; as far as priority in *individual* language development is concerned, DiVesta (1966) has shown that in qualifier elicitation from children of various ages the Positives of familiar opposites (*good, big,* etc.) typically appear earlier and hold higher frequencies than the Negatives (*bad, little,* etc.). As to sequencing of such pairs in language production, note first that in stating opposites one usually goes from Positive to Negative (we say *strong-weak* rather than *weak-strong*) and then that familiar idiomatic phrases tend to follow the same rule (thus *the pros and cons of it,* but definitely not *the cons and pros of it*).

THE POLLYANNA PRINCIPLE: *across all languages and levels of units, it is statistically universal that affectively Positive forms and constructions are more diversified, more frequently used, and more easily processed cognitively than affectively negative forms and constructions.* The greater *diversity* of Positives shows up nicely in our cross-linguistic semantic differential data on (now) some 30 language-culture communities around the world—in the eight-octant space defined by Evaluation, Potency, and Activity factors (which system is itself a human universal), the $+ + +$ octant (Good, Strong, and Active) is much more densely populated with concepts than the $- - -$ octant (Bad, Weak, and Passive). There is much evidence that the Positive members of pairs of word-forms are significantly more frequent in usage than their Negative counterparts. Perhaps the most striking evidence for the Pollyanna Principle is offered in a paper by Osgood and Hoosain: measuring the times required for simply saying appropriately "positive" or "negative" to single words from all sorts of pairs presented randomly, there was a highly significant difference of about 50 ms. favoring Positives. In other words, it is easier to "simply get the meaning of" affectively Positive words than of affectively Negative words, and this even when usage frequency was deliberately biased in favor of the Negatives. Table I.1 also summarizes these non-defining characteristics of human languages.

How May Human Languages Have Originated?

This is a question that has intrigued speculative philosophers of all periods—and it is as purely speculative as anyone could hope, since there is little likelihood that any of the hypotheses will ever be tested empirically. How did some genius man-ape "get the idea" of communicating with others of his kind by means of vocalizations having distinctive referential properties, thereby enabling him to influence their behaviors?

"Ding-dong", "Bow-wow", "Pooh-pooh", "Yum-yum" and "Babble-lucky" Theories

The *"ding-dong" (mystical) theory* assumes that meanings are somehow inherent in words and that objects have the power to evoke the words that refer to them; the process of language origin is simply that man-ape sees object DING, DING causes him to say "dong", and "dong" contains the meaning *ding*. This has its roots in the primitive (?) human tendency toward *reification of words:* like little buckets, words are assumed to pick up their loads of meaning in one person's mind, carry them across the intervening space, and dump them into the mind of another.

The *"bow-wow" (imitative) theory* assumes that animals and many other things make or have characteristic sounds and that our man-apes had a spontaneous tendency to imitate noises heard; language originates simply via generalization of the meaning of dog-produced "bow-wow" as a perceptual sign to man-aped imitative "bow-wow". Suggestive evidence would be the use of imitative sounds in most tribal ceremonies and the commonness of onomatopoeia across human languages. This theory has a grain of probable truth as a *"starter"* on the path toward vocal-auditory language.

The *"pooh-pooh" (interjectional) theory* assumes that, like ape, man-ape has a repertoire of unlearned vocal expressions of affect (grunts, groans, screams), that these are nonrandomly occasioned by the situations he is in, and that these situations (as complexes of perceptual signs) have meanings for him; the "idea" of language originates in the transfer of the meaning of a situation to the vocal interjection as a sign of that situation. Thus man-ape A breaks the thong he is using to tie his stone axe-head to its handle-stick and mutters a disgusted "pooh-pooh"; and later he says "pooh-pooh, pooh-pooh, pooh-pooh" to ridicule man-ape B for tripping clumsily over a log—and soon the whole tribe is going around "pooh-pooh"-ing each other! This theory also seems quite reasonable as a "starter".

The *"yum-yum" (gestural) theory* proposed by Sir Richard Paget assumes that our man-ape was a fluent and total gesture-maker (with noisy mouth-gestures accompanying other bodily gesturings and posturings) and that his gesturing behavior followed Zipf's principle of least effort; language originates as the least effortful and least interfering *vocal* parts of the gesturing are substituted for the total. Imagine two hungry man-apes squatting beside a grubby rotten log: if they keep rubbing their tummies they can't keep on digging for juicy grubs, but they can keep on "yum-yum"-ing (except when swallowing!)—so the vocalizations became the signs.

The *"babble-lucky" (associational) theory.* This is E. L. Thorndike's "dubbing" of his own theory of the origins of language. It assumes that man-apes already had strong tendencies for vocalic play ("babbling", like human infants), that they already existed in social groups and were surrounded with various natural and artifactual objects, and that they had the cognitive capacities for symbolizing the meanings of such entities; language evolves as a result of chance associations of certain random babbles with certain objects and events, these *happening* to be observed and imitated by the group, and thus becoming socially standardized (hence the "lucky"). Imagine that a bright man-ape spies some clams along the lake shore and happens to babble "uk-uk"; he brings some back to the cave-dwelling, calling "uk-uk-uk!" as he comes; the other, less gifted, man-apes imitate him, while observing and feasting on the clams—and "uk" thus comes to refer to CLAM object and all that it signifies. But maybe this theory is *too* chancy and too susceptible to social confusion (what with some man-apes in the group "uk-uk"-ing, others "yum-yum"-ing, and still others "whiss-whiss"-ing about the same clams); most critically, it remains simply a theory of "wording", with nothing to say about "sentencing" (see Thorndike, 1943).

Criteria for Language Primitiveness?

Is it possible that some prehuman simian species like Pithecanthropus had a human-type language? If so, we would expect it to have been more primitive than existing human languages, which presumably have evolved from simpler origins. It seems most unlikely that humanoids suddenly started talking as they dropped from the trees. Unfortunately, unlike skulls and tools, languages leave no traces in or on the earth, so there is no *direct* evidence available on language evolution. But what about *indirect* evidence?

Among the many thousands of extant human languages, are there some less and some more "evolved"? The Old Look answered "yes": it was suggested that there were stages in development—from isolating languages like Chinese, through agglutinating languages like Turkish, to highly inflecting languages like . . . of course! . . . Latin; this notion was dropped when it was realized, with some embarrassment, that most modern Indo-European languages, along with English, were *less* inflecting, *more* isolating, than Latin. The New Look answers with a resounding "NO!": ethnolinguists have found the languages of culturally primitive (near stone-age level) peoples fully as complex as those of highly civilized (??) peoples "like us"; complexity of language-based conceptual systems (for kinship relations, mythology, etc.) appears to vary quite independently of levels of technological development. The very question of "relative primitiveness" of extant human languages is meaningless without criteria—but what should we look at?

Structural simplicity vs complexity?
Size of vocabulary?
Efficiency in communication?
Degrees of concreteness?
Ease of learning?

Any or all of these *might* be criteria for "primitiveness", but as far as I am aware there is no systematic cross-language evidence available.

A "Naturalness" Theory of the Origin of Languages

The general notion underlying my own speculations is this: *both in the evolution of the species and in the development of the individual human, the cognitive structures which interpret sentences received and initiate sentences produced are established in prelinguistic experience, via the acquisition of adaptive behaviors to entities perceived in diverse action and stative relations.* I suppose one might also call this an "article of faith". However, it follows from two assumptions that would rather obviously seem to be true: (1) that humanoids, *before* they had language, must have had capacities for cognizing the significances of events going on around them and for learning to behave appropriately in terms of such significances—if the species were to survive; (2) that children of contemporary humans, *before* they have language, display exactly the same capacities for acquiring the significances of perceived events and reacting with appropriate intentional behaviors. Specification of these prelinguistic capacities involves hypotheses deriving from Representational Neobehaviorism, so a bit of behavior theory is in order.

First, *a sign-learning principle.* Just like apes (and even rodents) before, it seems likely that humanoids developed the capacity for "getting the meanings of" wholistic perceptual signs of things prior to the capacity for analyzing out the distinctive features which make the differences in meanings. This behavioral principle may be stated as follows: *when a percept which elicits no predictable pattern of behavior* (e.g., the "uk-uk"-ing) *has repeated, contiguous, and reinforced pairings with another percept which does elicit predictable behavior* (the clams), *the former will become a sign of the latter as its significate, by virtue of becoming associated with a mediation process, this process* (a) *being some distinctive representation of the total behavior produced by the significate and* (b) *serving to mediate overt behaviors to the sign appropriate to* ("taking account of") *the significate.* Such a principle has been implicit in all of the speculations above (except the "ding-dong" theory) about the origins of language, e.g., the "X"'s in Thorndike's "babble-lucky" theory. The representational mediation process that comes to be associated with a sign (perceptual or later linguistic) as a dependent event in the nervous system is its *significance* (in comprehending); the same process as an antecedent event is the *intention* behind the overt behaviors mediated by a sign (in expressing).

Second, *a feature-learning principle.* The crucial componential characteristic of human languages [see (15)] can also be shown to have its prelinguistic, and even preprimate, origins. Just as behavioral acts are composed of sets of overt responses, so must the representational processes derived from them be composed of sets of mediator components. *To the extent that pairs of signs elicit reciprocally antagonistic mediator components, these antagonisms will become differences that make a difference in meaning* (i.e., bipolar semantic features). A paradigmatic experimental demonstration (see Lecture II, pp. 29-32) will illustrate how even the humble rat will come to "pay attention" to those environmental differences that make a difference in meaning. And so, most certainly, did prelinguistic man-ape and so does prelinguistic child.

Third, *the "emic" principle in Neobehaviorism.* Not only are organisms and things mobile with respect to each other, but environmental contexts keep varying. Thus, for man-ape both the retinal size and hue of ANTELOPE percept must have varied as he stealthily followed his prey through the long afternoon; similarly, for human infant the retinal size and hue of MOTHER-FACE will vary with her comings and goings from dawn into twilight. But antelope eventually gets caught and eaten, and mother eventually coddles and comforts baby, so such sets of signs must become associated with a common *significance* in comprehending. This is the basis for the constancy phenomenon in perception—long familiar to psychologists; it is also the basis for the phone/phoneme distinction, whose discovery made linguistics a science.

So we can phrase the "emic" principle as follows: *sets of physically variable signs associated with a common mediation process will be differences that* DO NOT *make a difference in meaning in comprehending but DO make a difference in selecting among the alternative behaviors mediated by that common mediator in expressing.* Just as the particular phones of a given phoneme are contextually conditioned, so would neither human child nor man-ape in behaving toward a desired APPLE emit biting and then grasping movements (all in thin air) before first approaching and reaching for it. Thus there is *a syntax of behaving,* just as there is a syntax of talking—and, again, the former is clearly prior to the latter in both individual and species development and hence can serve as the cognitive model.

And fourth, *the "ambiguity" principle of Neobehaviorism.* When percepts are constant, but the mediators associated with them are variable, we have the conditions for *ambiguity*—the same sign having more than one meaning. Convergent contextual signs usually provide for *disambiguation*—selection among the alternative meanings. A child may be ambiguated by a fuzzy black something on the floor (BALL OF THREAD or SPIDER?)—until it *moves!* A man-ape may have been ambiguated by a colorful rustling behind some bushes (GIRL-APE or SABER-TOOTH TIGER?)—until it *growls!* This is strictly analogous to linguistic ambiguity—homonomy and more generally polysemy. The "ambiguity" principle, then, would be that *signs associated with more than one mediation process are semantically ambiguous; convergence with other contextual signs typically serves to disambiguate by modulating the probability of one as against any other of the alternative meanings.* These principles will be elaborated in Lecture II.

Finally, *some speculations about naturalness in sentencing.* These behavioral principles of prelinguistic cognizing lead to what I have called a Naturalness Principle for sentencing, namely: *that the more sentences produced or received correspond in their surface structures to the cognitive structures developed in adaptive prelinguistic perceptuo-motor experience, the greater will be the likelihood and ease of producing and comprehending them.* This principle has many potentially testable implications for what should be universal—in the development of language by the young of our species, in the processing of language by the adults, as well as in the evolution of language by the species itself.

Consistent with Greenberg's (1963) evidence (a) that for all three extant language types (*VSO, SVO* and *SOV*) the subject noun-phrase (S) is expressed prior to the object noun-phrase (O) in simple, active, affirmative, declarative sentences and (b) that the SVO type is dominant (SVO, 60%; SOV, 30%; VSO, 10%) across the world, I assume that *the structures of simple prelinguistic cognitions are tripartite in nature and are most naturally "SVO" in the ordering of their semantic components,* thus [ENTITY$_1$–RELATION–ENTITY$_2$].

I also assume that *there are two basic types of SVO cognitions: those representing Action Relations, where* ACTOR–ACTION–RECIPIENT *is the natural ordering in cognizing* (because of the characteristically $^+$Animate (and often $^+$Human) semantic coding of Actors as against the $^-$Animate (or at least relatively passive) coding of Recipients); *those representing Stative Relations, where* FIGURE–STATE–GROUND *is the natural ordering* (because of the gestaltlike $^+$Salience of Figures and $^-$Salience of Grounds). Thus, both for human children and for our hypothetical man-apes en route to language, one would expect prelinguistic cognizings like MAN KICK DOG (Action) and DOG ON BLANKET (Stative) to be more natural than DOG KICKED-BY MAN or BLANKET UNDER DOG. If the underlying Naturalness Principle is valid, then one would expect the earliest sentencings—by contemporary child and by now-extinct man-ape—to be Active (rather than Passive) and Figure-ative (rather than Ground-ative).

The Naturalness Principle also make predictions about the ordering of clauses in complex, conjoined sentences—namely that where there is a natural order in prelinguistic experience with complex events, this order in sentencing will be either required or preferred across languages. We already have considerable evidence—generally confirmatory—to be reported later (see particularly Lecture V, pp. 127-132).

Results of this sort are most encouraging, and support the general notion that the cognitive structures developed in prelinguistic perceptual experience do in fact provide the "most natural" cognitive bases for comprehending and producing sentences—both in the evolution of language in the human species and in the development of its contemporary children. But, of course, neither this nor the demonstrably intimate parallelism between nonlinguistic and linguistic cognizing means that such prelinguistic capacity in itself constitutes "a language". It lacks three of the criteria for *anything* being a language—nonrandomly recurrent signals in some channel, reciprocality in sending and receiving such signals, and combinatorial productivity—precisely because such prelinguistic cognizing cannot be *abstracted* from the perceptual and motor chains that bind it to reality.

Things and Words

Orientation

My title is a deliberate, and appropriate, reversal of the title of Roger Brown's well-known early book (1958) on psycholinguistics. I say "appropriate" because the most gross working principle underlying the general theory of cognizing and sentencing I am presently writing on (*Toward an Abstract Performance Grammar*, Osgood, in preparation) is this: *both in the evolution of the species and in the development of individual humans, the cognitive structures which interpret sentences received and initiate sentences produced are established in prelinguistic experience, via the acquisition of adaptive behaviors to entities perceived in diverse action and stative relations.* In what follows I will also be making the following assumptions: (1) that the "deep" cognitive system is essentially semantic in nature, with syntax involved solely in transformations between the structured semantic system and the surface forms of sentences produced and received; (2) that this "deep" cognitive system is shared by both nonlinguistic (perceptual) and linguistic information-processing channels; and (3) that sentencing (comprehending and producing) in ordinary communication is always context-dependent, influenced probablistically by contemporary linguistic (conversational, discoursive) and nonlinguistic (situational, social) factors.

A Capsule Life-History of Behaviorism

Since many of you may have mainly affective stereotypes about behaviorism—as well as be entirely unfamiliar with its more recent and complex variants—I feel that this brief orientation is necessary. At the outset it must be emphasized that Behavior Theory, or behaviorism, is *not* the same thing as Learning Theory; rather, BT *includes* LT, but along with innate structural and functional determinants of behavior as well. One might even, and quite appropriately, say that learning theory is to behavior theory in psychology what syntax is to grammar in linguistics.[1]

Primitive Single-Stage ("Empty Organism") Behaviorism

Behaviorism had its origins in British Associationism, but in its primitive stages it was peripheral stimuli and responses that were associated rather than the central meanings or ideas. What I will call the "Classic Behaviorism" of the 1930s and 1940s was one of the stepchildren of logical positivism and a hypothetico-deductive theoretical system, modeled quite explicitly on physics: antecedent (input) and subsequent (output) *observable events* in some natural or experimental situation were to be identified with the *abstract constructs* (overt Ss and Rs) with which the underlying postulates (principles) of the theory were expressed; these postulates, particularly in their dynamic interactions, were to lead to certain *deductions* (explanations or predictions) which could be unambiguously *confirmed* or *disconfirmed*—disconfirmation (in principle if often not in practice) leading to revision of the postulates. It was this type of theory building that gave impetus to the evolution of behaviorism.

As an aid in exposition, I will make use of the notion—NOT of a Little Black *Box,* but of a Little Black *Egg,* this being more appropriate for biological entities. The evolution of Behaviorism can be viewed as increments in the number and complexity of the theoretical mechanisms that are put *into* the Little Black Egg. In revulsion against what could fairly be called the "junkshop theorizing" that characterized much of late nineteenth-century psychology, around the turn of the century a group of American behaviorists (Watson, Weiss, and Kantor), and later Skinner, went to the other extreme: *there is nothing whatsoever inside the Little Black Egg that is the proper business of an objective behaviorist!* This was not strictly true, of course; even the most adamant Skinnerian would admit that it is not external stimuli (Ss) and overt movements (Rs) that are associated in learning—which would obviously

---

[1] I am quite aware that one of the impacts of the Chomskyan "revolution" in linguistics was to create a "revulsion" against associationism in general and behaviorism in particular, on the part of many psychologists as well as linguists; nevertheless I urge you to "struggle through" this updated background with me so that you will be in a better position to evaluate what follows.

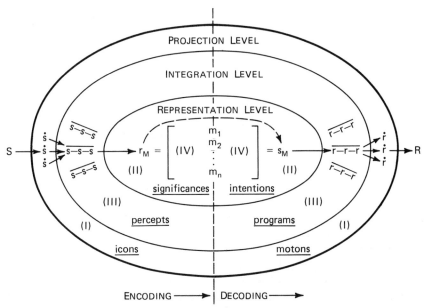

Fig. II.1. The Little Black Egg of Behavior

be nonsense—but rather the patterns of neural events at the more central termini of the sensory (s's) and motor (r's) projection systems.[2] So what Single-Stage Behaviorism really should be called is $\dot{s} \rightarrow \dot{r}$, not $S \rightarrow R$, psychology. Only the outer layer of the Little Black Egg (Roman I's in this figure) was filled, however.

Although Primitive Behaviorism proved to be a healthy antidote for the loose mentalism that it largely replaced during the 1920s, it was severely limited in the problems it could handle. Rats replaced humans as subjects—or humans were reduced to rat-level performances. But even at the "rat level" of human behavior replicable phenomena began appearing that were impossible for a single-stage theory to handle. One such was *semantic generalization*—where, having learned to make some novel response like finger-flexion to some word like JOY on a prior list, the same response would occur on a subsequent list to *semantically* related words like GLEE but not to *phonetically* related words like BOY—therefore generalization in terms of similar *meaning;* another was *semantic satiation*—where rapid seeing/saying repetition of a word, like CANOE-CANOE-CANOE . . . , produces a loss of meaningfulness, but rep-

---

[2] I also remind the reader that behaviorists—just like linguists with their phrase-structure "trees" of NPs, VPs, Ns, As, Vs, and even #s—have shorthand symbols for the constructs in *their* theories; I shall identify the symbols as they are introduced.

etition of a nonsense overt response having the same shape, NÚKA-NÚKA-
NÚKA . . . , does not. Both of these phenomena were very embarrassing
for a theory that dismisses "meaning" as a mentalistic ghost.

Classic Two-Stage ("Mediational") Behaviorism

Insufficiencies of this sort were the "why" of the evolution into Classic
Two-Stage Behaviorism, best exemplified in the theorizing of Hull (1930,
1943) and Tolman (1938, 1948). What was the "what"? As indicated by
Roman II's in Fig. II.1, Hull put into the Egg a replica (some might
prefer to say a "graven image"!) of the peripheral S-R ($\dot{s}$-$\dot{r}$) relation, but
for reasons that will become apparent, here reversed as $r_M \dashrightarrow s_M$ [where
the use of lower-case letters (r and s) indicates unobservable (hypothetical) responselike and stimuluslike events, the subscripts indicate merely
"mediational", and the dashed arrow indicates an automatic, unlearned
dependency relation]. The mediating process itself *is* a single, albeit
complex, event (presumably in the cortex), but as a *dependent event* (in
comprehending) it is functionally a "response" and as an *independent*
(antecedent) *event* (in expressing) it is functionally a "stimulus". For
Tolman, the equally hypothetical mediation process was called (anticipating a theory of meaning) a "sign-significate expectancy". What both
Hull and Tolman had done, in effect, was to break the S-to-R relation
into two, *separately manipulatable,* associations, $S/\dot{s} \rightarrow r_M$ and $s_M \rightarrow \dot{r}/$
R, the former involved in comprehending and the latter in expressing.
This greatly amplified the explanatory and predictive power of behavior
theory.

But what was the "how" of the anchoring to observables? Here is a
paradigmatic demonstration and, following, a Hullian explication:

> A rat is in a glass-fronted box that has an electrifiable grid for a floor
> and a turnable ratchet-device on a side wall; a buzzer is sounded
> intermittently, always followed in 5 sec. by shock. On early trials our
> subject "pays no attention to" the buzzer, but is galvanized by the
> shock into waltzing about on its hind feet, clawing at the walls,
> squeaking and no doubt undergoing autonomic glandular, heart-rate,
> etc., changes—in the course of which the ratchet is turned, shutting off
> the shock; a bit later the rat *begins* waltzing to the buzzer and moving
> in the general direction of the ratchet, promptly turning it when the
> shock comes on; and, finally, our subject waits near the ratchet, standing
> up and turning the ratchet *before* the shock comes on, thus avoiding it.
> (And our rat still later may become a bit cocky, delay too long, and get
> shocked again!)

In Figure II.2, the shock-*significate* (using Tolman's terminology), $\dot{S}$, is
associated single-stage (innately and/or via past learning) with the waltz-

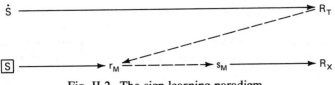

Fig. II.2. The sign-learning paradigm

ing, clawing, etc., which I symbolize as R_T (total behavior to the thing signified); the buzzer-*sign*, $\boxed{S}$, gradually acquires *some* of the behavior (notice, *not all*, e.g., not the frantic clawing) produced by the significate, clearly indicating the anchoring of mediating (r_M) to observable (R_T) behavior; but since these *overt* mediators drop out, while the mediated behavior, R_X (turning the ratchet), remains, we assume that this adaptive behavior is now being mediated by unobservable *covert* "replicas" of the overt mediators, the $r_M \rightarrow s_M$ process. This is the basic mechanism for development of two-stage (mediational) behavior out of single-stage behavior, and note that in Tolman's terms this mediating process is the *signficance* of the sign—the buzzer comes to "refer to" the shock— hence the symbol r_M for Tolman, as later for Osgood, would stand for a "meaning" response, not simply a "mediating" response.

Three-Stage ("Integrational, Mediational") Neobehaviorism

There were two very general, and significant, insufficiencies of the solely "mediational" theories of Classic Behaviorism, and they both came down to the fact that the principles of such theories dealt only with S → R associations. The first gross insufficiency was incapability of handling the phenomena of *perceptual organization,* so amply documented in the literature of Gestalt Psychology (e.g., the phenomenon of perceptual *closure*). That such phenomena are functions of experience, as well as having their innate determinants, is clearly indicated by the extensive evidence for an inverse relation between the frequency-of-usage of words and their tachistoscopic thresholds—the more frequent in experience, the lower the threshold. But since it is S-S learning that is involved here, no strictly S-R-type theory could handle it. The second gross insufficiency was inability to handle the phenomena of *behavioral organization,* the formation of central motor programs for complex behaviors like piano-playing and talking—as argued so forcefully by Karl Lashley in his Hixon Symposium address (1951). But since such behavioral organization involves R-R learning, again no strictly S-R theory could handle it.

By the mid-1950s I had become convinced that something else had to be put into the Little Black Egg if a behavior theory—of language performance, certainly—was to make any claim to adequacy. But, again hewing to the parsimony principle, this "something" had to be the minimum necessary. As indicated by Roman IIIs in Fig. II.1, I proposed an Integration Level of processing between the Projection and the Representational Levels, on both sensory and motor sides of the equation. Since projection systems are essentially isomorphic and unmodifiable by experience ("wired in"), surface *stimulations* (Ss) can be viewed as being in one-to-one relation with more central patterns of sensory signals (ś, ś, ś in Fig. II.1), or what I would now call *icons,* and surface *respondings* are similarly related to patterns of more central motor signals (ṙ, ṙ, ṙ), or *motons.* I further assumed that these signals at the central termini of the sensory and motor projection systems have connections with neurons in the still more central sensory and motor integration systems (the newly postulated Integration Level)—probably in what are called the sensory and motor "association areas" of the brain. The former (s-s-s) I would now call *percepts* and the latter (r-r-r) *programs* (after Lashley). Note that the relations *between* projection-level signals and integration-level events are *not* assumed to be isomorphic, but the relations *among* integration-level events *are* assumed to be modifiable by experience—*hence S-S (s-s) and R-R (r-r) learning.*

Without implying any particular neurology of the matter, the following functional principle was proposed for learning at the Integration Level: *the greater the frequency with which icons (ś, ś, ś) or motons (ṙ, ṙ, ṙ) have co-occurred in input or output experience, the greater will be the tendency for their post-projectional (s-s-s) or preprojectional (r-r-r) correlates to activate each other centrally as percepts or programs, respectively.* What it says, in effect, is that redundancies in either sensory input or motor output will come to be reflected by *evocative integrations* ("closures" resulting from higher co-occurrence frequencies) or *predictive integrations* ("tunings up" resulting from lower co-occurrence frequencies) in the nervous system.

This hypothesized three-level functioning of the nervous system would provide higher organisms with what might be called "Three Mirrors of Reality" on both encoding (sensory) and decoding (motor) sides of the information-processing coin:[3] on the comprehension side, (1) a mirror of *what is,* by virtue of unmodifiability via experience (ś, ś, ś), (2) a mirror of *what ought to be,* by virtue of predictive closures on the basis of past redundancies of often scanty information (s-s-s), and (3) a mirror of *what is signified,* by virtue of the representing relation of r_M; on the production side, and always via feedback loops, (4) a mirror of *what is intended* as

---

[3] It should be noted that, for good reasons that will become clear as we move along, I reverse the usual usage of "encoding" and "decoding"—the former putting information *into* the mediational code and the latter taking information *out of* the mediational code.

a communicative act (s_M), (5) a mirror of *what is programmed* ($\overline{r\text{-}r\text{-}r}$) for skilled execution, and (6) a mirror of *what is actually done* ($\dot{r}$, $\dot{r}$, $\dot{r}$). An intriguing example of the interaction between Mirrors (1) and (2) in my own experience is what happens when, due to power failure, the old banjo clock on my living room wall stops (and, because it can't be reset, we have to wait until time catches up); every so often I will glance at the clock 'to see what time it is', *see the second-hand moving* (my mirror of *what ought to be*), say to myself "that can't be", look again 'to inspect it', and see *that it is NOT moving* (my mirror of *what is*)!

The Componential Nature of Representational Mediators

Looking back at Fig. II.1, it will be noted that there is a IVth "level" in my Little Black Egg—which is not really a level but rather an elaboration on the nature of representational mediation processes. On both the encoding and the decoding sides of the mediational coin, the $r_M \rightarrow s_M$ process is assumed to be *componential* in nature. Just as the total behaviors made to things signified are typically a *set* of overt responses which together constitute an "act", so also are the mediation processes derived from these overt behaviors, and now elicited by the signs of things, a *set* of mediator components. *Thus r_M (in comprehending) and s_M (in producing) are summary symbols representing meanings-as-wholes, and they are analyzable into sets of mediator components* [m_1, m_2, . . . m_i . . . m_n]. Such mediator components are strictly analogous to *semantic features;* this, I think, is the entrée of Neobehaviorism to a theory of meaning and reference—and, with structuring of the semantic system (Representational Level), ultimately to a theory of sentencing (which is what my forthcoming *Toward an Abstract Performance Grammar* will elaborate in documented detail).

Just as the phonemes and sememes of linguistic theory are componential in nature, being exhaustively analyzable into sets of *distinctive features* (see, e.g., Jakobson, Fant, and Halle, 1963), so is it postulated in Representational Mediation Theory that global mediation processes (r_Ms) are exhaustively analyzable into sets of *distinctive mediator components* (r_ms). Note also that both phonemes and mediator components are *abstract entities,* unobservable in themselves but necessary as theoretical constructs for interpretation of what *is* observed: one never hears or produces the phoneme /k/, but rather always some contextually determined *allophone* of /k/ (e.g., with flattened lips in *key* and rounded lips in *coo*); analogously, one never hears or produces the meaningful distinction carried by a mediator component (r_m) but rather it is always a semantic distinguisher within some contextual set (r_M) which conveys the whole meaning of a form (e.g., some common affective feature is distinguishing *rage* from *annoyance, joy* from *pleasure,* and *yearning* from *expectation,* but we can only call it vaguely $^+$Potency).

Figure II.3 gives a componential elaboration of the global mediation process ($r_M \rightarrow s_M$). It also illustrates three other crucial aspects of this Neobehavioristic theory: (1) that a shift in a single mediator component can completely *shift the total meaning,* and hence the function of the mediation process in behaving—thus the change from component m_i to m_j, as shown in this symbolic representation, occasions the shift in *significance* (r_{M_1} to r_{M_2}) and hence in *intention* (s_{M_1} to s_{M_2}) of the entire process, all other components remaining constant; (2) that signs associated with the *same* global mediation process (here, $\boxed{S}_1$, $\boxed{S}_2$, and $\boxed{S}_3$ with r_{M_1}) will have the same *significance,* and hence be functionally equivalent, and similarly, the behaviors associated with the same global mediation process (here, $\boxed{R}_1$, $\boxed{R}_2$, and $\boxed{R}_3$ with s_{M_1}) will express the same *intention,* and hence be functionally equivalent; (3) that signs and behaviors associated with *different and incompatible* global mediation processes (here $\boxed{S}_2$ and $\boxed{S}_3$ as well as $\boxed{R}_2$ and $\boxed{R}_3$) will necessarily be *ambiguous* as to their significance (in comprehending) and as to their intention (in expressing).

For language as well as other behavior, differentiation of the effects

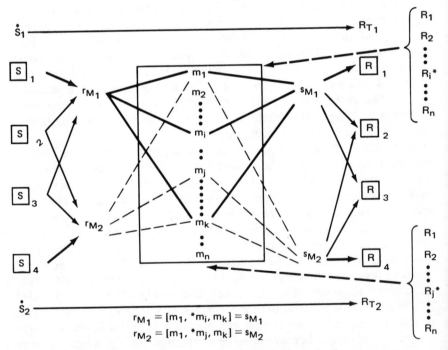

$$r_{M_1} = [m_1, {}^*m_i, m_k] = s_{M_1}$$
$$r_{M_2} = [m_1, {}^*m_j, m_k] = s_{M_2}$$

Fig. II.3. The componential nature of representational mediator processes

of signs upon dependent behaviors [(1) above], functional equivalences among signs as well as behaviors [(2) above], and ambiguities of both signs and behaviors [(3) above] are precisely the phenomena that require postulation of central mediating processes having the functional properties of $r_M = [m_1, m_2, \ldots m_i \ldots m_n] = s_M$. The two mediation processes displayed in componential terms at the bottom of Fig. II.3 are *distinct as wholes* because their derivational histories are from *different* significate-behavior relations, $\dot{S}_1 \rightarrow R_{T_1}$ vs. $\dot{S}_2 \rightarrow R_{T_2}$, as shown by the dashed $R_T \dashrightarrow r_m$ arrows.

Another paradigmatic type of experiment—conducted by Doug Lawrence (1949, 1950) with the humble rat as subject, and entitled "Acquired Distinctiveness of Cues", but in principle applying equally to the child acquiring its phonemic and semantic systems—would seem to be in order at this point, since it illustrates Figure II.3.

> In a simple T-maze, with the upper "arms" at the choice-point having both BLACK VS WHITE walls and CHAINS VS NO-CHAINS (soft curtain) distinguishing right from left sides (but with random right-left locations across trials), members of one group (of the four actually used) are rewarded with food-pellets at the end of the "arm" if they choose the BLACK side and punished by sudden loss of support (being dropped into a net) at the end of the "arm" if they choose the WHITE side. In Fig. II.3, BLACK would be $\boxed{S}_1$ (acquiring a "hope" significance, distinguished by our M_i) and making $\boxed{R}_1$ would be expressing an "approach" intention; while WHITE would be $\boxed{S}_4$ (acquiring a "fear" significance, distinguished by our m_j) and making $\boxed{R}_4$ would be expressing an "avoidance" intention). For this group the CHAINS VS NO-CHAINS locations are random with respect to this differential reinforcement, and hence must become signs having ambiguous significances ($\boxed{S}_2$ and $\boxed{S}_3$), generating ambivalent, cancelling intentions toward behaving ($\boxed{R}_2$ and $\boxed{R}_3$). Being reasonably bright little fellows, these rats rapidly learn to get food and avoid falls. The crucial thing in this experiment is this: after this training experience, *they will learn to approach* WHITE *and avoid* BLACK (reversing the significance of the cues) *much more rapidly than to approach* CHAINS *and avoid* NO-CHAINS (shifting from originally irrelevant to now relevant cues).

In other words, in this paradigmatic situation (and many experiments bear this out), *the humble rats have learned to "pay attention to" those differences that make a difference in meaning*—here anticipated reinforcement ("hope") vs anticipated punishment ("fear")—*and to "disregard" differences which do not make a difference in meaning*. In this connection, it is interesting that, although many linguists and most psycholinguists assume that phonemic and semantic feature distinctions must be acquired via experience (given the obvious fact that languages differ in just *what* features will come to "make a difference"), I have searched in vain for any theoretical explication of the crucial "how" of such learning.

The present theory offers two interrelated functional principles here. The first is the basic sign-learning paradigm for global meanings (which is probably prior to the acquisition of distinctive features in both species and individual development): *when a percept which elicits no predictable pattern of behavior is repeatedly paired with another which does* (e.g., SIGHT OF COOKIE followed by EATING COOKIE), *the former will become a sign of the latter as its significant, by virtue of becoming associated with a mediation process* (r_M/s_M) *that distinctively represents the behavior produced by the significant* (R_T) *and therefore serves to mediate overt behavior appropriate to* ("taking account of") *the significate* (R_X, e.g., salivating and reaching for perceived COOKIE OBJECT). This principle suggests how, bit by bit, LAD (Language Acquisition Device in the argot of linguists and many others) acquires what he "knows" about his *world*. The statement assumes that we are dealing with primary (usually perceptual) signs, but these in turn become *surrogate significates*—having "prefabricated" mediation processes as predictable response patterns — in later linguistic sign learning (e.g., heard "cookie" now paired with COOKIE percept). And, bit by bit, LAD acquires what he "knows" (semantically) about his *language*.

The second is the *feature-learning paradigm,* which—once a componential conception of the mediation process replaces an undifferentiated global conception—is a logical extension of the sign-learning paradigm: *to the extent that differences in signs as stimuli* (perceptual or linguistic) *are associated with reciprocally antagonistic differences in behavior, the central representations of these differences* ($+r_{m_i}$ vs $-r_{m_i}$) *will become those semantic features which distinguish among the significances of signs* (first perceptual and later linguistic). The Lawrence research on "Acquired Distinctiveness of Cues" above illustrates both global sign- and distinctive feature-learning paradigms—but are they feasible for human children? Shannon Moeser and her colleagues (Moeser and Bregman, 1972; Moeser and Olson, 1974) report that children acquire an artificial language easiest when the "words" (nonsense syllables) refer *consistently* to nonlinguistic entities in a perceptual-object reference field and the syntax of the "sentences" is lawfully related to the semantic classes which differentiate the perceptual reference field.

The Intimate Parallelism of Nonlinguistic and Linguistic Cognizing

William James characterized the mental state of the newborn infant as "a bloomin', buzzin' confusion". He was thinking of the infant's awareness of the external environment, but we could similarly characterize the infant's awareness via feedback of its own behavior as "a bumblin', fumblin' chaos". How, in behavior theoretic terms, is order brought out of perceptual confusion and behavioral chaos? On the *perceiving* side, we may first note that the infant is born with certain gestaltlike dispositions—innate tendencies to perceptually group stimulus elements having similar sensory *quality*, spatial *contiguity, continuity* of contour, and *common fate* as organism and environment move in relation to each other (thus the flesh-colored, spatially contiguous and contoured stimuli emanating from the infant's own chubby hand as it moves as a whole in front of its eyes, and similarly the more patterned stimulation of the mother's face). As Donald Campbell (1966) astutely observes, first perception and then language tend to follow Aristotle's advice and "cut Nature at her joints". And this advice is also followed on the *behaving* side: the infant comes equipped with many reflexive behavior units (like sucking to appropriate stimulations of the lips, fixating and tracking figural visual stimuli with the eyes, and grasping when the palms are suitably stimulated); these, along with an array of vocalization patterns, are to become components in the complex behavioral skills of childhood and adulthood.

Order Out of Chaos: Integrations and Representations

Given such innate "building blocks", the mechanisms postulated in three-stage Neobehaviorism also operate to bring order out of chaos in prelinguistic, and later linguistic, perceiving and behaving. Redundancies in *icons* (stimulus patterns) and *motons* (response patterns) give rise, through operation of the Integration Principle, to *percepts* (s-s-s) and *programs* (r-r-r)—which can fairly be called perceptual and motor skills, respectively; but these skills, in themselves, are meaning-less. Still further reduction of confusion is brought about via the association of percepts with *significances* (r_{M}s) and of *intentions* (s_{M}) with programs for behaving, following the basic Sign- and Feature-Learning Principles just stated. In this way percepts and programs become *meaning-full*. Prelinguistically, this development is evidenced by *appropriateness* in behaving toward the signs of things—the "representing" or "taking account of" criterion (thus reaching and salivating at the *sight* of the baby bottle, ducking the head when the *visual image* of an object increases rapidly in retinal size); linguistically, this development is prerequisite for the shift from phones to phonemes (differences that make a difference in *meaning*).

The "Emic" Principle in Neobehaviorism

(1) *Icons and percepts variable; significances constant.* By virtue of the fact that both things and organisms are mobile with respect to each

other, along with the fact that environmental contexts are changeable, *it follows that the distal signs of things* (and the icons and percepts they produce) *will be variable through many stimulus dimensions*. The "emic" principle is represented symbolically in Fig. II.4. Thus MOTHER'S FACE will vary in retinal-image size as a function of distance from the child and in both brightness and hue as a function of time of day, from midday through twilight. However, there are stable features, like the pattern of identifying facial features and their relations, and, since the signifying ($\dot{S} \rightarrow R_T$) relation will be constant regardless of these variations (eventually mother cuddles child), *there will be extension of the common representational process*, $(r_M \rightarrow s_M)$ *across such classes of distal signs*. Therefore, these will be percept differences which do *not* make a difference in meaning. *This common significance* (r_M) *is the constancy phenomenon*— familiar to psychologists—the "thingness" and "thatness", and in this example the "whoness", in perception. The heavy *convergent* arrows relating a variable set of perceptual signs to a common significance (r_M) represent this constancy paradigm. In behavior-theoretic terms, this constitutes a *convergent hierarchy* and indicates the functional equivalence of the set of signs with respect to the common mediator —they all signify the same entity.

(2) *Intentions constant; programs and motons variable*. The heavy *divergent* arrows relating the common *intention* (s_M) to a variable set of responses constitutes a *divergent hierarchy* and indicates the functional equivalence of the set of different responses with respect to the common intention (these responses are *not* necessarily equivalent with respect to other stimulus antecedents, as will be seen momentarily). This is the

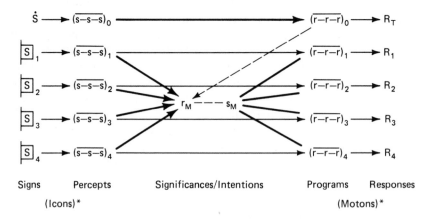

*Not diagramed to reduce complexity

Fig. II.4. The "emic" principle in behavior theory

behavior-theoretic representation of the fact that the same intention may be expressed in a diversity of ways (e.g., one may express an interpersonal "recognition" intention by vocalizing "Hi, there!", by an upward bobbing of the head plus a smile, by a salutelike forward wave of the hand, and so on). It should be pointed out that this combination of convergent and divergent hierarchies of functionally equivalent classes of signs and behaviors with respect to common mediators is *not* a special case, but rather *the general case in cognizing*.

(3) *Control and decision in Neobehaviorism.* We are now in a position to show how these two types of hierarchies interact in adaptive behavior. Let $\boxed{S}_1$ be the perceptual sign of a desired APPLE on a table some distance away (small retinal image), $\boxed{S}_2$ its percept at a bit more than arm's length, $\boxed{S}_3$ at crooked arm's (normal inspection) distance, and $\boxed{S}_4$ at a few inches from the face (very large retinal image); correspondingly, let R_1 be a locomotor response of approaching, R_2 a response of reaching for, R_3 a response of grasping, and R_4 a response of mouth-opening and biting. Now note that each of the *percepts* (s-s-s$_1$ through s-s-s$_4$) is associated *both* with the common "apple" significance (the "thatness") *and* with the distinctive response appropriate to the distance of an object having the real size of an APPLE-object (the "thereness"). Both of these associations are crucial for effective behavior (no one in his right mind "reaches for" the source of a percept signifying a RED-HOT COAL or "bites at" the percept of an APPLE on a table six feet away).

The *convergence* of the distinctive percepts (s-s-s 's) plus the common "apple-getting" intention (s$_M$) upon alternative responses (Rs) determines the smooth sequencing of the observed behavioral act—locomoting toward the distant APPLE (R_1), reaching for it when almost near enough (R_2), grasping it and bringing it to crooked arm's distance (R_3) (perhaps inspecting it briefly for possible bugginess!), and only then initiating a biting response (R_4). This is what I mean by *control* in Neobehaviorism. On the other hand, *divergence* among alternative responses—either different meanings (r$_M$s), e.g., HOT COAL VS APPLE, RIPE VS ROTTEN APPLE, HARD APPLE VS SOFT TOMATO, or different instrumental responses (Rs), as here—aways requires *decision*. In Neobehaviorism, as in Classical Behaviorism, "decision" is a probablistic function of the numbers and weights (habit-strengths) of convergent associations.

Why an "Emic" Principle?

Just as the emic principle was the conceptual "breakthrough" that made a science of linguistics possible, so I think an analogous principle makes Neobehaviorism feasible as a science of behavior, including language behavior. Not only does it provide an answer to Chomsky's (1959) critique of Skinner on the matter of inadequate definitions of "stimulus" and "response" (here defined as the *functionally equivalent* classes of signs having the same significance and behaviors expressing the same intention), but it further demonstrates the intimate parallelism between nonlinguistic and linguistic cognizing. Just as classes of physically different phones (as received) "converge" upon common phonemes (differences in sound that make a difference in meaning) and these "diverge" into classes of contextually determined phones (as produced)—and similarly for morphs to morphemes and most relevantly semes to sememes—so do classes of signs "converge" upon common meanings (in comprehending) and these "diverge" into classes of contextually determined behaviors (in expressing).

But more than this, one can claim that there is a *syntax of behaving* just as there is a syntax of talking—and the former is earlier in development. For a child to make biting, then grasping, then reaching responses in that order (all in thin air) as he approaches the desired apple would be just as "ungrammatical" as it would have been for Caesar to announce "vici, vidi, veni"! And note the strangeness of *he ate the apple, grabbed the apple, and opened the cupboard* as compared with the naturalness of *he opened the cupboard, grabbed the apple, and ate the apple*. There is increasing evidence that conjoined clauses ordered in terms of naturalness (i.e., in orders corresponding to prelinguistic experiencing of related events) are easier to process than when ordered otherwise. There is also a *semantics of perceiving* just as there is a semantics of word-combining in sentencing—and again, the former is earlier in development. The child reaches for a BALL OF BLACK THREAD on the floor and suddenly it spreads and starts moving—a sudden shift to SPIDER-object meaning occurs, along with a radical shift in programs for behaving!

The "Ambiguity" Principle in Neobehaviorism

(1) *Icons and percepts constant; significances variable.* The signs discussed above and diagramed in Fig. II.4 are *unambiguous;* one significance-intention mediation process has very high probability for all members of the constancy set of signs and all other alternatives have negligible probability. Figure II.5 represents in behavior-theoretic symbols the converse situation: a single sign ($\boxed{S}_Y$), and its resultant icon and percept ($\dot{s}$, $\dot{s}$, $\dot{s}_Y$ and s-s-s$_Y$ sketched in here for reasons that will become apparent) is associated with a *divergent* set of significances— and hence is *ambiguous* in meaning. This is the condition for *perceptual homonymy.* Just as most words in a language are to some degree polysemous (including homonymy)—*he went to the* BANK, *it was a* LIGHT

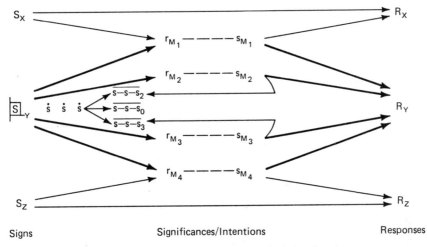

Signs   Significances/Intentions   Responses

Fig. II.5. The "ambiguity" principle in behavior theory

one, the SHOOTING *of the hunters was terrible*—so too are most nonlinguistic signs polysemous, not only the familiar ambiguous figures like the Necker Cube, but also the meanings of facial expressions of men in a picketline.

(2) *Intentions variable; programs and motons constant.* On the other side of this behavioral coin (the right side of Fig. II.5) we have represented the fact that observed communicative behaviors may be ambiguous as to the intention behind them—to the listener/recipient, of course, not the speaker/initiator. Thus, linguistically, "he was a *Colt* until this year, but now he's a *Bear*" as spoken is quite ambiguous (to a non-"sportsaholic", at least!) and the intention behind "*can* you open the window?" is ambiguous as to being a request or an inquiry about the listener's physical competence; nonlinguistically, the combination of a tight-lipped smile with the shaking of a fisted hand is ambiguous as to whether the intent is to threaten or to express successful completion of some effortful task.

(3) *The disambiguation of perceptual and linguistic ambiguities.* Given the ubiquity of ambiguity for signs in both linguistic and nonlinguistic channels, why aren't we hopelessly ambiguated most of the time? As indicated by the S_X and S_Z in Fig. II.5, potentially ambiguous signs (and responses by others) are nearly always *disambiguated by other contextual signs*—which may be either perceptual or linguistic in their relations to the signs and responses in question: *linguistic/linguistic—he* ROWED *to the bank, it was a light* PLAY, *and the shooting of the hunters* BY THE NATIVES *was terrible* are essentially unambiguous; perceptual/

linguistic—when my friend exclaims "duck!" in a barnyard, I'm likely
to respond by looking around for that bird, but passing by a busy sandlot
baseball field I'm likely to "duck" my head; *linguistic/perceptual*—as is
notoriously the case on television, interpretations of facial expressions
(e.g., of the men in the picketline) can be easily modulated from "rage"
to "determination" by the parallel commentary of an announcer; *per-
ceptual/perceptual*—the tight-lipped smile plus shaking of a fisted hand
by a boxer will be interpreted as "threat" just before the fight but as
"prideful satisfaction" just after his winning it.

Perceptual patterns vary in their degrees of ambiguity, as of course do
linguistic forms, from the near-infinite potential meanings of nonsense
signs to completely unambiguous single-meaning signs (see Osgood,
1953, Chap. 5). Now look at Fig. II.6A. For most of my students, these
two forms approach *infinite* ambiguity: interestingly, when I say of A(1)
"this is a fat janitress washing the floor, as seen from behind" and then
of A(2) "this is a soldier and his dog passing by a hole in a picket fence",
they find it almost impossible to interpret them any *other* way—as if one
little r_M had suddenly shot out to a probability of 1.00! Figure II.6B is a
sketch of the kinephantoscope used by Walter Miles (1931) to generate
a large number of alternative perceptual meanings of roughly equal
strength: as the "fan", brightly illuminated from behind, revolves, its
sharply etched shadow may be reported as "pirouetting" (clockwise or
counterclockwise), then suddenly as "arms stretching out and pulling
in", then as "arms flapping in front" (or in back), as "turning sideways
and then coming back", and so forth. Significantly, when the experimenter gives the above quotes as *linguistic suggestions,* the observer finds
it almost impossible to inhibit shifting to what he is told to perceive.

Figure II.6C(1) is one of the best-known, reversible figure-ground
displays, with "vase" and "identical twins looking at each other" as the
highest probability alternatives (although there are others—e.g., "two
bosomy ladies holding a conversation beneath a balcony"!): as shown in
Figs. II.6C(2),(3), the probability and persistence of the "vase" vs
"twins" meanings can easily be influenced by adding contextual cues
(the S_X vs S_Z in Fig. II.5). Figure II.6D shows (2) the famous Necker
Cube, which in two-dimensional outline form keeps flipping back and
forth between (1) the "from the side" and (3) the "from above" solid
percept integrations: there are studies demonstrating that *satiation* on
one of the solid forms inhibits *that* meaning of the subsequently shown
ambiguous two-dimensional form, the other alternative typically appearing first and persisting for longer periods than is the case for control
subjects. As far as I know, the most interesting experiment here remains
to be done—to see if one can satiate ambiguous *percepts* similarly with
words (e.g., repeating "block" vs "tower" here, or "vase" vs "twins"

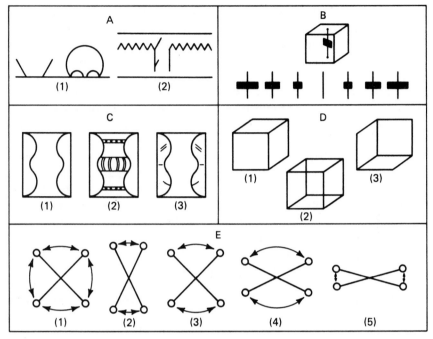

Fig. II.6. Some perceptual ambiguities and their disambiguation

above); positive results would strongly support the case for an "intimate parallel" between nonlinguistic and linguistic processing.

(4) *The effect of meaning upon salience in perception and language.* The final sequence in Fig. II.6E illustrates what Gestalt psychologists have discussed as the competition between "restraining" (peripheral) and "cohesive" (central) forces in determining what one perceives; in my terms this would be competition of *icons* (mirrors of *what is*) and *meanings* (mirrors of *what is signified*) in the determination of *percepts* (mirrors of *what ought to be*). In the ordinary phi-phenomenon, if two spatially separated lights go on and off alternately at an appropriate rate, they are perceived as a single light moving back and forth. Brown and Voth (1937) developed an apparatus in which two *pairs* of lights are alternately flashed, each pair being at the ends of two bars whose angular relation can be varied (*see* Osgood, 1953, pp. 206–208): when the bars are at right angles to each other, Fig. II.6E(1), and hence the distances among them being equal, the observer is equally likely to see *either* a single bar "tilting" vertically (like a baton held upright in the hand) or "teetering" horizontally (like a see-saw); when an observer is first shown

the display with the lights vertically aligned, Fig. II.6E(2), he *always* sees a rapid "tilting"; as the angle between the bars is gradually increased, the observer *persists* in seeing "tilting" *through* the equidistance 90° angle, Fig. II.6E(3), and well past it, Fig. II.6E(4)—holding on to his existing perceptual interpretation—unil at some point, Fig. II.6E(5), he suddenly shifts to seeing a rapid horizontal "teetering" (and the same happens if we go in the opposite direction, of course).

My neobehavioristic interpretation of this phenomenon would be that the pattern of icons ($\dot{s}$, $\dot{s}$, $\dot{s}$)s set up by the stimulations of Fig. II.6E(2) yield a shifting pattern of percepts ($\overline{s\text{-}s\text{-}s}$)s which has the unambiguous significance (r_{M_2}) of A BAR TILTING BACK AND FORTH; as the angle passes through and well beyond 90°, the persisting *feedback from this meaning* (s_{M_2})—see the feedback arrows in Fig. II.5 —maintains the salience of this percept ($\overline{s\text{-}s\text{-}s}$)$_2$ despite its increasing deviance from the iconic input, until the discrepancy becomes too great (mirror of *what is* vs mirror of *what ought to be!*)—and there is the sudden shift *in meaning* as well as in percept to A BAR RAPIDLY TEETERING BACK AND FORTH.

What about meaning and salience in language behavior? Salience of visual verbal units can be indexed by their tachistoscopic thresholds. In 1974 Rumjahn Hoosain and I reported a series of experiments designed to demonstrate the salience of words and wordlike larger units (having distinctive meanings as wholes) as compared with other units:

(1) monosyllabic words (*salt, mend,* etc.) had significantly lower thresholds than monosyllabic morphemes having much higher frequencies of visual usage (*sult, ment*), and the same held for multisyllabic words (*dashing, harmony,* etc.) and nonwords (*famness, henette*);

(2) wordlike nominal compounds (*stock market, stumbling block, real estate,* etc.) had significantly lower thresholds than ordinary noun phrases (*street market, copper block, city estate*) but the latter had only slightly lower thresholds than nonsense compounds (*shade market, sympathy block, post estate*);

(3) most significantly for present concerns, although prior presentation of both ordinary noun phrases and nonsense compounds lowered the subsequently tested thresholds for their single constituent words markedly (by reducing the number of alternatives), prior presentation of *nominal compounds* did not lower thresholds for *their* constituent words at all—the word-forms *stumbling* and *block* were presented N-times *physically* but they did not have their usual meanings in the compound *stumbling block*, hence the feedback ($s_M \rightarrow \overline{s\text{-}s\text{-}s}$) was *not* that associated in prior experience with tuning up either *stumbling* or *block* percepts. More anon on this study.

The "Deep" Cognitive System Shared by Things and Words

In introducing the Discussion section of my "Where Do Sentences Come From?" in the Steinberg–Jakobovits edited volume on semantics (1971), I stressed the complete insufficiency (as an answer to this question for a performance theory) of the symbol *S* that tops every "tree" in a generative grammar. *S* represents the set of all grammatical sentences in language *L* that can be generated by successive application of the rewrite rules of that language; however, this fails to meet the pragmatic criterion that sentences produced be appropriate to contextual conditions—humans don't produce sentences *ad libitum*. The reason is that such a grammar does not, *and need not* (being a *post hoc* description), provide any account of selection among alternative rewrite rules possible at each node in a "tree"—including, crucially, final selections from the lexicon. And, of course, a linguistic competence grammar has nothing to say about nonlinguistic perceptual cognizing.

Evidence for Interaction between Perceptual and Linguistic Channels

Casual (but convincing) observations. Imagine how flabbergasted you would be if, while riding up in an elevator, the only other occupant were to suddenly say "Pick it up!". Commands of this sort imply some appropriate nonlinguistic context (a dropped banana peel, say!). Similarly, pointings, lookings, head-bobbings and the like normally accompany conversings—often substituting for phrases ("I could SLITTING MOTION ACROSS THROAT the bastard!") or even whole clauses ("They've got our car back in the shop again, SO PRAYERFUL HAND POSTURE PLUS EYES LOOKING HEAVENWARD). It is also significant that nonlinguistic gestures typically parallel linguistic stress ("I will nót/HAND-BROUGHT-DOWN-SHARPLY wear that ridiculous tie!") and appear utterly ludicrous if displaced from stress points ("I will nót wear that ridiculous tie/ SAME-GESTURE!"). In a paper titled "The Relationship of Verbal and Nonverbal Communication", Mary Ritchie Key (1974) provides many illustrations of such interactions.

Redundancy deletion provides further evidence for this intimate interaction. Although anaphoric pronouns (*the three little bearded old men* becoming simply *they* in later sentencings), reflexives and quasireflexives (*John cut himself; one black ball hit another*) and other such linguistic devices serve to reduce redundancy, nonlinguistic devices often serve the same purpose—upon asking my wife where our poodle Pierre was during a Christmas shopping spree, she simply smiled and pointed to him on Santa's lap! Jerry Morgan (1975) provides many illustrations of how, in ordinary conversations, one uses the other's utterances as bases for redundancy deletion—example, PERSON A "What does Trick eat for breakfast?"; PERSON B "Bananas."—and Morgan's paper (titled "Some Interactions of Syntax and Pragmatics") nicely illustrates the recent shift of interest on the part of many linguists away from studying sentences-in-isolation toward studying sentences-in-context. The dependence of listeners on nonlinguistic context for selecting among literal or nonliteral intentions of speakers provides a nice illustration here: As written, out-of-context, *can you take Pierre out for a walk?* is ambiguous as to the intent of the "speaker"—is it a literal inquiry as to competence or an indirect request? When I ask this of my wife when she's down with a bad cold, *can you* is probablistically interpreted as *are you able to,* but when she's feeling fine and knows I'm very busy preparing a lecture, *can you* is interpreted as *please.*

Some experimental evidence. Early studies by the late Theodore Karwoski and his associates, including myself as an undergraduate at Dartmouth (e.g., Karwoski, Odbert and Osgood, 1942), made it clear that auditory-visual-verbal *synesthesia* is not a freak phenomenon in people whose "sensory wires are crossed", but rather a fundamental characteristic of human thinking, involving lawful translations from one modality to another along dimensions made parallel in cognizing—auditory LOUD going with visual NEAR rather than FAR (and similarly for the words *near* and *far*), auditory TREBLE being visually UP and BASS being DOWN (as well as verbally *high* and *low*).

In a paper of mine (1960) titled "The Cross-cultural Generality of Visual-Verbal Synesthetic Tendencies", I reported data indicating that—when Anglo, Navajo, Mexican-Spanish, and Japanese subjects "rated" words like *happy, lazy, excitement, weak, grey,* etc., by simply pointing to binary visual alternatives on cards (e.g., a COLORFUL vs a COLORLESS design, a BLUNT vs a SHARP form, a LIGHT vs a DARK circle, a VERTICAL vs a HORIZONTAL line, a LARGE vs a SMALL circle, and so forth)—there is high cross-cultural agreement on visual-verbal "metaphors"; *happy* is "universally" COLORFUL, LIGHT, and LARGE, but *weak* is T::N, LIGHT, HAZY, and CROOKED.

Using a somewhat modified version of this binary pictorial task, Sylvia Sheinkopf (1970) was able to demonstrate that anomic aphasics perform very much like normals—pointing appropriately to the visual alternatives when given the test words—despite their manifest difficulties in naming and word-finding (here, they were unable to even describe the visual forms). There are other subject populations, of course, for whom a valid Graphic Differential—valid in the sense of yielding semantic profiles correlating with those obtained with the usual verbal Semantic Differential—would be a most useful instrument, for examples, nonliterates, normal members of illiterate cultures and children younger than six years. After much testing and pruning of visual polarities used in earlier studies, Patrice French (1977) has come up with a 15-scale Graphic Differential which seems to satisfy this requirement.

Evidence for Parallel Processing Across Channels

Ordinary communicative competences. The ordinariest of human communicative abilities—and those most often used in one form or other in research with young children—are Simply Describing and Simply Acting Out, and both involve parallel processing of semantic information in the shared cognitive system. In *Simply Describing,* the meanings of nonlinguistic perceived states and events must be encoded "up" into this "deep" semantic system (comprehension) and then these cognitions are decoded "down" into semantically equivalent verbal expressions (production); in *Simply Acting Out,* the meanings of linguistic words and sentences must be encoded into the same semantic system (comprehension) and then these cognitions are decoded out into nonlinguistic behavioral operations upon appropriate entities in the environment (production). A speaker's everyday reportings ("Hey! There's a great big, wolf-like dog on the lawn!") and directings ("The book I want is that thick red one on the third shelf.") are instances of Simply Describing— as are the rapid-fire descriptions of a sports announcer. A listener's behaving appropriately to everyday commands ("Get me the big pliers on the tool shelf in the cellar!") and requests ("Please pass me the gravy bowl.") are instances of Simply Acting Out. But my favorite example is this: two coeds, walking along a campus path, see a third girl approaching with a *mini*-mini-skirt on; after she has passed, one says to the other, "She also dyes her hair!". The use of anaphoric *she* implies a prior cognition (which could only be perception based) and the *also* identifies it as something like [THAT GAL / IS WEARING / A REALLY SHORT SKIRT].

Undoubtedly the most basic competence, as well as earliest in individual human development, is *communication of affect* (feeling), and here we have extensive evidence for sharing of the same primitive semantic system. It was M. Brewster Smith who first, in 1960, pointed out to me the essential identity of the factors, Evaluation (E), Potency (P), and Activity (A), we were finding for American English speakers using the Semantic Differential, to Wundt's three dimension of feeling (Pleasantness, Tension, and Excitement); Schlosberg in 1954 had named them Pleasantness/Unpleasantness, Attention/Rejection, and Activation/ Sleep, and in a paper of my own (based on labeling of posed live expressions in a demonstration/experiment at Yale in the early 1940s) I was to name the same three factors Pleasant/Unpleasant (E), Controlled/ Uncontrolled (P), and Activated/Unactivated (A)—see Osgood (1966).

Over the past near-twenty years, our Center for Comparative Psycholinguistics has collected data from (now) 30 language-culture communities around the world, using comparable SD instruments, and the evidence for universality of the E-P-A affective meaning system is impressive (see Osgood, May, and Miron, 1975). Reciprocal facial gesturing by speakers and listeners is the most common parallelism of nonlinguistic and linguistic channels—smiling with the happy utterances, looking astonished with the surprising utterances, looking sorrowful with the sad utterances—and it is quite unsettling in ordinary conversation if either speaker or listener "dead-pans" it (interestingly, one of the clearest clinical signs of abnormal dissociation is inappropriateness of facial/verbal expression-pairings).

Extraordinary parallel processing in psycholinguistic experiments. Early research reported in Osgood, Suci, and Tannenbaum (1957, pp. 275–284) had demonstrated that the E-P-A values of phrasal adjective-noun combinations (e.g., *shy secretary, treacherous nurse, breezy husband*) were predictable to a fairly high degree from the measured affective meanings of their single-word components via the congruity formula of Osgood and Tannenbaum. Hastorf, Osgood, and Ono (1966) found that affective meanings of different posed facial expressions of an actor (CEO sans little mustache!), when fused in a stereoscope, could also be predicted from the meanings of the separate expressions; Ono, Hastorf, and Osgood (1966), using the same posed facial expressions, were able to show that the more *in*congruent the expressions paired in the stereoscope were, the greater the likelihood of the viewer experiencing binocular rivalry (e.g., COMPLACENCY/RAGE yielding more rivalry than DISMAY/REPUGNANCE).

In his doctoral thesis (1967) Dogan Cuçeloğlu used 60 "outline faces" (all combinations of four eyebrow types, three eye types, and five mouth types), these "faces" being rated for degrees of likeness to 40 emotion-names by high school subjects in American, Japanese, and Turkish cultures; factor analyses in all three groups yielded Pleasantness, Activation, and Control as the three dominant factors, with MOUTH-CURVED-UP VS MOUTH-CURVED DOWN, with WIDE-OPEN VS CLOSED EYES, and with DOWNWARD-BENT ⌣⌣ VS UPWARD-BENT ⌢⌢ EYEBROWS as the most distinctive facial features for E, A, and P, respectively.

Inescapable Conclusions

The evidence I have summarized here for intimate interactions between these channels in both ordinary communication and diverse experimental situations as well for parallel processing in both channels in both ordinary communicative competences and extraordinary psycholinguistic experiments—leads back to the assumptions I made near the beginning of this lecture, but now as inescapable conclusions: (1) that the "deep" cognitive system is semantic in nature, (2) that it is shared by both nonlinguistic (perceptual) and linguistic information-processing channels, and (3) that sentencing in ordinary communication is always context-dependent. I would view the shift in recent years of linguists toward Functionalism and Pragmatics as steps toward developing *linguistic theories of performance*. However, there is little in this recent philosophical, linguistic, and psycholinguistic (for that matter) literature that offers any *theory* of how nonlinguistic signs and contextual cognitions can have meanings and interact with language-based cognitions. Such a theory *is* central to the Abstract Performance Grammar that I will be developing throughout these lectures.

The Paradigm Clash in Psycholinguistics: Revolution or Pendula Swings?

Orientation

The pre-1950 history of the relationship between linguists and psychologists concerned with language can be characterized as having been either nil or contentious—witness the exchanges between linguist Paul and psychologist Wundt around the turn of the century (cf. Blumenthal, 1970). Like all sweeping generalizations, this one has its exceptions, of course: the first edition of Leonard Bloomfield's famous *Language* in 1933 was explicitly within a behavioristic framework (*see* the preface), although there was little detailed use of psychological notions; on the other side, German psychologist Karl Bühler's *Sprachtheorie* (1934) described linguistic phenomena, about which he was exceptionally well-informed, from a psychological point of view. Nevertheless, relations were remote and scholarly rather than intimate.

During the early 1950s, however, there was a drawing together of descriptive linguists and behavioristically inclined cognitive psychologists on a more cooperative, interactive basis. Recently I gave my own retrospections on the development of relations between linguists and psychologists, in an invited address at a New York Academy of Sciences conference (Osgood, 1975); it was titled "A Dinosaur Caper: Psycholinguistics Past, Present, and Future", and—in part to demonstrate that we should never take out pet theories, or ourselves, *too* seriously—I will occasionally insert excerpts from this address.

> My theme for psycholinguistics over the past quarter-century is frankly *marital*—engagement, abduction, marriage, divorce, and reconciliation. Since this history is inevitably personal, an introspective little dinosaur (there were little dinosaurs, you know) will, of necessity, be the main character. . . . The year 1950 found him at Illinois, busily at work on both the (learning theory) nature of meaning and the

(semantic differential technique) measurement of certain aspects of it. But first . . . a confession: At this time—except for the work of Charles Morris in semiotics—this young dinosaur didn't have the foggiest idea of what scholars in other fields were thinking and doing about language and meaning. Specifically, as to linguistics, he had only the vague notion that these were strange, bearded, birdlike creatures who inhabited the remoter regions of libraries, babbling away in many exotic languages and constructing dictionaries for them—hardly fit companions for a robust, rigorous, and objective young dinosaur!

His awakening came in the summer of 1951 when—sparked by Jack Carroll—the Social Science Research Council sponsored a summer conference of linguists and psychologists at Cornell University. By some fluke the youthful dinosaur was invited to participate (I often wonder how the course of my own scientific life would have run if this "fluke", and all that followed from it, had not happened.) In any case, that summer was an eye-opener: not only were the linguists there *neither* polyglots nor lexicographers, but they *were* robust, rigorous, and objective, maybe even a bit more so than the young dinosaur!

THE ENGAGEMENT. As a result of that summer's meeting, the SSRC established a new Committee on Linguistics and Psychology in October of 1952. This turned out to be a very lively little committee. One of its first steps was to plan and sponsor a research seminar on psycholinguistics, this being held during the summer of 1953, not by chance, on the campus of Indiana University, when and where the Linguistic Institute was also having its summer session. A monograph resulted from this seminar, *Psycholinguistics: A Survey of Theory and Research Problems* (1954), and the thrust of the continuing SSRC Committee on Linguistics and Psychology is evident in many other projects and seminars it supported during the late 1950s: a "Southwest Project on *Comparative Psycholinguistics*" (centered at The University of New Mexico, summer 1954); a conference on *Bilingualism* (Columbia University, 1954); another conference on *Techniques of Content Analysis* (University of Illinois, 1955); yet another on *Dimensions of Meaning— Analytic and Experimental Approaches* (1956) (it was at this one that our dinosaur first met young Noam Chomsky and got the impression that he was brilliant, but, alas!, *not* convinced that meaning was the central problem for students of language); a very impressive, large-scale conference on *Style in Language* organized by Tom Sebeok (Indiana University, 1958); a summer seminar on *The Psycholinguistics of Aphasia* (Boston Veterans Administration Hospital, 1958); and a conference on *Language Universals* (Dobbs Ferry, N.Y., 1961). Many of these activities resulted in book-length publications.

According to one impartial chronicler, A. Richard Diebold, Jr. (writing in 1965), "within a year or two of its appearance, [the Psycholinguistic Monograph] became the charter for psycholinguistics, firmly establishing the discipline's name. It so successfully piqued the interest of linguists and other behavioral scientists that the volume itself was soon out of print, and also became notoriously difficult to obtain secondhand, or even in libraries." (p. 208). And he notes that one of the graduate-student participants, Sol Saporta, was in 1961 to edit the first " . . . long-awaited reader, *Psycholinguistics: A Book of Readings* . . . [which was] also a testament to the fact that there [was] an ever-growing number of university courses variously titled 'psychology

of language', 'psycholinguistics', 'linguistic psychology', etc." (p. 208).
According to another observer, Howard Maclay (1973), "The Formative
Period was characterized by extremely good relations between psychologists and linguists. This happy state of affairs had two major
sources: a common commitment to an operationalist philosophy of
science, and a division of labor that prevented a number of potential
difficulties from becoming overt . . . linguists were assigned the 'states
of messages', while psychologists assumed responsibility for the 'states
of communicators' and also, by default, 'the processes of encoding and
decoding'." (pp. 570–571). Ah, happy, eager dinosaur! Now reaching
maturity, he had participated in the full kaleidoscope of these SSRC
activities, and Spring was turning into what *had* to be a Golden Summer.

THE MARRIAGE. While the mature dinosaur was at the Center in Palo
Alto in 1958–1959, George Miller, Eugene Galanter and Karl Pribram
were also there and were working on their *Plans and the Structure of
Behavior,* to be published in 1960; it was heavily influenced by Chomsky
and included a chapter on "Plans for Speaking". This was followed by
Miller's important paper titled "Some Psychological Studies of Grammar" (1962) and soon thereafter by a small flood of papers by Miller,
his students, and others testing the psychological reality (in terms of
effects upon processing time, memory and the like) of grammatical
structures and transformations. The consummation of this intimate
relation between linguists and psychology was symbolized by two
chapters in the *Handbook of Mathematical Psychology* (1963), written
jointly by Chomsky and Miller: "Introduction to the Formal Analysis of
Natural Languages" (Chomsky and Miller) and "Finitary Models of
Language Users" (Miller and Chomsky). This marriage between linguistics and psycholinguistics in the 1960s might better have been called
an *elopement*—or perhaps even an *abduction*—because it was a very
one-sided affair. The intuitions of generative linguistics were to provide
a theory of Competence and the wifely psychologists were to cook up
experiments on Performance designed to demonstrate empirically the
validity of such a theory of how the mind works in sentencing.

By the end of the 1950s the distant mutterings of a scientific
revolution were in the air, impelled by Chomsky's generative and
transformational grammar, certainly in linguistics and possibly in cognitive psychology, too. In the preface to his *Psycholinguistics* (1961),
Sol Saporta was to say: " . . . all attempts by psychologists to describe
'grammaticality' exclusively in terms of habit strength [etc.] . . . seem
inadequate . . . to account for some of the most obvious facts of
language." (p. v). In 1959 Chomsky wrote a carefully documented and
scathing review of Skinner's *Verbal Behavior* (1957)—never responded
to by Skinner himself—and this was to have cumulative impact on many
psycholinguists. Perhaps because our dinosaur was confidently mature,
had a much more complex behavior theory, and, indeed, had written a
highly critical review of Skinner himself (Osgood, 1958, titled "A
Question of Sufficiency") he was not particularly disturbed and kept
right on nuzzling among and munching away at his semantic daisies.

By 1966 the conflict between competing psycholinguistic paradigms
had reached what Thomas Kuhn (1962) terms the "crisis" stage in
scientific revolutions. In the spring of 1966, at the University of
Kentucky, there was a conference with an innocent-enough sounding

topic, *Verbal Behavior and General Behavior Theory.* Particularly in the session on Psycholinguistics, the prepared papers by "revolutionaries" Bever, Fodor, Garrett, and McNeill constituted a frontal attack on behaviorism and associationism generally. As the discussant of these papers, I found myself in the unfamiliar and unenviable role of defending The Establishment. The title of my discussion, "Toward a Wedding of Insufficiencies", is indicative of my ambivalence in this role. And I was beginning to realize that I *was* a dinosaur!

Paradigm Clash in Psycholinguistics

It was clear that the claims being made by the protagonists of the Chomskyan paradigm as to the inadequacy of S-R Behaviorism were not restricted to psycholinguistics, but rather included all of the phenomena of verbal behavior which were being considered at the conference. The Kentucky conference was a bit schizophrenic in its reaction to this attack, and this was evident in the remarks of the general discussants in the final session: Some participants seemed genuinely bewildered and uncertain about the true status and future of Behaviorism; other participants, already converts to the new paradigm, were obviously delighted with the turn of events; and some seemed to be unimpressed by, or perhaps rather oblivious to, the claims being made.

There are many facets to the controversies developed in the Kentucky Conference and elsewhere in the 1960s, but I will concern myself only with the three which I consider to be the most crucial in the paradigm conflict as it affects the viability of Neobehaviorism.

I. *Is representational mediation theory capable in principle of providing an account of symbolic behavior in general and of meaning in particular?* Mediation theory of this representational type has been the only serious attempt to deal with semantic processes in S-R terms, and any psycholinguistic theory which fails to handle the role of meaning in behavior is certainly insufficient in principle. The burden of Fodor's argument (1965, 1966) about the status of the construct r_M is that it is demonstrably inadequate, since " . . . once we grant a one-to-one relation between r's and R's, we insure that the former lack the 'surplus meaning' characteristic of terms designating *bona fide* theoretical entities." (1965, p. 81).

II. *Is any theory based on associationistic laws capable in principle of handling the abstract properties of language behavior?* According to Bever, Fodor, and Garrett (1968, p.582), "certain kinds of conceptual competences fall outside the explanatory power of associationism, given the kinds of constraints on learning principles that have traditionally defined associationism.'' If representational mediation theory is, at base, a variant of associationistic theory—as I must agree it is—then its failure in such cases would mean insufficiency in principle.

III. *Is representational mediation theory capable of incorporating what generative grammars characterize as the competence of native speakers of a language?* Chomskyans claim that it is essential to understand the nature of *what* is acquired by LAD (Language Acquisition Device) before trying to study *how* it is acquired or used in adult language performance. The *what,* of course, is claimed to be linguistic competence and, according to Palermo (1971, p.152), such a ''characterization of the *language* gives a characterization of the *mind* of the human who speaks the language.'' Although I would disagree with this way of putting it, it is certainly the case that any adequate theory of language performance must, in principle, be able to account for the kinds of competence described by an adequate linguistic theory or grammar.

These issues strike deep at the capacity of neobehavioristic theories, expressed in S-R terms and embodying associationistic principles, to handle the abstract entities and structures which are essential to the explanation of what is observed but are not themselves observable. As Garrett and Fodor say (1968, p. 451), and I agree, these are *not* merely ''an exchange of terminology''. To be sure, there are those linguists and psycholinguists who turn slightly green and lurch for the nearest exit when confronted with Ss and Rs (particularly little ss and little rs); but they should recognize that there are those psychologists and other psycholinguists who do the same when confronted with *NP*s and *VP*s organized into complex phrase-structure trees. Choice among symbol systems is not at issue here. Nor is any charge involved that behavioristic interpretations of language phenomena are at present insufficiently elaborated. I don't think anyone expects a complete and detailed explication, behaviorally or otherwise, of Man's most complex accomplishment at this stage in the game. The questions concern sufficiency *in principle.*

Issue I: Can Meaning Be an r_M?

In his original critique (1965), Fodor agreed (1) that r_M is *functionally characterized* (i.e., a hypothetical construct having, in theory, response-like properties as a subsequent and stimuluslike properties as an antecedent event) and (2) that r_M is not equal to but rather *a proper part of* R_T (i.e., avoiding the simple substitution fallacy). He then proceeded to set up what he considered to be an irresolvable dilemma: either a particular r_M must bear a one-to-one relation to a particular R_T (in which case the difference between mediational accounts and single-stage accounts of reference comes down to a "trivial" matter of observability) or a particular r_M may bear a one-to-many relation with several R_T (in which case the signs which elicit that particular r_M must refer ambiguously to more than one significate).

In my reply (Osgood, 1966) I accepted the first horn of the dilemma but denied the validity of Fodor's conclusions about the consequences of accepting a one-to-one relation between r_M and R_T. The essence of my argument was that (1) by virtue of their *componential nature*, r_Ms bear unique relations to their R_Ts *only as wholes*, the same components or features entering into many R_T/r_M relations, and (2) by virtue of the *functional separation* of encoding ($\boxed{S}$ $\to r_M$) and decoding ($s_M \to R_X$) phases of the mediation process and the *convergent and divergent hierarchies* in these phases, there are many-to-one and one-to-many relations respectively between peripheral signs and mediators and between mediators and peripheral responses, linguistic or otherwise.

Point (1) relates to the status of r_M as a theoretical construct—whether it has the "surplus meaning" characteristic of bona fide theoretical entities. Point (2) relates to the constraints on mediation—whether or not it is a simple, linear chaining process. Both bear on what will come to be seen as the underlying issue—the question of *functional equivalence* among types of stimuli and responses.

Status of r_M as a Theoretical Construct

Prerequisite to my arguments in the debate with Fodor was a distinction between two quite different kinds of mediation theory—a distinction which Fodor (1965, 1966) recognizes but, I believe, misinterprets: a *nonrepresentational type*—that is, "meaning*less*" in the sense of not providing any account of meaning in behavior—developed directly out of single-stage Skinnerian Behaviorism; a *representational type*—that is, "meaning*ful*" in the sense of being essentially a behavioral theory of meaning—developed out of two-stage Hullian Behaviorism.

Both models shown in Fig. III.1 provide for the *nonobservability* of the mediating process—a nontrivial characteristic demand by the facts of symbolic behavior. But here similarity ends. Whereas formation of the representational mediating process is *historical* (occurring during original learning of the meanings of signs), formation of the nonrepresentational mediator is *contemporary* with its (subvocal) utilization *as* a mediator in each performance situation. Whereas representational mediators could be entirely *central*, cortical events, having no formal resemblance to their overt behavioral sources (which I think is almost certainly the case), nonrepresentational mediators are explicitly assumed

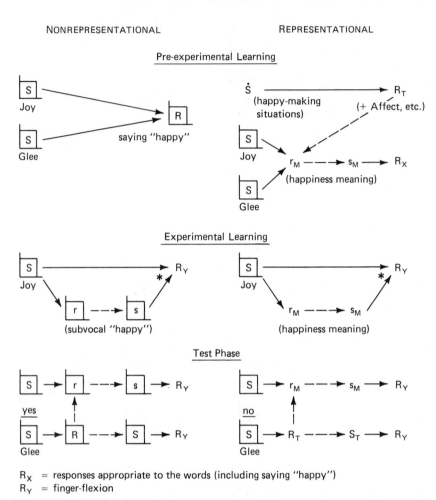

R_X = responses appropriate to the words (including saying "happy")
R_Y = finger-flexion

Fig. III.1. Nonrepresentational and representational mediation accounts of semantic generalization

to have formal resemblance to their overt sources, being equally *peripheral* occurrences albeit with greatly reduced amplitude. Correspondingly, whereas representational mediators can be semantically componential (cf. Fig. III.3), nonrepresentational mediators by their very nature could at best only be phonetically componential. And finally, whereas representational mediators are meaningful in nature, by virtue of their explicit anchoring in nonlinguistic behavior, nonrepresentational mediators are inherently meaningless, never escaping from the verbal trellis of surface linguistic responses. Fodor's (1965) critique effectively demonstrated the insufficiency *in principle* of nonrepresentational mediation theories as far as any account of meaning or reference is concerned. If I am right, then Fodor has done Neobehaviorism a service—by pruning out one of its less powerful alternatives!

Now, I do not think that Fodor would wish to argue that the phonemes and the other "emes" of linguistics are theoretically vacuous constructs—although, of course, he might. To do so, he would have to demonstrate that anywhere one uses the notion of the phoneme as an explanatory device he could substitute some concrete, observable phone—but *what* phone? This seems to be precisely what he believes to be the consequence of accepting a one-to-one relation between r_M and R_T—that one can substitute R_T for r_M in mediation paradigms and thereby eliminate any theoretically interesting differences between two-stage and single-stage behavior models. However, the one-to-one relation is between r_M and those reaction *components* of a class of R_Ts that have been differentially reinforced in the discrimination of behaviors to instances of the significate in question from instances of other significates.

The Functional Equivalence Question

Fodor (1966) begins his reply to Osgood (1966) and Berlyne (1966), all in the *Psychological Review,* with the following statement: "My discussion of Professor Osgood's criticisms will be very brief, for it appears that he and I agree . . . that a one-to-one correspondence obtains between the presumed implicit responses *and the gross stimulus-response connections they mediate. . . .* Transitivity guarantees that you may have arbitrarily many mediators in the box without jeopardy to the present argument *so long as they are in one-to-one correspondence with one another and with input and output states. A chain can connect only two points, however many links you add.*" (1966, p. 412, italics mine). There is a complete shift here from the one-to-one relation which I do and must accept—that between R_T and r_M—to several others which *I explicitly rejected in my response to his original critique.* There is nothing in representational mediation theory that postulates a one-to-one relation between any particular antecedent sign and a given r_M (this is typically a many-to-one convergent relation) or between s_M and any particular subsequent response (this is typically a one-to-many divergent relation). If we apply the same argument to any particular feature or component of r_M, e.g., m_1, then precisely the same many-to-one-to-many situation holds, nor is there any implication that the various components of r_M (m_1, m_2, . . . m_n) are linked to each other by one-to-one relations as in a "chain"; to the contrary, these components of r_M are assumed to be a *near-simultaneous* bundle of implicit reactions to a sign, independent one of the other.

Fodor's position appeared to come down to two assertions about functional equivalence: (1) That if one assumes the classes of signs,

$\boxed{S}$ s, and the classes of responses, $\boxed{R}$ s, mediated by the same r_Ms to be functionally equivalent, then " . . . this is tantamount to supposing them to be *instances of the same response"*; Fodor was here referring to the *mediating* function of r_M and not its representing function. (2) That unless one assumes that signs ($\boxed{S}$ s) are functionally equivalent to significates (Ss) and that mediators (r_Ms) are functionally equivalent to their source behaviors (R_Ts), we must have ambiguity of reference; here Fodor is referring to the *representing* function of r_M. We are now at the crux of this particular debate, so let us inspect the argument carefully.

Fodor correctly notes the distinction between stimulus or response *types* and *tokens,* but he draws incorrect conclusions from it. *Whereas all response tokens of the same type constitute "the same response", all response types mediated by the same* s_M *do not constitute "the same response".* The rodent intention (s_M) "to obtain food" may be expressed by various tokens of the "bar-pressing" type *in the context of a Skinner Box,* by various tokens of the "running" type *in the context of a maze,* and by various tokens of the "digging" type *in the context of a city dump;* "bar-pressing", "running", and "digging" are all functionally equivalent responses with respect to the "food obtaining" significance-intention process (a particular $r_M \longrightarrow s_M$ mediator), *but they clearly are not "the same response" by virtue of the fact that they are contextually conditioned.*

With regard to Fodor's assertion (1) —that assuming functional equivalence among the signs and responses mediated by the same r_M is tantamount to assuming them to be "the same" stimuli and responses, hence reducing mediation theory to single-stage theory—I accept the claim of functional equivalence but reject as false the implied consequences. Perception of the APPLE object and the heard word "apple" may be functionally equivalent with respect to eliciting a common meaningful reaction, but they are hardly "the same stimulus", as is clearly indicated by the fact that one may REACH FOR the object but hardly the word (i.e., they are not tokens of the same stimulus type); likewise nonlinguistic REACHING FOR and linguistic "asking for" are functionally equivalent with respect to a common intention, but they are hardly "the same response" since they occur in different total stimulus contexts. Representational mediation theory cannot be reduced to single-stage theory by this means.

Turning now to his assertion (2) —that we must have ambiguity of reference unless we assume functional equivalence between sign and significate and between mediator and source, and if we do we are back in the one-to-one bind—I reject this claim of functional equivalence along with the implied consequence for theory. If sign and significate are functionally equivalent, then they must be shown to be substitutable for each other with respect to the same response (either r_M or R_T); but *sign* does not elicit R_T, but rather r_M (which Fodor earlier admitted was not the same as R_T) and *significate* does not elicit r_M, but rather R_T. I may cry "ouch!" and undergo an "emergency" reaction to a pinprick, but hardly to the *word* "pinprick"; I may say "sharp" to the verbal sign "pinprick" in an association test, but hardly in response to being pinpricked. Identity of responses to sign and significate is the absurdity of the (Pavlovian) substitution theory of meaning. Via exactly the same arguments, r_Ms are not functionally equivalent to their R_Ts—they are not elicited by the same stimuli.

Does this mean that we are impaled on the other horn of Fodor's dilemma—ambiguity of reference? Not at all. Signs would refer ambiguously to different significates only if the *same* mediator derives from *different* behavior types produced by different significate types. The componential one-to-one representing relation between r_Ms and R_Ts— which I must accept—rules out such ambiguity of reference, but it does *not* permit reduction of Osgoodian representational mediation theory to Skinnerian single-stage theory.

Issue II: The Case of the Invisible Element

Bever, Fodor, and Garrett (1968) claimed that certain conceptual competences violate what they call "the terminal meta-postulate" of any theory of learning that could be "associative" in nature—namely: "Associative principles are rules defined over the 'terminal' vocabulary of a theory, i.e., over the vocabulary in which behavior is described. Any description of an n-tuple of elements between which an association can hold must be a possible description of the actual behavior." (p.583). Freely translated, this would seem to say that any associative theory (description, explanation) of learning cannot contain any elements that are *abstractly* related to what is observed. If such competences can be demonstrated, and if they cannot be accommodated by existing learning theory (which should be the case by definition), then learning theory is insufficient in principle. If, however, such competences *can* be accommodated by some existing learning theory, then we have a paradox: either the theory in question is not associative in nature *or* the proposed terminal meta-postulate is false.

A Mirror-Image Language

To illustrate the kind of competence they have in mind, Bever et al. describe a simple mirror-image language. Figure III.2 *A* shows a sample of "utterances" in this language, both "grammatical" ones (G) and "nongrammatical" ones (NG). The simplest system of rules which a

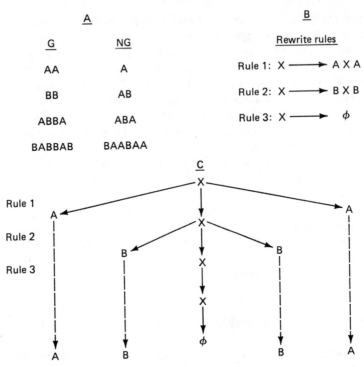

Fig. III.2. A grammar of a mirror-image language (after Bever, Fodor, and Garrett, 1968)

linguist (or a child) exposed to such a sample might extract as its grammar is " . . . precisely one which violates the terminal postulate . . . one which allows rules defined over elements that are precluded from appearing in the terminal vocabulary" (p.584). Note that the unordered rewrite (or expansion) rules for X (Fig. III.2 *B*) include one which rewrites X *out of existence* in the terminal expression—hence my calling this "The Case of the Invisible Element". Figure III.2 *C* represents the generation of one of a potentially infinite set of grammatical mirror-image utterances, ABBA. The length of an "utterance", of course, simply depends upon how long application of Rule 3 is postponed. Now many psychologists might be inclined to write this demonstration off as simply "a cute little trick", completely irrelevant to the real world of behavior, including language behavior. But it just so happens that rules of precisely this type also describe center-embedded sentences. I borrow an example from Bever (1968): *Insecticides exterminators manufacture fumigate apartments.*

Anticipating a Neobehavioristic Interpretation of Sentence Production

In what follows I will try to show that componential s_M (an intention) has the same property of "eliminating itself" in the process of decoding meanings into utterances and thus not appearing in the overt behavior it mediates. I will not be making any claims about sufficiency in detail at this point but merely a claim for sufficiency in principle.

Let us begin with probably the earliest and simplest type of "sentence" production—the development of spontaneous labeling of familiar environmental objects. Paradigm 1, *Naming,* in Fig. III.3 shows the perceptual form of the BALL object, $\boxed{S}_0$, as being encoded into a representational mediation process whose code-strip would include such basic features (componential r_m) as ⁺Concrete, ⁻Animate, ⁺Graspable, and so forth. Since particular human languages have *arbitrary* lexical rules—the particular vocalizations used to refer to sets of things and events—some form of *imitation* must be involved in learning these rules, at least in the early stages. So the top line in Fig. III.3 represents the imitative relation between the adult's form, heard "ball", and the child's approximation form, "baw". The critical relation (starred) between an automatic s_M pattern (intention) and an utterance represents *a semantic decoding unit;* as can be seen, such decoding units are independent of the classes of antecedent signs (whether perceptual or linguistic).

But now look at Paradigm 2, *Differentiating.* Here the child, a little

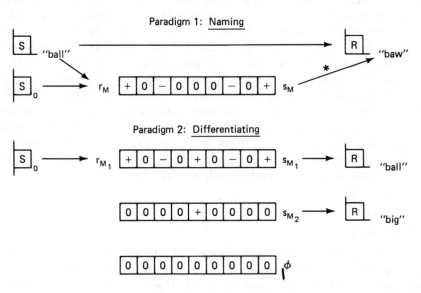

Fig. III.3. Early stages in semantic decoding

older and wiser now, is gazing at a BIG BALL—that is, big in perceptual contract with the sizes of most other ball objects in his prior experience— and has the urge as well as the opportunity to talk. His lexicon does not include any single decoding unit for the entire code-strip of features set up by this perceptual sign—nor does the adult lexicon, for reasons of a larger economy—and the child faces one of his early *syntactic* problems. Outputting of a subset of features to the lexicon (and hence into vocalizing "ball") eliminates most of the components of the set (shifting s_{M_1} to s_{M_2} in the semantic system), but s_{M_2} still includes a $^+$Relative Size feature ("large for an X") common to much prior perceptual and linguistic *encoding* experience in comprehending.

At some point we might expect a two-word utterance such as "ball . . . big!" Later in development, temporary holding of the output features corresponding to "ball" while first emitting the lexical item expressing the $^+$Relative Size feature—that is, saying "big" and *then* "ball"—will produce auditory feedback which *does* match the adult form and hence corresponds to the child's comprehension model. In the argot of learning theory, this matching is an instance of *secondary reinforcement* (it *sounds* right), and this is one of the conditions for learning the "rules" of one's language. The last line in Paradigm 2 shows an "empty" code-strip; s_M *has eliminated itself*. For the moment, LAD has no urge to talk—or at least nothing more to talk about!

What about mirror-image utterances, as represented by center-embed-ded sentences? Figure III.4 applies the same notions to the adult encoding of a sentence with a single center-embedding—appropriately enough, *intentions speakers express disappear*. Again for convenience in expo-sition, I have clumped the hypothetical features into units corresponding to words—although I am sure things are not this simple. Outputting the bundle of features corresponding to *intentions* (which can be immediately expressed) and the bundle corresponding to *disappear* (which must be temporarily stored in a buffer), we have reduced s_{M_1} to s_{M_2}. Now output-ting the signals corresponding to *speakers* and *express* (immediately expressable) and then finally those stored for *disappear* (now expressa-ble) we have reduced s_{M_2} to s_{M_3}. And since s_{M_3} is now "featureless", it can produce no further encoding and, in effect, *has disappeared* (like the $X \rightarrow \emptyset$ in Figure III.2C).

Conclusions

I have demonstrated that, in the process of utterance creation, represen-tational mediation processes are (a) hypothetical constructs (abstract elements) which (b) are essential in this theory for the discriminative selection of units of observable speech behavior, yet (c) never appear in the *contemporary* behavior itself, even though they are derived from

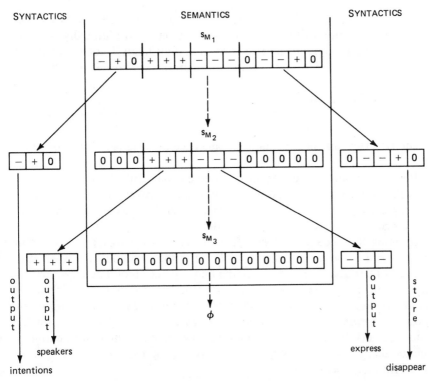

Fig. III.4. Hypothetical process for decoding a center-embedded sentence

overt behavior in the *history* of the organism. I would therefore claim that *in principle*—which the the issue—s_M has precisely the properties of X in the Bever et al. demonstration.

But if this is the case, then we do face the potential paradox with which I introduced this section: It would be most difficult to maintain that representational mediation theory is *not* associationistic in nature, given its basic Hullian operating principles. Is it possible that the Bever, Fodor, and Garrett meta-postulate is false? In searching for the *origins* of this meta-postulate about association theories in the Bever et al. paper on "A Formal Limitation of Associationism", all I find is the following statement: that certain conceptual competences fall outside the power of associationism, " . . . given the kinds of constraints on learning principles *that have traditionally defined associationism. Moreover, it can be shown that there are infinitely many such counterexamples* to the adequacy of associationistic accounts of learning. . . . *We assume* that the following meta-postulate is a necessary condition on any set of principles being called 'associative' . . . " (pp. 582–583, italics mine). No documentation of the constraints which have "traditionally" defined associationism is given, and of the "infinitely many" counterexamples only Lashley's (1951) paper on the problem of serial order in behavior is cited. So we seem to be left with "we assume" as the primary justification for this meta-postulate.

Issue III: The Role of Language Competence in Language Performance

Although Chomsky has repeatedly denied that grammatical derivations have anything directly to do with how speaker-hearers process sentences, he typically goes on to say (e.g., 1965, p. 9) that any reasonable model of language use will incorporate the generative grammar " . . . that expresses the speaker-hearer's knowledge of the language." Assuming that, more or less by definition of the field, psycholinguistic theories have as their goal the understanding and prediction of language *performance,* the issues here become, first, *what is the nature of linguistic competence?* and, second, *what constraints does it place upon the possible forms that performance theories can take?* (I remind you that this is a very brief and undocumented summary of much more extensive material available in the Chapter 2 of my in progress *Toward an Abstract Performance Grammar.*)

The Nature of Linguistic Competence

It appears that "knowing" a language comes down to being aware of the regularities in one's own language performances (and those of others) and being able to make judgments about potential samples of it. When the *real* speaker-hearers are *extraordinary* (e.g., specially sensitive and trained linguists), then this "knowing" can be systematized and becomes a characterization of what Chomsky has termed *linguistic competence.* Thus the *idealized* speaker-hearer—that uses only these rules and is therefore always grammatical (albeit usually a-pragmatic and often incomprehensible)—is a complex theoretical construction based on the "grammaticality" judgments of linguists about (usually) their own language performances. When the *real* speaker-hearers are *ordinary,* then their intuitions are called "acceptability" judgments and their behaviors in diverse language tasks are termed *linguistic performance.* There is thus no distinction *in kind* to be made between the cognitive capabilities contributing to what is called competence ("grammaticality" judgments) and those contributing to what is called performance ("acceptability" judgments). But since linguists are *not* ordinary speakers and are *not* independent evaluating instruments, it follows that *the intuitions which*

*create a competence theory cannot also be the ultimate determinants of
the validity of that theory*—this is the highroad to what I have called
"scholarly schizophrenia", be it an individual malady or one shared by
a group.

Constraints of Competence upon Performance Theories

We can trace here a brief history of decreasingly strong claims: Stage
(1), announced by Miller and Chomsky (1963), viewed linguistic competence as *an idealized model of linguistic performance.* But since, among
many other problems, the competence model has asymmetric rules
(expanding) whereas the performance model must have symmetric rules
for comprehending (contracting) and producing (expanding), in Stage (2)
competence came to be construed by most psycholinguists as *a central
component of a performance model*—with comprehending being handled,
not by any reversal of the rewrite rules, but by *analysis by synthesis.*
But it soon became obvious to most psycholinguists that such "spinning
through alternative generatings until a match is found for the input
surface form" would be incredibly inefficient. The present Stage (3), in
which linguistic competence is viewed as *an independent abstract system*
remote from performance, was brought about by the abject failure of the
Correspondence Hypothesis—that the psycholinguistic processing difficulty of sentences should be predictable from their derivational complexity grammatically. Thus, I would agree with Pylyshyn (1973, pp.45–46)
in his conclusion that " . . . the major contribution of the competence
theory is the isolation of an important class of non-behavioral evidence
to be considered by a broader psychological theory of cognition."

The Insufficiency of Representational Neobehaviorism Circa 1968

The reason for my not publishing in 1968 a paper titled "Is Neobehaviorism Up [sic!] a Blind Alley?"—which dealt with the three main issues
in the "paradigm clash"—(above)—was precisely that the drafting of it
had made me painfully aware of the insufficiency of my analysis of
sentencing. Although it did account for the "in principle" issue of having
abstract entities in an associationistic theory, it also revealed starkly the
inadequacy of a *structureless* semantic representational system. The
complex componential "code-strips" representing the meanings of whole
cognitions ("ideas") could only *arbitrarily* be "partitioned" into subsets
of components in encoding and decoding sentences; there was no way,
for example, that the meanings of *John loves Mary* and *Mary loves John*
could be distinguished. The question in the early 1970s was whether this
was, indeed, an insufficiency *in principle* or, with elaboration of the same
basic theory, it could be shown to be an insufficiency *in practice.* My

research and theorizing for the past near-decade have been devoted to this elaboration of theory, as will be seen.

On the Natures of Scientific Revolutions and Pendula Swings

Thomas Kuhn on Revolutions in the Physical Sciences

Since Thomas Kuhn's insightful little book on *The Structure of Scientific Revolutions* (1962) has achieved the status of being almost "required reading" for linguists, philosophers, and psychologists in recent years, I can be excused for presenting only the essence of his analysis.

At certain time-points in the history of any science one can identify an *established paradigm*. Such a paradigm is characterized by the near-universal acceptance by the practitioners of that science of a common set of underlying assumptions—metaphysical, methodological, theoretical, topical (what are the significant problems to be studied), and criterial (what standards are to be used in evaluating facts and theories). These function like a set of rules according to which the "game" of that science is to be played.

This process, while accumulating a great deal of data and enhancing the confidence of the scientists involved, inevitably leads to *anomalies*. Anomalies are observations which are not predictable from the theories generated within the particular paradigm at the time new facts appear. Since normal science is essentially a problem-solving business, and its practitioners are (with good reason) confident in the established paradigm, these regions of anomaly attract the most intensive effort of the most capable scientists. If the anomalies persist and multiply, then that science moves into a state of *crisis*. If the crisis is due to an insufficiency *in principle* of the paradigm, and the *extraordinary,* (nonnormal) *science* characteristic of crises keeps expanding the regions of anomaly, then the stage *is* set for revolution.

In their attempts to patch up a paradigm that is in principle insufficient, its loyal practitioners resort to increasingly *ad hoc* extensions—these typically becoming first clumsy, then absurd, and ultimately excrescent. The paradigm becomes less aesthetically pleasing, more ugly than elegant. Younger people in that science become increasingly dissatisfied and begin to debate the underlying assumptions of the paradigm—the previously unquestioned rules of the game—with their elders. But we still do not have a *scientific revolution*. Mere insufficiency is not sufficient. Scientists must have an *alternative paradigm* to shift their allegiance *to,* and this means a paradigm that makes different underlying assumptions and changes the rules of the game—usually the creation of a genius who can break through the "world view" provided by the old paradigm. To the extent that the new paradigm is successful, there is an accelerating shift from the old to the new—accompanied by often rancorous debate and increasing difficulties of communication, because of the often unexpressed differences in underlying assumptions.

On Pendula Swings

We must now inquire into another phenomenon in the history of science which may give one the *illusion* of revolutionary paradigm shift when in fact there is none. Fadlike shifts repeatedly occur on the underlying assumptions about science—about metaphysics, about methods, about theory construction, about what are significant topics, about relevant criteria, and many other matters—to which (following Esper, 1968) I shall give the collective name "pendula swings". Although these various pendula do not necessarily swing in parallel, they often do—e.g., a shift from metaphysical dualism to materialistic monism being paralleled by a shift from rationalism to empiricism in methodology—and what is especially interesting, and probably reflective of the generality of Zeitgeists, is the fact that the swings in interactive sciences tend to be somewhat in parallel, too, or at least this seems to have been true of linguistics and psychology.

In Table III.1 I've listed a number of these pendula, categorized roughly according to the primary types of implicit "rules" (underlying assumptions) in linguistic and psychological paradigms. Under ONE POLE I locate the radical Behaviorism identified with Watson and Skinner and the Descriptivism identified With Bloomfield; under OTHER POLE, with no pejorative intent, I locate the Structuralism identified with Wundt and Titchener and the Generativism identified with Chomsky. I am sure there would be arguments about both my assignments of pendula to facets of the sciences and about the implied locations of the respective paradigms at the termini of the pendula swings. But the main points I wish to make in this brief overview do not pivot on such details.

METAPHYSICS: Behaviorism and, I suspect, Bloomfieldian Descriptivism involved *materialistic monism* accompanied by a faith in ultimate *reductionism* (all mental events in principle can be reduced to neural events in the physical brain and these in turn ultimately to physics and chemistry); Structuralism and Generativism, on the other hand, are both *dualistic* (cf. Chomsky, *Language and Mind,* 1968) and at least open to *emergent* notions.

METHODOLOGY: Behaviorism and Descriptivism are both clearly *empirical,* the former being *experimental* and the latter being *distributional* in keeping with the natures of their materials; the methodologies of both

Table III.1. Some Pendula that Swing in Linguistics and Psychology

	ONE POLE Behaviorism Descriptivism	OTHER POLE Structuralism Generativism
	←——————————→	
METAPHYSICS:	monistic (materialism) reductionistic	dualistic emergent
METHODOLOGY:	experimental empirical distributional	introspective-intuitive rationalistic transformational
TOPICALITY:	nonhuman subjects associations phonology and morphology message characteristics multilanguage base	human subjects rules syntax and semantics cognitive determination unilanguage base
DATA:	observable behaviors quantitative surface structures	mental states & processes qualitative deep structures
DEVELOPMENT:	experiential species-general language-specific	nativistic species-specific language-general
CRITERIA:	objective behavioristic shared observables	subjective mentalistic shared introspections/ intuitions
THEORY:	inductive elementaristic synthetic peripheralist	deductive wholistic analytic centralist
GOALS:	prediction of performance descriptive adequacy	description of competence explanatory adequacy

Structuralism and Generativism are *rationalistic,* but with the former involving reports of private *introspections* and the latter reports of equally private *intuitions.* Generativism adds the power of *transformational* analysis.

The TOPICALITY category could be expanded almost indefinitely, and obviously the kinds of topics deemed most worthy of study within the paradigms are pretty much bound by which science one is talking about, so topics I have listed are only illustrative.

DATA: The raw data on which hypotheses must be tested are *observed behaviors* (including verbal-report behaviors) for Behaviorists and *sur-*

face structures of languages for Descriptivists—while both may (or may not) insist that these data be *quantitative* in nature; for both Structuralists and Generativists, on the other hand, one's own *mental states and processes* themselves constitute the raw data, and they are essentially *qualitative* in nature.

CRITERIA: These are the important pendula which relate to the admissibility of evidence for or against competing theories; the Behaviorist revolution against Structuralism and the Descriptivist revolution against what might be called Grammarianism were both closely tied to a swing from reliance on *subjective* criteria (introspections and evaluative judgments about how people ought to talk, respectively) to reliance on *objective* criteria (observed behavior and actual talk, respectively); Generativism in linguistics involved a definite return swing of these pendula—toward reliance on *subjective* criteria (of what can and cannot be said grammatically in a given language), with decisions among competing theories depending upon *shared intuitions* (usually engendered by compelling sentential examples vs counterexamples), and with the statement that the whole operation is *mentalistic* being claimed as a virtue.

THEORY: The Behaviorist and Descriptivist extremes of the pendulum relating to the nature of theories can be characterized as largely *inductive* (generalizations about sets of related facts) and *elementaristic* (aimed at identifying the nature and number of elements at each hierarchical level), with each higher level of units assumed to be *synthesized* from combinations of the units at each lower level, and also largely *peripheralist*; both Structuralism (and Gestaltism) and Generativism tend more toward the other poles of these pendula—being more *deductive* (rationalistic predictions from interlocking sets of abstract entities), *wholistic* (images, thoughts, or sentence-meanings being viewed as emergent wholes), *analytic* (in the sense of lower-order units only being analyzable in terms of their functions in the larger wholes), and certainly *centralist* (emphasis being on the states and processes which intervene between observable inputs and outputs).

GOALS: The goal of Bloomfieldian linguistics was precisely what gives name to its paradigm—what Chomsky has called *descriptive adequacy*— this in sharp contrast to the goal of the Generativists—*explanatory adequacy,* i.e., to characterize that *competence* of speakers of any language which enables them to produce and understand a potentially infinite set of novel sentences; on the psychological side, we also have a clear split here—the goal of Structuralism being to arrive, via shared introspections, at a *descriptively adequate* (valid) characterization of the contents of consciousness in the adult human mind and that of Behaviorism being *the prediction* (explanation) *of performance* (be it of rats in mazes, of children in school, or of people producing and understanding sentences).

Transformational Grammar: A Revolution?

Pendula swings of the sort I have described are the stuff of which real scientific revolutions are made—the paradigmatic shifts in metaphysical assumptions, in accepted methods and criteria, in theory construction and in goals—but they go on continuously and do not *in themselves* constitute a genuine revolution. My characterization of the repetitive oscillations in assumptions, methods, and values of scientists as "pendula swings" may be a bit misleading, implying lack of any real scientific progress. The image of a progressively rising, *pendula spiral* would be more accurate: each swing toward a given pole is driven by felt insufficiencies in the paradigm at the other pole; in the course of the swing new problems are set, new insights are gained, and eventually new anomalies encountered; if the crisis period has generated more adequate theories within the old paradigm, and they can now handle the anomalies that gave rise to the crisis as well as their previous areas of apparent sufficiency, then a return swing starts and gains momentum. But the pendula do not all return to the same loci. What has been described here is thus a persisting state of oscillating *competition* between two (or more) viable paradigms in a science.

How Does One Recognize a Revolution When He May Be in One?

Under what added conditions can we say that a true scientific revolution, rather than just continued competition, has occurred? One condition is that *there must be a new paradigm,* in the sense of a well-motivated, internally coherent alternative theory that grows out of the changed assumptions ("rules of the game"). According to Kuhn (1962, pp.77–79), "the decision to reject one paradigm is always simultaneously the decision to accept another, and the judgment leading to that decision involves the comparison of paradigms with nature *and* with each other . . . to reject one paradigm without simultaneously substituting another is to reject science itself."

Another condition for scientific revolution is a convincing *demonstration that the old paradigm is insufficient in principle.* As I have already noted, mere insufficiency in detail or completeness (i.e., relevant problems which have not yet been explored within the paradigm) is *not* a basis for denying the potential viability of an older paradigm. As Kuhn (pp.144–46) points out, instead of competitive verification in terms of the number and significance of problems solved by two paradigms, demonstration of insufficiency in principle requires *falsification*—a clear negative result of a test which involves some fundamental and inherent assumptions of the paradigm in question.

A third condition which must be met is that, ideally, *the new paradigm must incorporate* (on its own terms, of course) *solutions to the problems the old paradigm could handle.* I say "ideally" because at any point in the period of a paradigm shift there will only be partial overlap in the problems handled by the competing paradigms—fewest at the beginning, where it is the anomalies for the old that are foci of attack by the new. But the new paradigm must *in principle* be capable of such incorporation. The reason for this is very clear: If the new paradigm is *only* capable of handling in well-motivated, coherent ways the phenomena which constituted the insolvable anomalies for the old paradigm, then what we have is not revolution *but partitioning into separate sciences.* This state of affairs could hold for Generativism vs Neobehaviorism—as extended to human cognizing generally—if a generative theory of human cognizing could *only* handle sentence comprehension and production, and a neobehavioristic theory *only* nonsentencing performance.

Evaluation of the Impact of Chomsky upon Linguistics

There is no question but the work of Chomsky and his students constituted a genuine revolution within the science of linguistics. It met all of the criteria that distinguish revolutionary paradigm shifts from ordinary pendula swings: (1) Chomsky's generative grammar provided a well-motivated alternative to the phrase-structure grammars of the Descriptivists. (2) Chomsky has presented convincing arguments that phrase-structure grammars are capable of attaining only descriptive adequacy, but in principle not explanatory adequacy. (3) Generative grammars, with their deep structures and transformational relations to surface structures, can handle phenomena of sentential relationships that could only clumsily be treated in the Descriptivist paradigm, but it incorporates the phenomena (e.g., hierarchial organization, phonology, morphology) for which the older paradigm did seem sufficient—at least in principle, even if syntax and, more recently, semantics have been the main thrusts of the Generativists. And, of course, (4) there has been nearly complete conversion of younger linguists to the new paradigm, along with the proliferation of introductory and advanced texts written within the new framework that is typical of scientific revolutions, according to Kuhn.

Probably as a result of the population explosion (including the sheer numbers of linguists) and the communications-technology explosion (including rapid multicopying of "hot-off-the-typewriter" mimeos, dittos, and xeroxes), pendula swings and even revolutions in science seem to be cycling faster and faster. We have already seen what look like *counterrevolutions* within the Chomskyan paradigm—and this in little more than a decade after its inception (with *Syntactic Structures,* 1957). However, most of the paradigmatic shifts that have characterized the post-*Aspects* (1965) period of counterrevolution in linguistics can be viewed as attempts to push even further the claim of explanatory as contrasted with descriptive adequacy.

One has been a shift in relative priorities, from syntax to semantics. By 1971 Maclay—in his "Overview" of the linguistics section of *Semantics: An Interdisciplinary Reader in Philosophy, Linguistics and Psychology* (ed. by Steinberg and Jakobovits)—was able to say that "all of the papers in this section fall within what we have called the third period of generative-transformational theory", which includes *generative semantics*. Since that time there has been a veritable explosion of papers and debates on generative semantics, but—interestingly—although it represents a shift in priorities, most of this work remains well within the Chomskyan paradigm as far as underlying rationalistic, logic-based, generative-transformational methodology is concerned. However, as Maclay (1971, pp.178–181) suggested, the work on generative semantics may be having a "domino" effect: first, the autonomy of syntax is questioned; then, "if no principled boundary can be drawn between [syntax and semantics] . . . there can be no distinct level of syntactic deep structure and the question of whether or not semantics is interpretive becomes irrelevant" (p.178); and once the existence of a deep-structure base is questioned, "the autonomy of competence may well be the next victim" (p.180). Implied in this developmental sequence, of course, is the ultimate substitution of an elaborated (generative) *semantic component* for the deep structure of the *Aspects* syntactic component, leaving the latter responsible solely for transformations upon information from the "deep" semantic component in the mediation between surface and deep structures. This, as will be seen, is exactly the direction my own performance theory has moved.

There have been other extensions in the search for explanatory adequacy that have been developing more or less in parallel with the generative semantics thrust. One of these is an extension of concern to explaining the *logical* (and, as it turns out, *psycho-logical*) *presuppositions and implications of sentences*—the nagging question always being whether the readily demonstrable phenomena are to be considered intra- (i.e., part of the grammar) or extralinguistic. Another shift in priorities has been from interest in language as an abstract object to language as a means of social communication, now referred to as *sociolinguistics*. And yet another correlated shift toward explanatory adequacy has been away from the use of context-free (abstracted, textual) and toward context-dependent (ordinary conversational) sentential materials as the more relevant data for linguistic analysis.

Two related trends—toward viewing sentences as "speech acts" and as obeying certain "conversational postulates"—have their source in philosophical studies of language: (1) From the writings of Austin (particularly his *How to Do Things with Words,* 1962) has come the interest of linguists in *speech acts* (as epitomized in philosopher Searle's

1969 book with that title) and here the extended search for explanatory adequacy has been to incorporate the social intentions underlying a speaker's utterances [cf the papers in *Syntax and Semantics: Volume 3, Speech Acts* (1975, ed. by P. Cole and J.L. Morgan)]. (2) Coming directly from the writings of H. Paul Grice—see his "Logic and Conversation" in the same collection on *Syntax and Semantics* above—has been linguists' interest in *conversational postulates;* concern about, e.g., "Sincerity Conditions" (note the strangeness, but not ungrammaticality, of *I promise to pay you back, but I don't intend to*) and "Reasonableness Conditions" (reasonable requests, for example, are for things the speaker really wants done, that he knows the hearer can do and would be willing to do, and so forth).

The price of such extension for linguistics might, quite simply, be *loss of identity as a scientific discipline.* Howard Maclay, at the conclusion of his "Overview" to the linguistics section of the Steinberg and Jakobovits (1971) volume, put it this way: "It is evident that linguistics cannot profitably expand until its domain comes to include everything about human beings that is in some way connected to the acquisition and use of language," and he continued with the speculation that the next development will be a *contraction* of the boundaries of linguistics as a science.

However, there is another real possibility: The search for explanatory adequacy has led to the quasi-incorporation of a variety of social science disciplines (broadly speaking). Given the way new specializations develop in academia from closely interacting "modules of knowing" originating in quite separate "departments", a *diffusion* of linguistics is also likely—into Philolinguistics, Psycholinguistics, Sociolinguistics, and . . . Communolinguistics? . . . while leaving a "hard core" Linguistics consistent with Maclay's speculation above. As a matter of fact, this seems to be "in process" at the present time. As far as psychology is concerned, just as the Chomskyan revolution against Descriptivism entailed a movement toward this field [to the extent that Chomsky (*Language and Mind,* 1968) could refer to linguistics as "a branch of cognitive psychology"], so does much of the counter-revolution represent a much further movement in this direction—to the extent that the concerns of the "Young Turks" are becoming practically indistinguishable from those of many psycholinguists.

Evaluation of the Impact of Chomsky upon Psychology

Chomsky's carefully documented and highly critical review (1959) of B. F. Skinner's *Verbal Behavior* was aimed primarily at the insufficiency in principle of Skinner's attempt to extend his single-stage version of behaviorism to language performance. However, Chomsky clearly intended the review to be a critique of behaviorist conceptions of cognitive processes in general. Although a few "replies" to this review have appeared, they were a decade late (Suppes, 1969; MacCorquodale, 1970) and Skinner himself has never countered Chomsky's attack—thus fostering the impression that behaviorists *had* nothing to say in their defense. The MacCorquodale response did recognize the "paradigmatic clash" but did little to respond to the Chomsky review on these terms. In part, at least, this seems to be because MacCorquodale did not do his "homework" on generative linguistics as thoroughly as Chomsky did his on Skinnerian behaviorism.

In terms of the conditions I suggested for distinguishing a genuine scientific revolution from mere pendula swings in a competition between opposing paradigms, I think one is forced to conclude that—at least, up to this point in time—the impact of the Chomskyan TGG upon cognitive psychology generally, and even upon psycholinguistics particularly, cannot be characterized as a revolution. Although there has been large-scale conversion *away from* behaviorism in any form and *toward* the rationalism and mentalism of Chomsky, this condition is not in itself sufficient, as Kuhn notes, and can better be viewed as a "revulsion" than as a revolution. The other three identifying conditions for a scientific revolution clearly have not been met.

(1) *There has been no attempt to incorporate solutions to problems successfully handled by the old paradigm.* These would include solutions for (explanations of) diverse verbal conditioning phenomena (e.g., acquisition and extinction of verbal habits, semantic generalization and discrimination, spontaneous recovery, and the like) and diverse verbal learning phenomena (e.g., verbal operant behaviors, serial learning, transfer and retention, and the like), to say nothing of development of the perceptual and motor skills involved in learning phonetic codes.

(2) *To date there has been developed no new paradigm for psycholinguistics.* By this I mean, in the sense of a principled, internally coherent theory of language *performance.* Generative grammar itself has not proven to yield predictions about performance in any obvious (direct) way, or any nonobvious way for that matter, and the combination of this with the revulsion against behaviorism in any form has resulted in what could fairly be called a state of "a-theoretical chaos" in psycholinguists. Much of the research being reported is the purest empiricism, devoid of anything but vague testimonials to rationalism couched in lay mentalistic terminology, and certainly not tests of deductions from any general theory of language performance. There are a plethora of mini-theories, of course—about memory for ideas, about the organization of semantic

memory, about linguistic processes in deductive reasoning, comparing sentences with pictures, drawing inferences, and the like. Such proliferation of mini-theories is a state of affairs characteristic of a time of crisis in a science.

(3) *The old paradigm has not been shown to be insufficient in principle.* This, it will be recalled, requires demonstration of the failure of a theory in a situation where one or more of the basic tenets of its paradigm are entailed—thus, falsification of its predictions in a situation where they must be made. I believe this can be demonstrated—and, indeed, has been—for all *nonrepresentational* (meaningless) versions of behaviorism (mediational or otherwise), however.

All this is *not* to imply, of course, that the Chomskyan revolution in linguistics has had little impact on psycholinguistics and cognitive psychology more generally. The sharply increasing curve of citation of Chomsky's writings is in itself mute testimony to the impact. It is doubtful if psychologists would have involved themselves so soon in the complexities of sentencing had it not been for this impact (cf. my own presidential address to the American Psychological Association in 1963, "On Understanding and Creating Sentences").

Needless to say, the elderly dinosaur was following these developments with great interest, and even the casual observer could see the brightening gleam in his eye and the increasing vigor with which he flicked his tail. By the early 1970s he had discovered a new field of semantic daisies—one that grew in a wondrous variety of little bands (which he called "cogs") made up of chains of linked blooms—and he fed upon them with relish while he refurbished and expanded the shrine for his paradigm. The denouement of the Competence/Performance distinction had paved the way (some might say paradoxically) for a new, more balanced, and potentially very productive relation between linguists and psycholinguists in what Maclay (1973) has called The Cognitive Period of the 1970s.

And in the Midwest this old dinosaur and his cogophile companions had also been moving happily into the new relationship. He contributed a paper titled "Where Do Sentences Come From?" to the Steinberg–Jakobovits collection; his main point was to demonstrate that there is an intimate interaction between nonlinguistic and linguistic channels in the process of Simply Describing ordinary events, and hence that these channels must share some deeper cognitive level that cannot, in principle, be characterized by purely *linguistic* constructs and rules. With one of his friends, Meredith Richards, he even invaded the heartland of the linguistic domain by publishing an article in *Language* (1973) titled "From Yang and Yin to *and* or *but*", in which laws of cognitive congruence and incongruence were used to predict the discriminative use of these conjunctions in simple conjoined sentences of the form X is ADJ_1 _____ ADJ_2—a frame which, linguistically speaking, will accept either *and* or *but*.

In the spring of 1972, back from several long trips around the world in connection with the continuing cross-cultural project—which had become something like a dinosaur having a bear by the tail!—what we call our Cog Group at Illinois began to hold regular idea-suggesting and critiquing sessions. We are trying to build a fresh conception of "where sentences come from and go to"—or, going back to Watt's (1970) notions, you could say that we are trying to build an Abstract Performance Grammar on psychological as well as linguistic bases. These Cog Group sessions have been exciting for the old dinosaur, downright rejuvenating, in fact. And they've been good intellectual fun for all—particularly, I guess, when the old fellow tries to put his baby booties back on and intuit how his prelinguistic world was structured cognitively!

Structure and Meaning in Cognizing

Orientation

The major work for which these Lectures are an "anticipation" will be titled *Toward an Abstract Performance Grammar,* this being taken from the well-known article by W. C. Watt ("On Two Hypotheses Concerning Psycholinguistics", 1970). He questions whether the deep *mental grammar* (MG) could be equated with a *competence grammar* characterized by any *linguistic grammar,* deriving from the intuitions of linguists about relations among sentence in a language. He then goes on to state that the deep mental grammar must be equated with an *abstract performance grammar* (APG) which is *not* characterizable by any purely linguistic grammar. His main argument is that the competence grammar which systematizes intuitions of linguists maximizes one economy criterion (deep syntactic relations between sets of sentences having different surface structures—e.g., x, y, where x are full passives and y truncate passives) and the APG that systematizes language performance maximizes another (" . . . a premium on economy of derivation of individual sentential paradigms" (p.187), x and y independently, in order to most efficiently satisfy pragmatic demands of communication). But aside from casual reference to the language performances of ordinary speaker-hearers (particularly children), Watt is quite vague about how an APG is to be characterized (and thus we are left with MG $\equiv$ APG = ?). This book, and these Lectures, will be an attempt to reduce somewhat the "emptiness" symbolized by that ? mark.

For the mental grammar I will substitute the notion of a *"deep" cognitive system*—the "where sentences and other perceived events *go to* in comprehending" and the "where sentences and other intentional behaviors *come from* in expressing". As you will see, my APG is essentially semantic in nature, but it is a highly *structured* semantic processing system. This lecture will introduce you to the structural mechanisms I think must be postulated for an abstract performance grammar—that is, a theory of language *performance*. I will also have something to say about the source and identification of semantic features. The general—and I guess one could say "radical"—thrust of the theory embodies such underlying notions as the following:

(1) that the "deep" cognitive system is essentially semantic in nature, with syntax involved solely in transformations between this structured semantic system and the surface forms of sentences produced and received;

(2) that the structures developed and utilized in prelinguistic cognizing determine the most "natural" cognitive structures for later sentence understanding and creating;

(3) that the more surface forms of sentential inputs and outputs correspond to these "natural" structures, the more easily will they be processed;

(4) that this "deep" cognitive system is shared by both linguistic and nonlinguistic (perceptual) information-processing channels, which continue to interact throughout adult communicative activities;

(5) that the most basic ("primitive") dynamics in cognizing, and hence communicating, are psycho-logical (affective) rather than logical (denotative);

(6) that sentencing (comprehending and producing) in ordinary communication is always context-dependent, influenced probablistically by contemporary linguistic (conversational, discursive) and nonlinguistic (situational, social) factors;

(7) that the only way to extract what is universal in human communicative behavior from what is unique to particular languages and cultures is via cross-linguistic and cross-cultural studies utilizing demonstrably comparable methods.

The most gross notions of this APG appear in the postulation of *three levels* of cognitive processing on both encoding and decoding sides of the behavioral equation. To refresh your memory, I refer you to the "Little Black Egg" (Fig. II.1). Structurally, the Projection Level reflects the *isomorphic* relations between peripheral receptors and effectors and their correlates in the sensory and motor projection areas of the brain— *icons* in encoding (comprehending) and *motons* in decoding (expressing); functionally, these relations are *unmodifiable by experience*, "wired in". Structurally, the Integration Level represents the more central organization of icons into *percepts* (in comprehending) and motons into *programs* (in expressing), and organization at this level is *not* assumed to be isomorphic; functionally, both sensory and motor integrations are assumed to be *modifiable by experience*, the cohesiveness of sensory percepts and motor programs varying with the frequencies and redundancies of co-occurrence of the icons (sensory signals) and motons (motor signals) in perceiving and behaving respectively—thus sensory and motor *skills,* including language skills. Structurally, meaningful mediation processes at the Representational Level are related to antecedent percepts as their *significances* (in comprehending) and to subsequent programs for behaving as the *intentions* behind them (in expressing); functionally, these relations are established in experience. Now let me give you just one illustration of the complexity of interactions across these levels.

Salience of the Word in Cognizing—and Why

For a long time I have argued that the word has special status as a psycholinguistic unit—it is Janus-faced, being simultaneously the largest characteristic unit at the meaning*less* sensory integration level and the smallest characteristic unit at the meaning*ful* representational level—but until quite recently (in a series of experiments with my then research assistant, Rumjahn Hoosain, in 1973), I hadn't done anything about it experimentally. Way back in 1957, Greenberg defined the "word" as the smallest meaningful unit that accepts almost unlimited insertion *at* its boundaries—but not *within* its boundaries—hence lending itself to combination with other words to generate a potentially infinite variety of sentences.

Many experiments with the tachistoscope have testified empirically to *an inverse relation between usage-frequency of words and their thresholds for recognition*—the more frequent the usage the shorter the duration of tachistoscopic exposure required. This relation holds for usage-frequency of word *forms,* not for word *meanings* (or senses); at the sensory integration level, the word is a relatively "empty" perceptual form, capable of multiple semantic codings dependent upon context.

Morphemes, Words and Nominal Compounds as Units

In linguistic analysis it is the *smaller* unit, the *morpheme,* that is usually considered to be the minimal form having a meaning; if morphemes also function as salient units in perception, then one would expect language users to recognize the morphemic components of words (e.g., the *de + ceit + ful*) prior to recognition of the words they compose (here, *deceitful*)—this because, being components of many words, morphemes *must* have higher overall frequencies than any particular words they appear in.

What about units *larger* than the word? *Nominal compounds* (like *stumbling block, real estate,* etc.) are the most wordlike, in that their meanings are not simple fusions of the ordinary meanings of their constituents—this in contrast to *ordinary noun phrases* (cf, *he's the stumbling block in this organization* with *stumbling over the block he went sprawling*). Note that, consistent with Greenberg's definition of the word, one can make insertions at the *boundaries* of nominal compounds (*he's an old stumbling block*) but not *within* (**he's a stumbling old block*)—this again in contrast to ordinary noun phrases, where either type of insertion is acceptable (either *that's an old rusty block* or *that's a rusty old block*). If nominal compounds *do* function just like ordinary noun phrases in *perception,* then the tachistoscopic recognition thresholds of the two types should be undifferentiable from each other.

A Series of Interlocking Experiments

In a series of interlocking experiments, Osgood and Hoosain (1974), "Salience of the word as a unit in the perception of language", present evidence *contrary* to both of these expectations—about the perceptual salience of morpheme units (smaller than the word) and ordinary noun phrases (larger than the word) as compared with "wordlike" nominal compounds. All I can do here is spin through a series of displays, with just enough commentary to give a general impression of the results—so I urge you to read over Osgood and Hoosain (1974) for details on methods, results, and theory.

What you should pay attention to, and compare, on *all* the following tables are, not the *guessing thresholds* (columns 2), but the durations in milliseconds of tachistoscopic exposure required for the first of two successive correct recognitions of the stimulus—and these *recognition thresholds* are always given in the column 3s. Let's look first at words vs morphemes (Experiment I). Table IV.1 (I vs II) compares monosyllabic nonword morphemes with words containing those morphemes. Here the mean for morphemes is 19 ms and that for words only 16 ms, and with 27 of 32 subjects going this way, the result is significant at the 0.001 level (one chance in a thousand of being due to chance)—despite the greater length of the words. In Table IV.1 (I vs III) we compare the same morphemes with monosyllabic words of the same length (e.g., *ment* with *mend*) and the mean difference in exposure times is slightly less (19 vs 17 ms), but with 26 of 32 subjects going the predicted way it is still significant at the 0.001 level. Table IV.1 (IV vs V) compares *multisyllabic* nonword combinations of morphemes (like *famness*) with multisyllabic words (like *dashing*); the mean difference in exposure time for recognition was tremendous—36 ms for morpheme combinations vs only 15 ms for

Table IV.1. Thresholds for Words and Morphemes

	1	2	3	4	
I. Monosyllable nonword morphemes					
ment	130	14	19	mant	(3)
mani	17	15	20	male	(3)
fide	76	13	17	tide	(5)
para	29	13	19	pars	(6)
voke	18	14	18	voice	(3)
sist	129	14	18	mist	(3)
cuse	76	16	20	curse	(4)
sult	407	12	19	suit	(7)
Grand mean		14	19		
II. Words containing the morphemes					
mental	41	13	15	menial	(4)
manifest	17	12	14	—	(2)
fidelity	6	15	16	finally	
paradox	3	14	17	pardon	(2)
provoke	15	13	17	provide	(6)
resist	33	18	18	—	
accuse	28	16	17	—	
insult	21	13	14	—	
Grand mean		14	16		
III. Monosyllabic words					
mend	49	14	18	hand	(3)
				mand	(3)
mane	10	14	19	name	(5)
pile	50	13	16	pills	(3)
pave	14	13	16	prove	(3)
poke	13	14	16	pose	(3)
seat	124	13	20	nest	(4)
fuse	7	14	14	—	
salt	100	13	14	—	
Grand mean		14	17		
IV. Multisyllabic nonword morpheme combinations					
famness	135	25	45	famous	(9)
roofism	63	24	35	—	
planial	194	20	23	—	
framive	179	13	44	famine	(2)
artover	606	18	21	actover	(3)
grobion[a]	—	25	35	question	(4)
lossate	86	22	48	—	
henette	36	22	36	benette	(2)
Grand mean		21	36		
V. Multisyllabic words					
dashing	3	15	16	—	
subline	8	13	16	—	
plaster	16	13	14	plastic	(3)
frantic	12	14	16	frontier	(3)
article	153	13	14	artistic	(3)

Table IV.1. (*continued*)

problem[b]	178	13	11	—	
lobster	7	14	15	luster	(3)
harmony	23	13	13	—	
Grand mean		14	15		

[a,b]Grobion and problem are left out in computing grand mean thresholds.

Note—Estimated frequencies of usage per one million words (1), mean duration exposures for first guesses in milliseconds (2), mean duration exposures for correct recognitions (3), and most frequent misperceptions with frequencies in parentheses (4), for monosyllabic nonword morphemes (I), words containing those morphemes (II), monosyllabic words matched in length (III), multisyllabic nonword morpheme combinations (IV), and matched multisyllabic words (V).

multisyllabic words—this difference, with all 32 subjects going the same way, being significant at well below the 0.001 level.

In Experiment II we compared three-letter *trigrams* (nonmorpheme/nonword like *ple*) with three-letter *morphemes* (like *pre*) with three-letter *words* (like *pen*), here with *matched* frequencies of visual usage; as you can see in Table IV.2, trigrams are hardest to recognize, then morphemes, and words are easiest—and the differences across 29 subjects were all significant at the 0.01 level. Clearly throughout these comparisons, the more *uniquely meaningful* the forms the lower the recognition thresholds.

Now let's look at nominal compounds. Table IV.3 presents the data for 13 familiar cases (e.g., *looking glass, stock market, motion picture,* and *peanut butter*). There were 30 subjects, 15 having the compounds first and then the (randomized) single words that make them up and 15 having the single words first and then the compounds. The first thing to note (in column 1) is that the usage frequencies of nominal compounds are very low (only 1 to 7 per million) whereas those for their included words are very high (most AA, greater than 100 per million). Despite this, the first presentation mean differences for compounds (23 ms) vs words (18 ms) are rather small. Note, second, that having their single words presented first (even though randomized) greatly facilitated subsequent recognizing of the nominal compounds (from mean of 23 ms down to 17 ms), *but* having seen the individual words in *nominal compounds first* (at least two clear recognitions) *did not facilitate recognition of their included words one bit* (18 ms means for single words being presented *either* first or second).

We replicated the experiment just described, but using *nonsense compounds* (like *sympathy block, actor general, motion glass,* and *post estate*) and *their* constituent words; Fig. IV.1 compares the results: note,

Table IV.2. Trigrams, Morphemes, and Words

	1	2	3	4	
I. Trigrams					
ple	197	14	22	pie	(12)
pes	4	14	17	pas	(7)
tai	150	13	16	tal	(9)
etu	11	14	18	stu	(4)
ima	25	15	19	—[a]	(2)
ske	36	14	16	she	(6)
eam	293	15	20	cam	(5)
des	135	14	20	dis	(7)
fas	14	13	16	fan	(3)
neu	2	14	14	man	(3)
Grand mean		14	18		
II. Nonword morphemes					
pre	216	13	15	pro	(2)
geo	9	14	15	quo	(2)
tri	167	13	14	—	
epi	17	13	16	api	(3)
iso	24	14	17	isc	(3)
sym	33	14	17	—	
com	301	15	16	con	(2)
dia	75	13	20	dis	(17)
fam	16	12	15	fan	(5)
neo	3	15	19	men	(2)
				meo	(2)
Grand mean		14	16		
III. Words					
pen	161	13	15	pan	(11)
gun	5	13	15	man	(2)
				pun	(2)
tab	164	13	14	—	
ego	10	14	16	—	
jam	16	13	14	—	
six	17	13	14	mix	(4)
can	216	13	13	—	
die	29	12	17	dis	(11)
few	20	13	14	fen	(2)
nil	5	12	14	mil	(2)
				all	(2)
Grand mean		13	15		

[a]ime (2), ina (2), imm (2), ism (2).

Note—Estimated frequencies per one million words (1), mean duration exposures for guesses in milliseconds (2), mean duration exposures for correct recognitions (3), and most frequent misperceptions with frequencies in parentheses (4), for trigrams (I), nonword morphemes (II), and words (III).

Table IV.3. Words and Nominal Compounds

	I. Nominal compounds						II. Words						
	1	2a	2b	3a	3b	4a	1	2a	2b	3a	3b	4	
looking	1	23	16	27	17	looking	—	14	17	18	20	talking	(3)
glass						clean (3)	AA[b]	14	18	21	19	class	(4)
post	1	19	15	20	17	—	AA	15	15	21	21	past	(13)
card							A[c]	17	15	19	17	guard	(2)
town	1	17	13	22	17	—	AA	16	16	18	17	—	(9)
hall							AA	14	16	23	19	ball	
stock	2	20	14	21	16	stock	AA	15	15	19	18	stack	(4)
market						yard (2)	AA	17	17	18	20	—	
attorney	7	23	16	25	17	—	23	16	16	20	17	stationary	(2)
general							AA	14	15	16	17	quarrel	(2)
bowling	1	21	15	26	19	looking	1	15	13	16	17	looking	(2)
green						glass (2)	AA	14	17	17	17	queen	(3)
coast	1	20	16	24	17	—	A	16	20	17	24	closet, green	(2)
guard							AA	16	15	18	16	—	

	(1)	(2a)a	(2b)	(3a)	(3b)	(4)
real estate	4	20	16	23	17	—
motion picture	5	20	15	22	16	—
trap door	2	16	16	19	17	—
lieutenant commander	1	22	17	28	21	lieutenant colonel (5)
stumbling block	1	21	15	25	17	—
peanut butter	—	19	14	20	15	—
Grand mean		20	15	23	17	—

	(1)	(2a)a	(2b)	(3a)	(3b)	(II)
real	AA	14	16	15	17	—
estate	44	16	17	21	22	—
motion	A	16	16	20	20	notion (2)
picture	AA	14	15	15	16	pleasure (2)
trap	42	15	15	19	17	trip (5)
door	AA	15	17	17	19	dear (4)
lieutenant	33	14	13	16	15	limousine (3)
commander	32	15	16	18	17	—
stumbling	—	15	16	18	18	stimulus (2)
block	A	14	15	16	19	black (12)
peanut	7	14	16	16	18	penant, peasant (2)
butter	AA	16	15	19	19	bullet, butcher, butler (2)
Grand mean		15	16	18	18	

a Although guessing threshold times for the compounds include those where Ss reported seeing only one of the constituents of the compounds, such "partial" perceptions are not given in this column.

b Over 100 per million.

c Over 50 per million.

Note—Estimated frequencies per one million words (1), mean duration exposures for guesses in milliseconds for first presentation (2a) and for second presentation (2b), mean duration exposures for correct recognitions for first presentation (3a) and for second presentation (3b), and most frequent misperceptions (for both presentations combined), with frequencies in parentheses (4), for nominal compounds (I) and words (II).

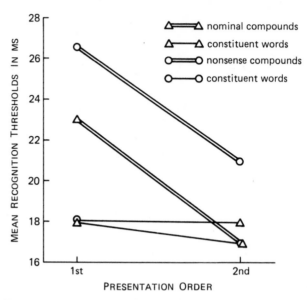

Fig. IV.1. Nominal vs nonsense compounds and constituent words

first, that while prior presentation of *nominal* compounds did *not* facilitate recognition of their included words (lower triangles), prior presentation of *nonsense* compounds *did* (lower circles); note, second, that for both prior and subsequent presentation order, nominal compounds (upper *triangles*) have markedly lower thresholds than nonsense compounds (upper *circles*). Is this due to the nonsensicality of the latter or the "wordlikeness" of the former? The answer was clear in another experiment. As shown in Table IV.4 when nominal compounds are compared with single words *matched for length and usage frequency,* there are no differences whatsoever in recognition thresholds —thus it was the "word-likeness" of nominal compounds.

What are the implications of all this? The most general one is that it is the *meaningfulness* of a perceptual form (linguistic or otherwise) that somehow makes it easier to recognize under conditions of reduced duration or intensity. More specifically still, the richer the semantic coding and the more uniquely that feature-pattern is tied to the particular form, the lower will be the threshold. But what (in theory) is the "how" of this? Figure IV.2 is a non-egglike version of our "little black egg". The crucial thing here is the *feedback* from the Representational (meaningful) Level to the Sensory Integration (perceptual) Level—shown by the dashed arrows from s_M to $\overline{\text{s-s-s}}$. Note that, whereas the feedback for *morphemes* is more amorphous (!), tending to strengthen a variety of forms rather indiscriminately, that for *words,* including "wordlike"

Table IV.4. Nominal Compounds vs Single Words Matched in Length and Frequency of Usage

I. Nominal compounds	1	2	3	4		II. Single words	1	2	3	4	
looking glass	1	19	22	—		misunderstand	4	17	19	misunderstood	(3)
post card	1	17	18	—		pregnancy	1	16	17	—	
town hall	1	16	18	—		selective	1	16	18	selection	(2)
stock market	2	16	20	—		encyclopedia	4	16	17	—	
attorney general	7	18	19	—		transcontinental	3	17	20	—	
bowling green	1	18	21	—		approximation	1	16	17	experimentation	(3)
coast guard	1	16	19	—		pessimistic	1	16	18	—	
real estate	4	15	17	—		bureaucracy	1	17	18	—	
motion picture	5	16	17	—		generalization	1	21	23	sterilization	(3)
trap door	2	17	17	—		extremist	2	17	19	extremely	(2)
lieutenant commander	1	21	23	lieutenant colonel	(2)	characteristically	1	20	21	characterization	(4)
stumbling block	1	20	21	—		acknowledgement	3	17	19	—	
Grand mean	17	19					17	19			

Note—Estimated frequencies of usage per one million words (1), mean duration exposures for correct recognitions (3), both in milliseconds, and most frequent misperceptions with frequencies in parentheses (4), for nominal compounds (I) and single words (II).

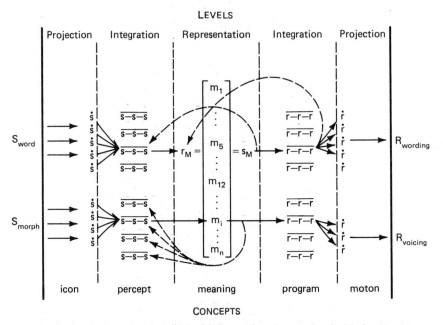

Fig. IV.2. A three-level model of information processing (with feedback)

nominal compounds, is much more distinctively facilitative for particular perceptual forms. Given the complex nature of human nervous systems, including rich feedback capabilities, and given the obvious fact that every time one *clearly* sees a word its distinctive meaning pattern is evoked (its r_M), it would seem quite reasonable that distinctness and richness of *meaning* should be a facilitative factor in language perception.

Structure of the Representational Level

The more recent, and finer, structural notions of APG_0 have been concerned with the minimal "machinery" required for information processing at the Representational Level. At least the following "mechanisms"—by which I mean structures assumed to be capable of certain functions by as yet unspecifiable means in the central nervous system—must be postulated: a LEXICON (LEX), an OPERATOR (OPR), a BUFFER (BUF), and a MEMORY (MEM). All of these are kinds of "memory," but of very different sorts, as will be seen. Figure IV.3 provides a sketch of this "structuring" of the Representational Level. During statements of the Structural Notions relating to each of the "mechanisms", I will refer

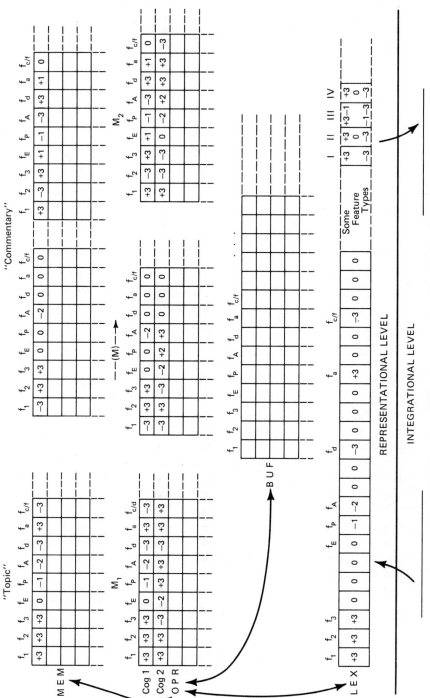

Fig. IV.3. Structure of the representational level—four "mechanisms"

you to this figure for visual inspection. For each postulated "mechanism"—LEX, OPR, BUF, and MEM, in that order—I will move from grosser to finer structural notions. The structural notion *numbers,* S I to S XIII, are those used in my APG (a 242-page "outline" which was available at the time of preparing this lecture), and are ordered from most *gross* to most *fine.*

The LEXICON

Grossly, *S I: the* LEXICON *is a semantic encoding and decoding mechanism, transforming analogically coded percepts* (perceptual and linguistic signs) *into digitally coded significances* (meanings) *in comprehending and transforming the same digitally coded information, now intentions, into analogically coded programs for behaving* (linguistically or otherwise) *in expressing.* These encoding and decoding relations are represented by the heavy arrows at the bottom of the figure. Use of the terms "encoding" and "decoding" seems entirely apropos here: on the input side, *meaningless,* analogically represented percepts of signs are being *en*coded into meaningful, digitally represented (but not necessarily binary semantic-feature sets (patterns of r_m components); on the output side, the same semantic-feature sets are being *de*coded (taken out of the semantic code) into motor programs that are *meaningless* in themselves. The LEXICON is a "process" rather than a "storage" memory, having the advantage that it can be used and reused at a very fast clip, "wiping itself clean" automatically by outputting its information either to OPR in comprehending or to the motor integration system in expressing; what is "stored" in LEX is a very large set of *relations* between signs (percepts) and the semantic feature codes they have acquired in sign learning.

More finely, *S V: the near-simultaneous sets* ("code-strips") *of semantic features, elicited* "upward" *in the* LEXICON *by the signs of entities* (later NPs) *and relations* (later VPs) *in comprehending or by transfer from the* OPERATOR *"downward" in expressing are the semantic representations of the components of perceptual cognitions and* (later) *the constituents of linguistic cognitions.*[1] Note the *bi*directional heavy arrow relating LEX and OPR. Note also that, while the LEXICON is a word-by-word semantic encoding and decoding device, the OPERATOR is a *constituent-by-constituent* processing mechanism (e.g. /THAT NASTY DOG/ IS CHASING AFTER / MY LITTLE KITTEN/). The perceptual signs of entities may be semantically complex just as must be the linguistic NPs that describe them (thus A BIG DIRTY BEACH BALL or even THE THREE LITTLE BEARDED OLD MEN), and the same holds for the perceptual signs of relations in events and their VP descriptions (thus LIMPED SLOWLY AND

---

[1] See Lecture V, particularly Functional/Notion IV, for elaboration.

PAINFULLY AWAY or IS SUDDENLY SHATTERED TO PIECES). Most finely, *S XII: in the* LEXICON *semantic features are ordered "left-to-right" (and "scanned") according to the overall frequency with which they differentiate the meanings of signs, both perceptual and linguistic; since all cognizing operates on "code-strips" outputted from the* LEXICON, *feature-processing order will be constant for* LEX, BUF, *and the components of OPR and MEM.* For efficiency of operation in the LEXICON, ordering the "scanning" of features according to the likelihood of their making differences in meaning seems entirely reasonable. The behavior-theoretic basis of this APG leads directly to this expectation (as well as to the conditions for shifts in the natural order). That this order should be constant for all "mechanisms" at the Representational Level also seems necessary for efficient operation—note, for example, that the essential feature-by-feature comparisons *across* the three components of the OPERATOR would be reduced to utter confusion if the within-component feature orderings were random.

The OPERATOR

Grossly, *S II: the* OPERATOR *is a tripartite mechanism that gives structure to functionally related sets of semantic outputs from the* LEXICON *or from the* MEMORY *and within which the dynamic interactions among such sets occur* (see later under Functional Notions). Like LEX, this OPR is a very short-term process memory, holding the semantic information from LEX or MEM only while the postulated cognitive interactions occur, and then outputting it either to MEM (in comprehending) or to LEX (in expressing)—thereby "wiping itself clean" for further operations. If inputs are from LEX, we refer to (fresh) "cognizing"; if they are from MEM, we refer (appropriately enough) to "re-cognizing".

More finely, *S VI: single perceived events or states* (later, linguistic clauses or "sentoids") *are represented in the* OPERATOR *as simple cognitions* (simplexes) *having tripartite form, the three components being the complete semantic representations of a pair of entities* (later, subject and object NPs), M_1 *and* M_2, *and the signed and directed action or stative relation* (later, VPs), --- (M) --> , *between them.* The symbol M refers simply to the "meaning" of a component (constituent), the embedded (M) indicating that relations usually have richer meanings than their direction and $^+$Associative/$^-$Dissociative signing. My postulation of tripartite structure for simple cognitions (in English sentencing, S → SNP + VP + ONP) rather than the bipartite structure of Chomskyan TGG (S → SP + VP) follows Greenberg's (1963) argument that tripartite structure for simple, active, affirmative declarative (SAAD) sentences is necessary for the demonstration of grammatical universals—a well as my own intuitions about the "natural" structuring of prelinguistic cognitions. The three major language types are SVO, SOV, and VSO (roughly 60%, 30%, and 10%, respectively, of the world's languages), there being only a handful of debatable VOS which reverse the S-before-O ordering.[2] Thus in this APG (as will be seen in Functional Notion IV) all underlying simplex cognitions are

$$[M_1 \ (SNP) \ \text{---} \ (M) \ \text{-->} \ (VP) \ M_2 \ (ONP)]$$

in form.

S VII: *all complex cognitions, involving multiple but related perceived actions or states* (later, conjoined clauses in sentencing), *are analyzable into concatenations* (complexes) *of simple cognitions, represented in parallel* ("vertically", as shown in the figure) *in the three components of the* OPERATOR; *semantically, all complexes are representable as conjunctions of congruent simple cognitions* (linguistically *and* and its elaborations) *or disjunctions of incongruent simple cognitions* (linguistically *but* and its elaborations). It is assumed that complexes *must* be so analyzed in order to be comprehended but *may* be synthesized in expressing, given certain efficiency and salience motivations of speakers (as we will see later). Both perceptually and linguistically, when fused in the OPERATOR, the concatenations of simple cognitions are "paraphrases" (semantic equivalents) of the complex cognitions they analyze. Thus, in comprehending, *the ball the boy hit broke the window* is "paraphrased" analytically as *the boy hit the ball* (and then) *the ball broke the window;* in expressing, *the ball the man bounced hits the plate* may be a synthetic "paraphrase" to Simply Describe (cf Osgood, 1971, "Where Do Sentences Come From?") THE MAN IS HOLDING TWO BALLS (AND) THE MAN BOUNCES ONE OF THE BALLS (AND) THAT BALL HITS THE PLATE.

The BUFFER

Grossly, *S III: the* BUFFER *is a temporary information-holding mechanism, receiving from OPR constituent code-strips that are prior in ordering to that which is "natural"* (as we'll see in detail under Functional Notions later) *and transferring these code-strips back to OPR as the displaced constituents are moved forward* ("leftward") *into "natural" order.* BUF is a memory of the familiar "storage" type, but very short term and displaying rapid fading over time. Given the many,

---

[2] The fact that there *are* some 10% of the world's languages of clearly VSO type directly refutes Chomsky's postulation of a bipartite (NP + VP) structure, since V and O are separated, and as far as I am aware he has never dealt with this problem.

particularly "optional", transformations in sentences produced and received, some BUFFER-like mechanism is essential for any performance model. Assuming, for example, that active constructions are more "natural" than passive ones, in order to comprehend *the window was broken by the ball,* both *the window* and *was broken by* constituent information-sets must be "stacked" in BUF until *the ball* information has been shifted to M_1 in the OPERATOR, and then retrieved. In effect, the ordering and reordering of semantic information in the interactions between OPERATOR and BUFFER constitute the *transformational* syntax of this APG, as will be detailed in Lectures VII and VIII.

More finely, *S VIII: the* BUFFER *is structured* ("vertically") *as a "push-down" storage for constituents of simplexes that are displaced from "natural" order, or for the constituents of whole cognitions that are "unnaturally" ordered in conjoined complexes.* As will be seen under functional analysis, such a "push-down" storage mechanism is postulated to guarantee the restoration of "natural" from given "transform" ordering. Whether this sort of BUFFER *always* guarantees naturalness of reordering will remain to be seen. There obviously are close relations between the role of the BUFFER as described here and Yngve's "depth" hypothesis (1960 and elsewhere); these will be explored later under my functional notions.

The MEMORY

Grossly, *S IV: the* MEMORY *is a mechanism for long-term storage of semantic information inputted from the* OPERATOR; *it is organized both in terms of the tripartite structure of the* OPERATOR *and the feature-ordering structure of the* LEXICON. This is a "real" memory in the lay sense—representations of past events (perceptual or sentential) being stored, decaying over time, and displaying the preservation effects of rehearsal. It is quite literally a *semantic memory* (all of its "entries" being code-strips of semantic features), but simultaneously it is *knowledge of the world,* by virtue of the propositional character of the whole cognitions that are stored (thus, a memory for "ideas"). Since in this APG *all* higher cognitive processes are operations on encoded semantic features, all "knowledge of the world" must be semantic in nature. However, since I also assume that distinctive semantic features (r_m/s_m components) are derived primarily from experience, rather than innately given, *semantic features themselves are simply the most generalized kind of "knowledge about the world"* (e.g., that there are Concrete vs Abstract substantives, Palpable vs Impalpable entities, Male vs Female organisms, and so forth).

More finely, *S IX: the* MEMORY *is structured* (*see* top of the Figure) *"horizontally" in terms of the semantic representations of the "topics" of processed cognitions* (M_1s), *each with its associated "commentary", the feature representations of the relations* (--- (M) -→ 's) *and related* (M_2s) *of the same cognitions.* This is admittedly a somewhat "iffy" notion, both in terms of "topics" being the basis for organization and in terms of not fusing relation (VP) with related (ONP) information as the "commentary", but rather storing these sets of information separately. This postulation does have a very strong implication: namely, that the "topics" of sentences (or perceived events, e.g., Actors and Figures) will be retrieved from MEM more quickly than the "commentaries" of sentences (or perceived events, e.g., related Recipients and Grounds)— and, indeed, that "topic" retrieval will be a prerequisite for prompt "commentary" retrieval. As a *propositional store,* this MEM is not unlike the "network" models recently proposed by Anderson and Bower (1973) and others; on the other hand, the *internal representations* (sets of semantic features) are more related to the "set-theoretic" models proposed by Smith, Shoben, and Rips (1974) and others.

Most finely, *S XIII: the* MEMORY *is organized "vertically" by topics* (M_1s) *from maximum Positiveness on the ordered semantic features* (+ + +. . . . +) *to maximum Negativeness* (− − −. . . . −) *and "horizontally" within topics* (M_1s) *from most to least frequently differential features in usage* (see S XII above). As a psycholinguist I find it inconceivable that there could be an alphabetized "encyclopedia" somewhere in the brain. However, the "vertical" organization postulated here guarantees that semantically related "topics", having the same higher-order, entailed features (e.g., *robin, sparrow,* and *hawk* all entailing *bird*) will be "close" in scanning.

Two "Molecular" Structural Notions

There are two notions that apply most directly to the very fine structure of semantic features, but also have ramifications throughout the whole APG system. These two postulations complete our roster of Structural Notions.

S X: *semantic features* (r_m/s_m mediator components) *are bipolar in nature and, in the general case, are continuously variable in intensity between zero* (neutrality, absence of a feature from a code-strip, r_M/s_M) *and some maximal value of one or the other of the* poles. Most semantic theories with which I am familiar make use of bipolar features (although not necessarily exclusively) derived on intuitive or rationalistic bases (e.g., ±Animate, ±Marital, etc.). This postulation is particularly well motivated in Representational Neobehaviorism by virtue of the derivation of mediator components from the behaviors made to things signified—*all reaction systems,* skeletal and autonomic, *appear to be reciprocally antagonistic in nature,* à la Sherrington. Semantic features are assumed to be continuously variable in intensity because the overt reactions from which they come are usually graded in amplitude; but, as I say, this is only "in the general case"—because (a) reactions made frequently and rapidly tend to become all-or-nothing rather than finely graded (e.g., the very rapid movements of the speech musculature) and (b) the physical, biological, and sociological natures of the world may just happen to be discrete (e.g., entities are either Concrete *or* Abstract, Male *or* Female, and Married *or* Unmarried).

S XI: *in the general case, semantic features have polarities that are nonarbitrarily signed, Positive and Negative, cognitively.* This notion is related to that of linguistic *marking* but I think, more general in nature. It is the Yang and Yin of things cognitive (see, e.g., Osgood and Richards, 1973). Although the linguistically *unmarked* is usually affectively positive and the linguistically *marked* affectively Negative (Greenberg, 1966; Boucher and Osgood, 1969; Hamilton and Deese, 1971), this is not necessarily the case (e.g., troubled–*un*troubled). This is one reason for the escape-clause, "in the general case", in this statement; another is that there are some features that seem to defy affective polarity assignment or are not identified by the usual linguistic marking criteria.

However, before turning to the Functional Notions of this APG, two structural characteristics must be emphasized: (1) In the total cognizing process—whether via perceptuo-motor channels (comprehending perceived events and behaving appropriately) or via linguistic channels (comprehending and producing sentences)—*percepts* at the Sensory Integration Level (meaningless forms) are the *input* to the Representational (meaningful) Level via the LEXICON and *programs* at the Motor Integration Level (meaningless in themselves) are the *output,* again via the LEXICON. (2) Note that everything that transpires at the Representational Level in this model is based upon transfers of, and operations on, *semantic feature-sets* that have been (either previously or immediately) inputted "upward" from the LEXICON—thus fully substituting the "semantic component" for the "syntactic (deep-structure) component" of the standard (Chomsky, 1965) Transformational Generative Grammar—as a step toward an Abstract Performance Grammar. This is a step not unlike, in effect, those taken recently by many linguists seeking greater explanatory adequacy, e.g., in Generative Semantics, Relational Grammar, Functionalism, and Pragmatics. What remains to be seen, of course, is the degree to which the language phenomena characterized by a TGG can also be handled (meeting descriptive, explanatory, *and* predictive* adequacy criteria) by an APG of the sort being developed here.

Functional Notions Relating to the LEXICON

Since the Sign- and Feature-learning principles of this theory were introduced in Lectures I and II, I can be appropriately brief here. All three functional notions relating to the LEXICON derive directly from Hullian Two-Stage Behaviorism—but, as elaborated into my own Representational and Componential Neobehaviorism.

A Sign-Learning Paradigm

Functional Notion I specifies the experiential source of the semantic feature "code-strips" into which the LEXICON encodes the perceptual or sentential signs of entities and their action or stative relations. *F I: when a percept which elicits no predictable pattern of behavior has repeated and reinforced pairing with another percept which does* (e.g., SIGHT OF COOKIE paired with EATING COOKIE), *the former will become a sign of the latter as its significant, by virtue of becoming associated with a mediation process* (r_M/s_M) *that distinctively represents the behavior produced by the significant and therefore serves to mediate overt behaviors appropriate to* ("taking account of") *the significate* (e.g., salivating and reaching for perceived COOKIE OBJECT). Keep in mind that r_M is a *summary symbol* for *sets* of mediator components ($r_m s$); given stimulus contiguity in time and strengthening via reinforcement, there is summation of the effects of repetitions into increasing habit strength associating the sign with the set of mediator components. Relating to the develooment of what might well be called "behavioral competence", this principle indicates how, bit by bit, LAD acquires what he "knows" about his world. The actual statement assumes that we are dealing here with *primary* (usually perceptual) signs, but these in turn become *surrogate* significates—having "prefabricated" mediation processes as predictable response patterns—in later linguistic sign learning (e.g., heard "cookie" now paired with COOKIE percept). And, bit by bit, LAD acquires what he "knows" about his language (at least, its semantics).

A Feature-Learning Paradigm

While F I concerns the acquisition of *global meanings* ($r_M s$), F II concerns the acquisition of more abstract *differences-that-make-a-difference in meaning* ($r_m s$), i.e., semantic features. It specifies the experiential source of the featural *components* of the "code-strips" LEX encodes and decodes. *F II: to the extent that differences in percepts are associated with reciprocally antagonistic differences in behavior, the central representations of these differences* ($+r_{m_i}$ vs $-r_{m_i}$) *in the* LEXICON *will become the bipolar semantic features which distinguish the significances of percepts* (of first perceptual and later linguistic signs). Note carefully that it is the *behavior-based* representational code that has this property of reciprocal antagonism, not the *stimulus-based* percepts themselves; although signs may have what we humans interpret as oppositional properties (e.g., BLACK VS WHITE, *male* vs *female,* etc.), it is the differential behaviors toward them (e.g., Positive vs Negative Affect, Approach vs Avoidance, etc.) that confers their oppositional semantic character. Note also that introducing this notion with *"to the extent . . . "* implies that the formation of semantic features is a continuously graded function of frequency, contiguity, and reinforcement factors.

Frequency and Recency Effects on Sign-Processing

Some of the implications of these factors for sign-processing are expanded in F III, and they all derive from Hullian-type behavior theory (1943). *F III:* (a) *the greater the overall frequency with which mediator components* ($\pm r_{m_i}$ = semantic features) *have been elicited in the* LEXICON *by signs, the shorter will be the latencies of their evocation;* (b) *the more recent the prior elicitation of sets of related components* (r_M "code-strips"), *the more available will be such sets for re-elicitation;* (c) *massed repetition of related sets of mediator components will result in reduced availability.*

The latency notion (a) derives directly from the habit-strength principle of Hullian (and most other) behavior theories; it is the functional basis for the order-of-scanning structural characteristic (S XII) of the LEXICON—and the "scanning" is therefore not *spatial* (as the word implies metaphorically) but rather *temporal,* in terms of the finely differential speeds of component reactions. Although the differences in latency will be very small in absolute terms—measurable in milliseconds—this is sufficient to provide for sequence in feature processing. Interestingly, the taxonomic "tree" structures that characterize some semantic feature systems (e.g., for nouns, at least fairly well) can be derived from this principle: since all higher-order features entailed in the strip-codes for lower-order exemplars (e.g., those for *bird* entailed in the meanings of *sparrow, robin, dove,* etc.) must be activated whenever the latter are encoded, it follows that features higher in the "tree" (more generalized, abstract) must have greater overall usage frequencies than any features below them. The facilitating (sensitizing) effect (b) of recent prior elicitation of particular meanings ("code-strips") is what is often termed the "recency effect". Activation of a feature pattern has the effect of raising its availability ("tuning it up") for a closely subsequent elicitation—a kind of "semantic readiness". This is one reason why sentences whose topics derive from closely preceding sentences are easier to process (and this is typically the case in ordinary discourse, conversational or written). I also assume that this is a behavioral basis for the temporal constraints on anaphora of all types—e.g., as the time and intervening material between the meaning of an NP *(the three little old men)* and its reactivation increase, the probability of an anaphoric PN *(they/them)* goes down and that of repeating the NP goes up.

The inhibiting (desensitizing) effect of massed elicitation of particular meanings (c) is well documented by the extensive literature on what is termed "semantic satiation". Repeated activation of a feature pattern in close succession has the effect of lowering its availability. Massed repetition of a word causes it to lose semantic intensity, and this loss of meaningfulness is familiar in everyday life (try saying the vivid "assassination" some 20 times!). Such satiation effects are presumably a basis for redundancy deletions and paraphrasings in ordinary language.

Semantic Feature Discovery Procedures

The LEXICON, reflecting the end-products of Functional Notions I–III, transforms percepts into "code-strips" of semantic features (r_m components)—but just what *are* these semantic features? Two grossly different feature-discovery procedures can be distinguished, and these reflect disciplinary backgrounds: *Intuitive,* or rational, methods are typically used by linguists, semanticists, lexicographers, and philosophers—it is part of their tradition. *Empirical,* or objective, methods are typically used by anthropologists and psychologists—it is part of *their* tradition. Let me first characterize and contrast these methods and then describe two empirical discovery procedures that I have been concerned with— all necessarily very concisely, so I again refer you to the references related to this lecture.

Evaluation of Alternative Discovery Procedures

Intuitive

Here the investigator utilizes (usually) his intimate knowledge of his own language as a native speaker, intuiting semantic features via the same strategies of substitution and contrast that have proven so successful at the phonemic, morphemic, and syntactic levels. Validity is sought by appeal to the intuitions of other (usually scholarly) native speakers; for example, the intuition that, in the sentence *John is eager to please, John* is semantically coded +Initiating (Source), as well as +Animate, +Human, etc., of course, whereas in the sentence *John is easy to please, John* is semantically coded −Initiating (Recipient)—and appropriately chosen paraphrases often reinforce the appeal, *it is easy to please John* but **it is eager to please John*.

Intuitive methods have the obvious advantages of generality across word-form classes and of making full utilization of the competence of sophisticated native speakers. They also have certain disadvantages: what may be compelling examples for one speaker may not appeal at all to another, as the delightful bickerings at linguistic symposia testify; what seems easy to intuit in one's own language may be difficult, if not impossible, to intuit in another's language, particularly an "exotic" one—in other words, intuitive methods would appear to be highly language and culture bound. There is also the problem of *naming* semantic features—not for obvious ones like ±Sex or Maritality, of course, but certainly for obscurely abstract ones like ±Ego/Alter-oriented for interpersonal verbs or my ±Initiating above—however, this is a problem shared by both intuitive and empirical methods.

Empirical

Here the investigator may also make use of his own intuitions as a native speaker (and, indeed he should), *but* they are used to devise appropriate linguistic tests and materials for *other ordinary speakers* and as aids in interpreting results. The strategies of substitution and contrast take the form of quantitative similarities and differences within the judgments about, or usages of, selected language items by these other speakers. Objectivitiy (across investigators) and reliabiliity (across repetitions) are tested statistically; validity is sought by checking empirically derived features against those obtained by others where available (e.g., via the componential analyses of cultural anthropologists) as well as against the intuitions of linguists and other investigators.

Empirical methods have the advantages of scientific objectivity and quantification, as well as offering the potential for application to languages of which the investigator is not a native speaker. But they, too, have their disadvantages: a method that works for certain types of features or for certain form classes (e.g., affective features for nouns) may not work for others (e.g., denotative features for interpersonal verbs)—i.e., generality of application is a significant problem; there also may be doubt about the feasibility of using *ordinary* speakers and the appropriateness of using *statistical* methods for discovering the very subtle distinctions made in semantics.

Semantic Differential (SD) Technique

The semantic differential was my first vehicle designed for the exploration
of semantic space and, although she has her limitations, she has proved
to be a worthy ship and has traveled far since she was constructed in the
early 1950s (see Osgood, Suci, and Tannenbaum, 1957)—and, I guess
her captain is better known for this ship than for anything else! Here I
can give you only the basic structure of this vessel, what features in
essence were discovered, and some evidence for their universality in
human languages.

Rationale, Method and Early Results

Let me first ask you to do the impossible—to imagine a hypothetical
semantic space of some unknown number of dimensions. With the help
of an analogy with the familiar color space we can at least *conceive* of a
three-dimensional space and then, in theory, generalize to any number
of dimensions. Like all self-respecting spaces, this semantic one has a
central *origin*—a locus of complete *meaning-less-ness* analogous to the
neutral grey center of the color space. We can represent the meaning of
any concept by a *vector* extending outward from this meaningless origin:
the *length* of the vector would represent the degree of *meaningfulness* of
the concept (RAGE having a longer vector than ANNOYANCE, for example),
this being analogous to saturation in the color space; and the *direction* of
the vector in the space, in analogy with both brightness and hue, would
represent the *nature or quality of meaning*. But to talk about "direction"
in any space implies the existence of some reference coordinates or
dimensions. What are the dimensions of the semantic space and are they
natural or are they arbitrary? This becomes an empirical, measurement
problem.

In ordinary, natural languages humans use substantives (nouns) to
refer to entities and qualifiers (adjectives) to differentiate among entities
in the same conceptual classes. All natural languages also provide ways
of quantifying—thus, *poodles are* VERY *pretty dogs, but bulldogs are*
QUITE *ugly*. Each item on a semantic differential form has the native-
speaker rate a concept (say, POODLE) on a 7-step scale defined by a pair
of polar qualifiers (here say, *pretty-ugly*), with the middle position on the
scale defined as *neutral* (that is, *either* or *neither* of the qualities) and the
three steps outward in each direction defined as *slightly, quite* and *very*.
Thus, when I rate *my* poodle, PIERRE, as +3, I am creating a little
sentence which says "Pierre is very pretty"—*Noun* (Be) *Quantifier*
Qualifier.

When a sample of people rate a sample of concepts against a sample
of scales, the SD generates a cube of data as displayed schematically in

Fig. IV.4. The rows of the cube represent qualifier scales, the columns represent the substantive concepts, and the slices, front to back, represent the native speakers doing the rating. Each of the cells in the cube has a value which can vary from +3 through 0 to −3. There are many ways we can carve up this semantic "cake" for analysis, and all of them presuppose—as do all linguistic and philosophical conceptions of meaning with which I am familiar—*that semantic similarity is indexed by similarity in distribution of usage*. Thus descriptive scales are similar to the extent that they are used the same way by subjects across concepts, concepts are similar to the extent that they produce the same kinds of "sentences" [SYMPATHY *(is) slightly hot* and DEVOTION *(is) slightly hot*], and we can even say that two speakers of a language possess similar semantic systems to the extent that the "sentences" they produce using the concepts and scales are similar.

Affective E, P and A, and Their Universality

During the 1950s we collected many such cubes of SD data and subjected them to factor analysis, with our main interest then being in the scale factors (i.e., the semantic dimensions of qualifying). We varied the type of subjects (college students, old people, IQ levels, political affiliations, and even normals vs schizophrenics), the samplings of scales and of concepts, an even the methods of factoring—and we kept getting the

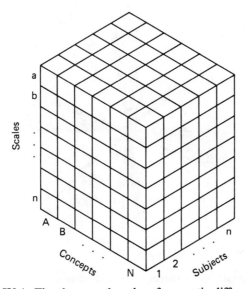

Fig. IV.4. The three-mode cube of semantic differential data

same basic factor system shown in Fig. IV.5. The vertical dimension clearly labels itself as Evaluation (E) in terms of the scales loading high on it, *good-bad, kind-cruel, honest-dishonest;* the horizontal dimension labels itself as Potency (P), *strong-weak, hard-soft, heavy-light;* and the back-to-front dimension, *hot-cold, fast-slow, active-passive,* seems to label itself as a kind of Activity (A) factor.

The factor-analytic model provides a framework of underlying dimensions within which both concept and scale meanings, and their modes of interaction, can be displayed. Figure IV.6 provides an illustration. The solid black lines represent the E-P-A factors and the fine dashed lines represent the projections of a concept point (COWARD) and the termini of a scale (*kind* and *cruel*) on these three factors. All scales are assumed to be straight lines through the origin, here shown as a bamboo-type line, and we get the locations of the termini from the loadings of scales on the same factors. Thus *kind* is very GOOD, quite Weak, and slightly Passive and *cruel* (reciprocally) is very BAD, quite Strong, and slightly Active. What happens when a subject rates COWARD on the *kind-cruel* scale? Geometrically, the answer is very simple: we just project the COWARD point at right angles onto the *kind-cruel* line (the arrow) and we find that this speaker said, "COWARDS are *slightly cruel"*. What goes on *cognitively* is a bit more complicated!

We refer to this E-P-A semantic structure as *the affective meaning*

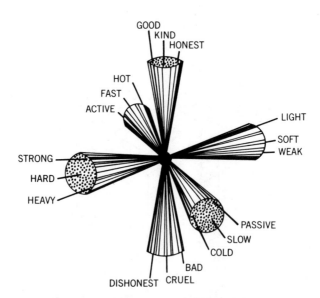

Fig. IV.5. The Evaluation (E), Potency (P), and Activity (A) structure of affective meaning

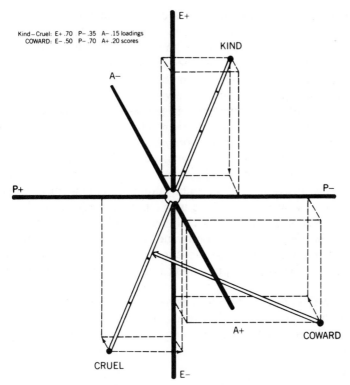

Fig. IV.6. Graphic representation of the rating of a concept on a scale in the semantic differential technique

system. It appears to be based on the way humans universally attribute primitive emotional *feelings* to the persons and things in their environments. However, up until 1960 nearly all of our research had been focused on humans sharing a common (American) culture and speaking a common (English) language. It was at least *conceivable* that the dominance of Goodness, Strength, and Activity was attributable to something peculiar about American culture or the English language—or both. So now let me shift from ethnocentrics to anthropocentrics (see Osgood, May, and Miron, 1975).

Universality of E, P, and A

Our sampling among the world's communities began in the early 1960s with six locations, widely diversified in both language and culture—these were Finnish, Arabic in Lebanon, Farsi in Iran, Kannada in Mysore, Chinese in Hong Kong, and Japanese. During the now 20-year life of this project we have extended our research to 30 human communities. You will note from Fig. IV.7 that we have over-representation of Europe and Asia, but under-representation of the Southern Hemisphere—and no involvement to date of communities in the two great communist countries, China and the Soviet Union. Since we were interested in gross differences in culture and language, we decided to maximize sociometric *equivalence* within communities—in all cases using teen-age male students in average high schools in urban settings.

The first step was *to obtain a sample of productive qualifiers* in each community. A set of 100 nouns was used as stimuli in a modified word-association test to elicit 100 adjectives from each of 100 teen-age school boys. The nouns were selected to be culture-common—mainly from lists developed by glottochronologists who study changes in word forms and meanings over long periods of time in families of related languages. Table IV.5 lists the 100 concepts that remained after careful translation checks. There are many abstract (TRUST, CHOICE, WEALTH) a well as concrete (HOUSE, CAT, MAN) concepts among the 100, and all are very familiar notions.

When the 10,000 qualifier tokens had been collected in each community (100 boys giving their first responses to the 100 nouns), they were shipped to Illinois and computer analyzed *in the native language* (that is,

Table IV.5. The 100 Culture-Common Concepts Used in Qualifier Elicitations

1. House	21. Bird	41. Cat	61. Success	81. Man
2. Girl	22. Hope	42. Poison	62. Snake	82. Wednesday
3. Picture	23. Heat	43. Tree	63. Hand	83. Chair
4. Meat	24. Map	44. Hunger	64. Mother	84. Guilt
5. Trust	25. Husband	45. Choice	65. Knot	85. River
6. Tooth	26. Rain	46. Noise	66. Life	86. Peace
7. Defeat	27. Truth	47. Need	67. Head	87. Hair
8. Book	28. Stone	48. Doctor	68. Thunder	88. Food
9. Lake	29. Pain	49. Anger	69. Luck	89. Danger
10. Star	30. Ear	50. Tongue	70. Author	90. Policeman
11. Battle	31. Respect	51. Horse	71. Music	91. Father
12. Seed	32. Laughter	52. Marriage	72. Sleep	92. Fear
13. Sympathy	33. Moon	53. Game	73. Future	93. Root
14. Progress	34. Courage	54. Color	74. Egg	94. Purpose
15. Cup	35. Work	55. Heart	75. Crime	95. Fire
16. Wind	36. Story	56. Friend	76. Sun	96. Rope
17. Thief	37. Punishment	57. Death	77. Belief	97. Power
18. Bread	38. Wealth	58. Smoke	78. Money	98. Window
19. Love	39. Woman	59. Freedom	79. Knowledge	99. Pleasure
20. Fruit	40. Cloud	60. Dog	80. Fish	100. Water

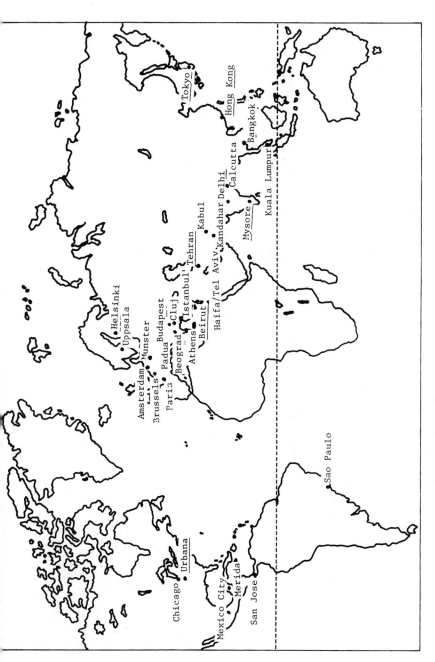

Fig. IV.7. Geographic distribution of language/culture communities in sample

blindly, untouched by American minds!). The qualifier types were first ordered in terms of their overall frequencies and diversities of usage across the 100 nouns and then were pruned in terms of their correlations in usage with all higher-ordered types—this last to maximize diversity of the semantic dimensions tapped. The top-ranked 50 qualifiers resulting from this process were shipped back to the field, where their opposites were elicited, and they were thence transformed into 7-step bipolar scales.

The second step was *collection of data for concept-on-scale factorizations.* Another group of teen-age male subjects in each community rated the same 100 culture-common concepts against the 50 bipolar scales. So imagine, if you will, some 30 data cubes like that I described earlier for American English. To determine the functional equivalence in usage (meaning) of scales in different languages *independent of translation,* we must put these cubes in a single mathematical space for analysis, and this requires that at least one of the three sources of variance (subjects, scales, or concepts) be shared. Subjects are obviously different and the scales are quite varied, so that leaves us with concepts. Although we are sure that the 100 concepts did not mean *exactly* the same thing in all of the translations into more than 25 languages, they are carefully *translation-equivalent* and the data can be ordered in their terms.

Figure IV.8 illustrates the design of our monstrous *pancultural factorization* of the scale mode. First we collapse the subject dimension of all our data cubes into the means across subjects for each item (concept-on-scale). Then, as the *upper* diagram shows, we organize the means horizontally by community blocks (50 scales each) and vertically by a constant order of the 100 concepts. And then every scale is correlated with every other scale. As the *lower* diagram shows, each *triangular* matrix along the main diagonal is the indigenous one for each community (L1 scales with other L1, L2 with L2, and so on); the *rectangular* matrices in the body of the total matrix are the intercommunity correlations (L1 scales with L2 scales . . . L1 with L23 . . . L22 with L23). This entire matrix for all communities is finally factored.

Now suppose that there is a very high correlation between scale #21 for AE (American English, *good-bad,* and scale #37 for JP (Japanese), *iwa-matsu*—meaning what, we deliberately have no idea. What does this indicate? It indicates that, regardless of the translation, we can conclude that the Japanese use their *iwa-matsu* to differentiate among the 100 translation-equivalent concepts in a way that is *functionally equivalent* to the way American use their *good-bad* scale. We are thus applying the psycholinguistic definition of similarity of meaning—similarity in distribution of usage—but now *across* languages.

The proof of this particular pudding, however, lies in the *results* of the factorization. If, despite some unknown variation in the meanings of

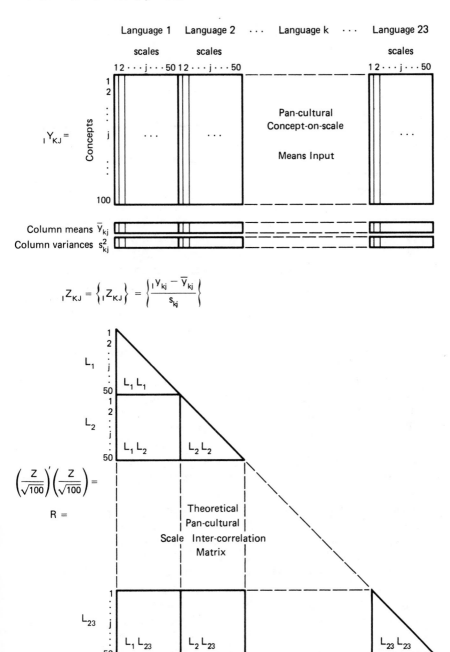

Fig. IV.8. Design of pancultural factor analysis for 23 language/culture communities

the 100 concepts, our old friends, E, P, and A come forth loud and clear *and* are represented by scales with reasonably high loadings for all communities, then we have demonstrated the universality of the E-P-A affective meaning system and are in business as far as the construction of comparable measuring instruments is concerned. On the next three tables the results for E, P, and A, respectively, (for 20 communities) are displayed—but only for the "positive" terms of the four highest-loading scales. We use two-letter, usually Locus/Language, codes for our communities—thus AE for American English, AD for Afghan Dari, BF for Belgian Flemish, CB for Calcutta Bengali, and DH for Delhi Hindi, but, where language and locus coincide, FF for Finnish, FR for French, and GK for Greek. Of course, in order to communicate these results here, all terms have been translated into English, but this had nothing to do with which scales appeared on which pancultural factors. A mere scanning of Table IV.6 is convincing as to the universality of the Evaluative factor, and you will note that the loadings are nearly all in the 0.80s and 0.90s. Scales translating as *good, beautiful, pleasant,* and *nice* appear repeatedly.

While the scale loadings for the Potency factor (Table IV.7) are somewhat lower (ranging from the 0.40s into the 0.70s), common strength and magnitude flavors are evident in scales translating as *big, strong, heavy,* and *tall.* But some generalizations of Potency into scales like *military, difficult,* and *brave* will also be noted. As is always the case, even for AE (American English), the Activity scales shown in Table IV.8 have somewhat lower loadings (ranging from 0.30s into the low 0.70s), but, with the possible exceptions of DH (Delhi Hindi), LA (Lebanese Arabic), and MK (Mysore Kannada), the Activity flavor is clear and is evident in the most common scales, *fast, quick, alive* (and *lively*), and *active* itself. Again some common generalizations will be noted—to *young,* to *noisy,* and to *red* and *bloody.*

This is rather convincing evidence for the universality of the affective meaning system—and it should be kept in mind that, although procedures were standardized at all critical points, our young subjects were free to produce *any* kinds of qualifiers and use them in *any* ways in rating concepts to create *any* kind of semantic space.

But why E, P, and A? One reason is that—humans being a kind of animal (just scan any day's newspaper for ample evidence)—the most important questions about the *sign* of a thing, today as in the day of the Neanderthal, are: first, *is it good or is it bad for me?* (does it signify a cute Neanderthal female or a saber-tooth tiger?); second, *is it strong or is it weak with respect to me?* (is it a saber-tooth tiger or a rat?); third, *is it an active or a passive thing?* (is it a saber-tooth tiger or merely a pool of quicksand that I can just walk around?) Survival of the species has depended upon answers to such questions.

Table IV.6. Pancultural Principal Component Factor Analysis. Factor 1: Evaluation

AE		AD		BF		CB		DH	
.94	Nice	.88	Good	.91	Good	.93	Beautiful	.83	Glad
.92	Good	.85	Well	.89	Magnificent	.93	Lovely	.83	Good
.90	Sweet	.84	Safe	.88	Agreeable	.91	Kind	.81	Ambrosial
.89	Helpful	.82	Lovely	.88	Beautiful	.91	Finest	.80	Superior

FF		FR		GK		HC		IF	
.88	Nice	.90	Pleasant	.93	Superb	.92	Lovable	.92	Good
.87	Pleasant	.89	good	.91	Good	.92	Good (not bad)	.89	Worthwhile
.86	Good	.88	Nice	.88	Friendly	.91	Good (not poor)	.88	Best
.81	Light	.86	Magnificent	.85	Useful	.90	Respectable	.88	Auspicious

IT		JP		LA		MK		MS	
.93	Valuable	.93	Good	.90	Sound	.78	Merciful	.93	Admirable
.92	Beautiful	.92	Pleasant	.90	Good	.76	Good	.93	Agreeable
.92	Desirable	.91	Comfortable	.90	Beautiful	.75	Delicate	.92	Good
.92	Good	.91	Happy	.89	Enlivening	.74	Calm	.92	Friendly

ND		SW		TH		TK		YS	
.91	Pleasant	.86	Good	.88	Useful	.91	Beautiful	.93	Pleasant
.91	Happy	.84	Nice	.87	Comfortable	.90	Good	.92	Good
.90	Good	.82	Right	.87	Right	.90	Tasteful (art)	.91	Lovable
.87	Nice	.82	Kind	.87	Loving	.90	Pleasant	.89	Beautiful

Note: Communities are represented by two-letter symbols, location indicated by the first letter and language by the second (AE for American English, BF for Belgian Flemish); where locus and language coincide and there is no ambiguity, the two letters simply stand for the language (thus FR for French, GK for Greek, and so forth).

Table IV.7. Pancultural Principal Component Factor Analysis. Factor 2: Potenc

AE	AD	BF	CB	DH
.68 Big	.55 Great	.57 Strong	.62 Huge	.47 Strong-of-its-kin
.68 Powerful	.45 Military	.57 Big	.60 Powerful	.47 Brave
.57 Strong	.40 Absolute	.54 Heavy	.55 Big	.46 Heavy
.57 Deep	.37 High, loud	.50 Deep	.54 Strong	.44 Difficult

FF	FR	GK	HC	IF
.60 Large	.68 Large	.60 Big	.76 Tall, Big	.62 Heavy
.59 Sturdy	.59 Strong	.59 Strong	.75 Big	.50 Severe
.51 Heavy	.57 Huge	.46 Brave	.72 Strong	.47 Thick
.40 Rough	.52 Heavy	.39 Difficult	.68 Significant	.42 Stout

IT	JP	LA	MK	MS
.68 Big	.66 Heavy	.51 Large	.44 Wonderful	.60 Giant
.55 Strong	.63 Big	.42 Strong	.41 Huge	.58 Big
.54 Wide	.59 Difficult	.41 Long	.41 Big	.55 Major
.49 High, tall	.56 Brave	.38 Heavy	.34 Great	.54 Strong

ND	SW	TH	TK	YS
.57 Big	.50 Difficult	.50 Heavy	.67 Big	.72 Big
.55 Heavy	.50 High	.49 Deep	.58 Heavy	.67 Bulky
.54 Strong	.46 Strong	.43 Old	.53 Large	.67 Strong
.48 Special	.45 Long	.42 Big	.51 High	.55 High, tall

Powers and Limitations

Let me now say something about the virtues and vices of Semantic Space Explorer I—which can be done without embarrassment, since she responds only to feeling, not reason! The *strength* of SD technique lies, first, in its adaptability to the very powerful procedures of multivariate statistics, in which factor analysis is a means of discovering semantic features and distance analysis is a rigorous means of specifying similarities and differences in meaning among concepts. It lies, second, in SD being a multidimensional, componential model—efficiently describing the meanings of a potentially infinite number of concepts (from simple word forms to complex ideas) in terms of a relatively small number of distinguishing features. But unlike most componential systems, its features are continuous rather than discrete and paradigmatic rather than hierarchical in organization (i.e., there is no logical entailment of certain features within others). I might also note that its dominant affective features, E, P, and A, are the same as those found to be dominant in human emotions and feelings.

The major *limitation* of SD technique is that it amplifies these universal affective features at the expense of obscuring equally ubiquitous deno-

Table IV.8. Pancultural Principal Component Factor Analysis. Factor 3: Activity

AE		AD		BF		CB		DH	
.61	Fast	.51	Fast, rapid	.69	Quick	.47	Alive	.47	Gay
.55	Alive	.41	Sharp	.65	Active	.43	Fast	.36	Thin (slim)
.44	Young	.40	Tender, soft	.42	Bloody	.43	Active	.34	Soft
.42	Noisy	.36	Narrow	.40	Impetuous	.38	Light	.30	Loquacious
FF		**FR**		**GK**		**HC**		**IF**	
.67	Fast	.61	Lively	.55	Quick	.68	Agile	.53	Active
.66	Flexible	.57	Fast	.52	Young	.54	Fast	.52	Exciting
.64	Agile	.56	Living	.39	Active	.49	Alive	.41	Fast, sharp
.52	Lively	.42	Young	.39	Thin	.46	Red	.31	Warm
IT		**JP**		**LA**		**MK**		**MS**	
.66	Fast	.48	Noisy	.35	Fast	.35	Loose	.56	Active
.47	Mortal	.45	Active	.31	Infirm	.34	Unstable	.46	Young
.47	Young	.44	Soft	.30	Thin	.33	Fast	.44	Fast
.40	Sensitive	.42	Fast	.29	Alive	.27	Few	.37	Soft
ND		**SW**		**TH**		**TK**		**YS**	
.72	Active	.66	Bloody	.56	Agile	.50	Fast	.63	Lively
.71	Fast	.63	Swift	.44	Fast	.47	Living	.54	Fast
.51	Fasinating	.62	Lively	.39	Thin	.43	Soft (flexible)	.45	Young
.48	Warm	.54	Sensitive	.28	Naughty	.42	Young	.41	Soft

Nonhuman). Why should this be so? Since in SD technique every concept must be rated on every scale, this means that, for examples, TORNADO must be judged *fair* or *unfair,* MOTHER must be judged *hard* or *soft,* and SPONGE must be judged as *honest* or *dishonest.* While the philosophers among you writhe, let me add the fuminous fact that, for each of the 100 concepts used in our cross-cultural "tool-making" studies, only a relatively few scales will be denotatively relevant for creating acceptable sentences. Only *metaphorically* will "sentences" like *tornados are very unfair, mother is slightly soft,* and *a sponge is quite dishonest* be acceptable. This pressure toward metaphorical usage means that, for most concepts, qualifying scales must be *rotated* in the affective space toward that factor on which they have their dominant loading—thus *fair-unfair* toward generalized Evaluation, *hard-soft* toward Potency, and *hot-cold* toward generalized Activity. This is why the SD cannot provide a *sufficient* characterization of meaning. Thus, for examples, the concept-pair NURSE and SINCERITY and the pair HERO and SUCCESS have near identical locations in the E-P-A space; yet, while I can say *she's a cute nurse,* I cannot say *she's a cute sincerity,* and, while I can say *our hero led them,* I cannot say *our success led them*—except metaphorically.

Semantic Interaction (SI) Technique

Because of this insufficiency of SD technique, in the mid 1960s—while on sabbatical in Hawaii, accompanied by a very bright, fresh Ph.D. of mine, Ken Forster—I began investing in Semantic Space Explorer II, the semantic interaction (SI) technique, working first with interpersonal verbs and later with emotion nouns. Since I must be very brief here, I refer you for details to my 1970 paper, titled "Interpersonal Verbs and Interpersonal Behavior".

In a nutshell, SI technique utilizes the *rules of usage of words in systematically varied syntactic combinations* (phrases, sentences) as a means of inferring the minimum set of features necessary to account for exactly those rules of usage. The "rules" are inferred from native-speaker judgments of combinations as being particularly fitting or *apposite* (like *plead with humbly,* where verb and adverb combine to intensify a Subordination feature), as being merely *acceptable* (like *plead with sincerely,* where the adverb simply adds a $^+$Morality feature to the pleading), or as being *anomalous* and hence unacceptable (like *plead with tolerantly,* where the verb and adverb have opposed signs on the Super/Sub-ordination feature). From arrays of many such judgments, we were able to infer, for example, that a feature which might be intuitively labeled Terminal/Interminal operates within the interpersonal verb domain: witness *attack suddenly* (apposite) vs *help suddenly* (acceptable) vs *console suddenly* (anomalous) as compared with *attack calmly* (anomalous) vs *help calmly* (acceptable) vs *console calmly* (apposite). The same feature appears for emotion nouns: witness *sudden surprise* (apposite) vs *sudden excitement* (acceptable) vs *sudden melancholy* (anomalous).

Not being fully satisfied with factor analysis as a feature identifying technique for such data—and with Ken Forster playing a computer like E. Power Biggs plays the organ—we tried a variety of analytic techniques, but we were not able to come up with appropriate and workable programs. Due to the load of our cross-cultural research with the SD technique—mainly in compiling comparable *Atlases* for some 620 diverse concepts for each of our 30 language-culture communities—the SI technique research had to be temporarily shelved. However, I think it is *potentially* a highly generalizable feature discovery procedure, without the inherent limitations of SD technique, and one that attempts to capture objectively the intuitions of linguists and philosophers.

By Way of Conclusion

Let me come back to the structure and function (so far as related to the LEXICON) of the Abstract Performance Grammar I am working on. I think it is fair to say that, *up to and including* the encoding and decoding functions of the LEXICON, my APG *is* a modern variant of Behaviorism—albeit a highly complex, centralized, and componential variant that focuses on the crucial role of *meaning* in communication. But once the constituent code-strips of little r_m feature components are forwarded "upward" from LEX to the OPERATOR—and all sorts of complex interactions occur within and between OPERATOR, BUFFER and MEMORY—the r_M code-strips lead a pretty wild life, more akin to computer-based artificial intelligence models than, certainly, to simple associative behaviorism. And it is this "wild life" that we will be exploring in the remaining lectures.

Naturalness in Cognizing and Sentencing

Orientation

Unless one makes the assumption that humanoids enjoyed a rather miraculous genetic mutation into full-blown linguistic capability more or less simultaneously with dropping from the trees and using tools, it would seem to be rather obviously true that, *before* they "had" language, humanoids must have had capacities for perceptually cognizing the significances of things going on around them and for learning to behave appropriately in terms of such significances—if the species were to survive. It seems equally reasonable to assume that, *before* children of contemporary humans "have" language, they must display exactly the same capacities for acquiring the significances of perceived events and states and reacting with appropriate intentional behaviors—and, of course, they do. These assumptions lead directly to the most general notion underlying my Abstract Performance Grammar (APG): namely, *that the basic cognitive structures which interpret sentences received and initiate sentences produced are established in prelinguistic experience, via the acquisition of adaptive behaviors to entities perceived in diverse action and stative relations.*

Now, this notion is essentially *axiomatic*—an "article of faith", if you will—and it does not *in itself* generate any testable hypotheses. However, it leads to what I call a Naturalness Principle for sentencing, and this *does* have multiple empirical consequences: namely, *the more sentences correspond in their surface forms to the cognitive structures developed in prelinguistic perceptuo-motor experience, the earlier they will be understood and produced by children and the more easily they will be processed in both comprehending and expressing by adults.* I should point out that specification of naturalness involves postulations deriving both from Representational Neobehaviorism and from psychological intuitions about *what is natural* in the cognizings of prelinguistic children—in contrast to linguistic intuitions about *what is grammatical* in the sentencings of adults. Since the little ones can't *tell* us anything about it, we often have to don the booties of our own babyhood and try to recapture these early experiences.[1]

In my last lecture three functional notions relating to the LEXICON were stated and elaborated—specifying the *sign-learning* (F I) and *feature-learning* (F II) principles of the developing APG, along with a principle governing *frequency, recency,* and *massed-repetition effects upon semantic availability* (F III). Although linguistically these notions relate to units smaller than the sentence (typically the meanings of word-forms), they are still aspects of Naturalness—in that they, too, display priority of prelinguistic cognizing. In this lecture we will explore the implications of the Naturalness Principle for the OPERATOR—how it organizes semantic information in both perceptual and linguistic cognizing and how this relates in sentencing to (1) ordering of the constituents of single-clause simplexes (F IV), (2) ordering of words within the constituents of simplexes, via interaction with the LEXICON (F V), and (3) ordering of simplex cognitions conjoined into multiple-clause complex cognitions (F VI). And, finally, we will see how all this relates to the MEMORY—both the storage and the retrieval of simplex and complex cognitions, whether derived from perceptual or linguistic channels.

Naturalness in Ordering the Constituents of Simplexes (F IV)

Now let me ask you to don the booties of your *very* early babyhood. It seems likely that we all begin independent life in a state of affairs much like that of prenatal experience—which might be characterized as one of rather complete semantic *Amorphousness*—but soon three very primitive semantic distinctions develop, and more or less simultaneously (cf, T. G. R. Bower, 1974, and elsewhere). These are what I will call *Substantivity, Directionality,* and *Stativity* and, in combination, they serve to define (in theory, of course) the structures of natural simplex cognitions in my APG.

Probably the most basic distinction is *±Substantivity.* This semantic feature distinguishes Entities (+), later generalized to NPs, from Relations (−), later VPs—which, of course, is the most gross distinction made universally in human languages. *+Substantive Entities* may be

---

[1] As I'm sure you have already noted, I quite frequently use the verbalized forms, *cognizing* and *sentencing,* instead of the more usual nominals, *cognition* and *sentence;* the reason is, quite simply, that both are dynamic *processes,* not static *states.*

either redundantly experienced *contoured* "things" (like OWN HANDS, MOMMY FACE, VOICES, APPLE-, COOKIE-, DOGGIE-OBJECTS) or redundantly experienced *uncontoured* "things" (like WALLS, CEILINGS, SKY, LAWN, BACKGROUND NOISES), and of course this featural property is relative, not absolute (e.g., COOKIE is figural relative to TABLE which is figural relative to WALL). ⁻Substantive *Relations* are not directly perceptible but rather *must be inferred from changes-in-state of* ⁺*Substantive Entities that are perceptible* (MOMMY-FACE GETS LARGER, i.e., MOMMY *comes toward* BABY; DADDY-HAND CONTACTS BALL AND BALL SHIFTS LOCATION, i.e., DADDY *pushes* BALL)—and one suspects that there may well be innate features relating to Space and Time operating here.

Similarly innate may be the gestaltlike predispositions to perceive both *contoured* entities as more salient than *uncontoured* backgrounds and entities *initiating* changes-in-state as more salient than entities *affected by* such changes. These predispositions naturally yield a ±*Directionality* distinction for both Entities and Relations. A third primitive distinction—driven by a basic difference in the kinds of Relations among Entities (which may or may not be innate)—is what I will call a ±*Stativity* feature, and it serves to define the two types of simplexes in my APG: *Stative vs Action cognitions.* Given the essential passivity (motoric ineptness, if you will) of the very young infant, I make the weak assumption that cognizing Stative Relations is probably prior to cognizing Action Relations. You might also note, however, that these two types of relations are cognitive representations of the two most fundamental and general kinds of environmental contingencies with respect to which any organism must behave appropriately—*spatial vs temporal contingencies.*

A Semantic Characterization of the Syntax of Simple Sentences

What is being proposed here, of course, is a *semantic characterization* of the most fundamental distinctions made by linguists in defining the constituent structures of simple sentences. (And I might note in passing that such a characterization is essential for an Abstract Performance Grammar that operates entirely on semantic information inputted from the LEXICON.) As shown on Fig. V.1, it is assumed that Prenatal Amorphousness is differentiated progressively: first in terms of a Substantivity feature (differentiating ⁺Entities from ⁻Relations); second, within ±Substantivity, into a salience-based Directionality feature (differentiating cognitively ⁺Prior from ⁻Subsequent Entities and ⁺Naturally-from ⁻Unnaturally-directed Relations between them); third, within both of these, a Stativity feature (differentiating ⁺Static states vs ⁻Static (i.e., Dynamic) actions).

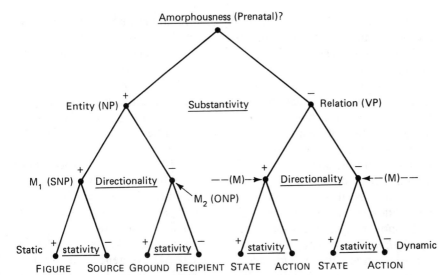

Fig. V.1. A semantic characterization of the constituent structures of simple cognitions

Thus, as shown at the bottom of this figure, we have the two basic types of simple cognitions in this APG: (1) *Stative Cognitions* [FIGURE / STATE / GROUND] and *Action Cognitions* [SOURCE / ACTION / RECIPIENT]. An example of a stative cognition would be THE CAT / IS ON / THE PILLOW (and you might note the naturalness of the sentence *the cat is on the pillow by the window* as compared with the utter strangeness of *the window is by the pillow under the cat*); an example of an action cognition would be THE CAT / JUMPED ON / THE PILLOW (and note the naturalness of the sentence *the cat jumped on the pillow for the toy mouse* as compared with the utter strangeness of *for the toy mouse the pillow was jumped on by the cat*)—but neither of these unnatural sentences is ungrammatical (and could, under certain motivational conditions for a speaker, be uttered). The general symbolism I use for natural cognitions (either stative or action) is

$$[M_1 - - (M) -\!\!\rightarrow M_2]$$

where the *M*'s stand simply for "meaning"—M_1s being the complete semantic "code-strips" for FIGURE or SOURCE entities (later SNP constituents) and M_2s being those for GROUND or RECIPIENT entities (later ONP constituents)—and where the directed dashed arrow stands for the STATE or ACTION relations (later VP constituents) between the entities [with the embedded (*M*) indicating that relations may be more richly coded semantically than simply as a directed state or action].[2]

This Naturalness Principle (F IV) makes a very strong claim about human languages—namely, *that regardless of the basic adult surface ordering of sentence constituents* (VSO, SVO, or SOV), *the prelinguistically based natural ordering of components in cognizing will universally be "SVO"*. First it should be noted that, of the world's extant languages, the distribution of basic types is estimated to be about 60% SVO, 30% SOV, and only 10% VSO; also, although there have been many spontaneous diachronic shifts from SOV types into SVO, as far as I know there are no recorded historic shifts in the reverse direction, in the absence of external pressures like occupation and cultural dominance. Secondly, note that Greenberg in his now-classic 1963 paper on "Some Universals of Grammar" found it—not merely "convenient" but—necessary to set up a *tripartite* typology of languages, based on the dominant order for simple, active, affirmative, declarative (SAAD) sentences in order to state many of the 45 universals (often statistical) he derived from his sample of 30 diverse languages. This tripartite system contrasts with the familiar *bipartite* (S → NP + VP) system of Chomskyan TGG; interestingly, the 10% VSO languages would break up the VP by interposing S— a problem which, as far as I am aware, has never been addressed by Noam Chomsky.

Critique

Of course, this postulation of "SVO" structure for prelinguistic cognizing raises some serious theoretical and empirical problems itself. Roughly 40% of human languages are *not* SVO in basic typology. Although VSO languages (10%) are found mainly in small and isolated groups of humans, SOV languages are spoken by many major societies, mainly (but not exclusively) in Asia. The Naturalness Principle seem to predict (a) that non-SVO languages will be somewhat more difficult to process and (b) that children acquiring them will, in the early stages, display strong SVO tendencies—evidence on (b) will be reported at a later point.

(1) *Why are there ANY SOV or VSO languages?* Although it is true that all languages provide speakers with means of transforming basic structures into orderings that better express their momentary communicative intentions—and that elites in cultures may try to distinguish themselves from the hoi polloi by using nonnatural structures (which, of course, the hoi polloi eagerly adopt!)—such an explanation

---

[2] Formal statement of F IV is given in Appendix A; this appendix is designed to facilitate cross-checking of references to these Functional Notions in my text.

seems insufficient. Note, first, that *S-before-O* is a universal ordering principle for all language types, this fitting the $\pm$Directionality feature above (Figures of states more salient than Grounds; Sources of actions more salient than Recipients). Note, second, that while Entities (Ss and Os) *are directly perceptible,* the stative or action Relations (Vs) *must be inferred* from the the stable (stative) or unstable (action) relations among entities. While dominant SVO-ers have opted for one Naturalness Principle (which locates the inferred Relations in their "relational" place), SOV-ers have opted for another (which highlights the perceptible Entities over the nonperceptible Relations), and the VSO-ers opt for yet another (which highlights the non-perceptible Relations over the perceptible Entities—which may explain their rarity!).

(2) *What about perfectly grammatical and acceptable simplex sentencings with fewer than or more than three constituents?* Here we must keep in mind that, in the sentencings of very young children, limitations in production capacity (not in cognizing) will limit utterance lengths [cf, Roger Brown's MLU data (1973) for Stage I speech], and, in the sentencings of adults as well as children, shared information in perceptual (as well as prior linguistic) channels will permit redundancy deletion by speakers.

   (a) *Single-constituent.* In everyday communication single-constituent sentences are frequent—in "namings", in "commandings", in "answerings", and so forth. The child points and says "Pierre!" (there is *Pierre* poodle-dog); the daddy says "Eat!" (you *eat* your cereal); the wife, when asked where the mustard is, says "on your bun" [the mustard is (already) *on your bun*]—and here redundancy deletion is obvious.

   (b) *Two-constituent.* Intransitive sentences are a case in point: in some cases deletion of redundant ONPs is also obvious [e.g., *the golfer putted* (the ball), *the sharpshooter fired* (his gun), *Arturo Toscanini conducted* (the orchestra)]; in many cases, however, deletion is ambiguous sans context [*John paddled* (the canoe? his son?), *Sam carved* (the roast? his initials?), *Peter believes* (in God? the story?)]; but many intransitives imply genuine bipartite cognizings, with no ONP involved (*Jane is sleeping, Sarah works hard, Paula died*). Actually, the only claim being made in F IV is that tripartite stative and action cognitions are the most *characteristic* structures in prelinguistic experience, and, for genuine bipartite intransitives, we would simply substitute a convenient ϕ for the M_2 (i.e., a semantically "empty" component).[3]

   (c) *Four (or more) constituents.* Any sentence type with four or more constituents raises the question as to whether it represents a simplex cognition (with fusion of information into the M_1, the $- - (M) - \rightarrow$, and/or the M_2) or the conjoining of simplexes into a complex

---

[3] My linguist assistant, S. N. Sridhar, and I are presently investigating the semantics of verbs that can function intransitively to see if there are language universals here.

cognition. Given the fact that NPs "hang" on VPs (as their arguments) the presence of two main verbs in a sentence is a clue that
two conjoined cognitions are involved (compare assertive *Mary* IS
pregnant with commentative *John* THINKS *Mary* IS *pregnant*). But
this is not an infallible clue: witness, first, trite verb phrases like *the
lad hopped-and-skipped down the walk* and *the man waxed-and-
polished his car;* but witness, second, increasingly debatable main-
verb/infinitive-verb fusions, ranging from obvious ones like *he used-
to-go to Miami* and *he ought-to-go to the lecture,* through debatable
ones like *he intended to give Sally a present,* into clearly conjoined
cognitions like *he found something to read* and *he is easy to please.*

A general processing-efficiency principle seems to operate here: *increasing the number of conjoined cognitions increases processing difficulty more than increasing the complexity of constituents within simplex
cognitions.* Forster and Olbrei (1973) reported data indicating that processing time for single-clause sentences is less than for otherwise matched
two-clause sentences—e.g., *the wealthy child attended a private school*
(simplex) vs *the dress that Pam wore looked ugly* (complex); Osgood
and Hoosain (in preparation), using 2-cog, 4-cog and 8-cog versions of
12 sentences—e.g., (*At Devonshire Academy*—the recall cue) *boys
create ballets and girls perform in plays* (2-cog) vs . . . *boys and girls
create ballets and perform in plays* (4-cog) vs . . . *boys and girls create
and perform in ballets and plays* (8-cog)—found that sentence recall
decreased significantly with number of cogs in complexes, and this for
both American English (SVO) and Iranian Farsi (SOV). So the moral for
human languages would seem to be: *pack as much information as
possible into simplexes!*

Bitransitive and Prepositional Simplexes

Cognizings and sentencings that involve three entities (or NPs) but only
one relation (or VP) put pressure on a theory that postulates an underlying tripartite structure for simplexes: the meaning of the third entity
must *either* be "absorbed" into one of the three OPERATOR components,
thereby preserving a simplex cognition, *or* it must be demonstrable that
the cognition is in fact complex, analyzable into two conjoined simplexes—which is most difficult when only one relation (VP) is involved!
Bitransitive and prepositional sentences—both of which appear to be
universal structures in human languages (and on one of which, bitransitives, we have considerable data)—provide test cases *par excellence.*

Naturalness Expectations and Some Relevant Linguistic Tests

Prototypical bitransitives are those in which a +Human agent voluntarily
transfers a ⁻Animate object to another +Human recipient. Putting oneself
back into the booties of early childhood, it seems intuitively clear (a)

that, when a prelinguistic child cognizes BIG BROTHER GIVE BALL TO BIG SISTER, the ball-object (the so-called DO) is perceptually "embedded" in the transfer relation between human source and human recipient—therefore (b) that the recipient (the so-called IO) is the *real* direct object (the M_2) in bitransitive sentences, contrary to the claims of traditional grammarians. This, of course, was the thrust behind the title of the Osgood and Tanz (1977) paper for the volume honoring Joseph Greenberg, "Will the Real Direct Object in Bitransitive Sentences Please Stand Up?".

What about prepositional cognizings? These constitute a large and varied class in which the third entity provides a kind of context, delimiting, specifying, qualifying, etc., one or another component of the cognition—but which one? Again donning one's booties, it would seem that it *could* be any one of the three components: M_1 (SNP), DOGGIE (WITH SHAGGY HAIR) IS CHASING OUR KITTY; $- - (M) - \rightarrow$ (VP), DADDY CUT OFF (WITH AN AXE) DEAD BRANCH; or M_2 (ONP), MOMMY WEARING DRESS (WITH A BIG RED BELT). Although PP phrases *can* be "absorbed" into any cog component, we will be interested primarily in VP vs ONP absorption.

In selecting sentential materials for research, we applied three linguistic tests:

(1) *Substitutability of single verbs for verb phrases.* The reasoning here was that, if such substitutions exist, "absorption" of the third entity into the relation component is supported. Thus, for bitransitives, for *made a promise to* → *promised (his wife)* but not for *gave a book to* →*booked (his wife);* and, for prepositionals, for *put in his pocket (my ball)* → *pocketed (my ball)* but not for *put in the saucer (his cup)* →*saucered (his cup).* In other words, there are many lexical gaps in any language.

(2) *Reversibility in the ordering of the two nonsubject NPs.* The assumption here was that the more acceptable ordering would indicate the component "naturally" incorporating the third entity. This test doesn't work for prototypic bitransitives, whose hallmark, of course, *is* reversibility, but (as we'll see momentarily) it does distinguish prototypic from nonprototypic bitransitives. For prepositionals, this test clearly fails in many instances; for one obvious example, *the cop chased the dog across the street* is clearly more acceptable (in American English) than *the cop chased across the street the dog—* yet, cognitively, the PP phrase *across the street* is certainly more related to the "chasing" than the "dog"—in contrast, say to *my poodle Pierre likes the dog across the street.*

(3) *Passivization.* Here the argument is that, if the two non-subject NPs can be *separated* in the transformation, then the third entity must be part of the VP, but, if they *cannot,* then the third entity must be part

of the ONP. This test seems to be the most effective. It neatly generates three types of prepositional structures: (a) *VP absorption* (where *some herbs / were put on the shelf / by the cook* is acceptable but not **some herbs on the shelf / were put by the cook*); (b) *ONP absorption* (where *a house with a view / was bought by the philosopher* is acceptable but not **a house / was bought with a view/by the philosopher*); and (c) *ambiguously either, but with a meaning shift* (given *the gardner helped the old lady across the street*, VP absorption in *the old lady / was helped across the street / by the gardner* serves to characterize the "helping" whereas ONP absorption in *the old lady across the street / was helped by the gardner* serves to characterize the "old lady").

We may now illustrate the application of all three linguistic tests to bitransitive sentences. The *substitutability* test (1) merely attests further to lexical gaps in American English—while for *made a promise to* → *promised* (sans the *to*), for *gave a bone to* is not $\overset{*}{\rightarrow}$*boned*. The other two tests both serve to distinguish prototypic "give" (direction *away from* actor) from nonprototypic "take" (direction *toward* actor) bitransitives — and note that it is consistently the prototypic "give" type that is the *least* constrained: thus, on the reversibility test (2), prototypic *John gave the bike to his daughter* reverses into the dative transform without changing meaning, but the dative form of nonprototypic *John took the bike from his daughter* reverses into *John took his daughter the bike,* thus shifting in deictic meaning to "giving"; and, on the passivization test (3), while both the basic and transform of prototypic "give" type can be passivized acceptably, only the basic form *(John took the bike from a neighbor)* can be acceptably passivized, the dative transform *(John took a neighbor the bike)* already having suffered the shift in deixis.

There is another very critical *difference* between prepositionals and bitransitives: note that in the former the preposition *must be retained* in phrase reversals (one cannot say grammatically *Mac put the table his knife*) while in the latter the preposition *must be deleted* (one can only say awkwardly *Mac gave to the policeman his knife*). We can also make a fine comparison of "identical" PP and BT surface structures: *Mac brought his knife to the dance* → **Mac brought the dance his knife* vs *Mac brought his knife to the dancer* → *Mac brought the dancer his knife.* This suggests that there is some basic difference between the ordinary prepositional *to* and the bitransitive *to*—and (as elaborated in the Discussion section of Osgood and Tanz, 1977) this difference comes down to the fact that the *to* in prepositionals is part of the ONP (M_2) whereas the *to* in bitransitives is part of the VP [– – (M) – →]. Thus, cognitively speaking, we have for the prepositional [Mac / brought / to the dance his knife] but for the bitransitive [Mac / brought his knife to / the dancer]. Adding more fuel to the fire illuminating the greater linguistic constraints on the transform, we have the following: *lexical* (cf, *John described the book to Mary* / **John described Mary the book*), for compound verbs (cf, *Sam turned over his wallet to the thief* / **Sam turned the thief over his wallet!*), and in allowing *pronominalizations* (cf, *John gave it to Luke* / **John gave Luke it* and *John gave it to him* / *?John gave him it*).

Some Cross-Language Linguistic Evidence

I can only summarize very briefly the evidence we now have on bitransitive sentencing (it is detailed in the Osgood/Tanz paper). For cross-language linguistic data we had both a 1973 independently initiated paper by Edward Blansitt and research by Philip Sedlak (1975) we initiated and supported, via the good graces of Joe Greenberg and the Stanford Universals Project.

Predictions #1 (from Osgood and Tanz, 1977) all concerned ordering of D (dative) vs O (objective) with respect to V. The overall prediction (a)—that, regardless of language type or marking characteristics, O will be closer to V than D—was *not* upheld as can be seen in Table V.1 here (a summary of the combined Sedlak and Blansitt data for 45 and 106 languages, respectively). However, we may note that, whereas SVO languages, the more likely to display variable order, have D closest to V most often (39% of the cases), as we move through SOV (31.5%) to VSO (16.5%) the percentage of languages having D closest to V goes down sharply. Now, keeping these facts in mind, witness how the predicted holding-in-BUFFER times for processing the transform dative increase (as indicated by the superimposed bars between the parts, *gave . . . a bath to,* of the theoretically basic relation), particularly for VSO: for SVO, natural *the janitor gave a bath to his nephew* to unnatural *the janitor gave his nephew a bath;* for SOV, natural *the janitor his nephew to a bath gave* to unnatural *the janitor a bath his nephew to gave;* and for VSO, natural *gave a bath the janitor to his nephew* to unnatural *gave*

Table V.1. Closeness of D vs O to V:
Sedlak and Blansitt Data (%s)
Combined

	D	=[a]	O
SVO	39.0%	38.5%	22.5%
SOV	31.5%	25.5%	43.0%
VSO	16.5%	28.5%	55.0%

[a]These include all variable-order languages.

the janitor to his nephew a bath. In other words, prediction #1 (b) from
theory is confirmed by this difference in (presumed) processing difficulty
of transform datives across language types.

Predictions #2 all concerned marking characteristics: (a) the general
expectation that D (being the "real" independent ONP constituent)
would be more frequently marked was supported by a consistent ratio of
2-to-1 in the predicted direction; (b) that D-marking should be relatively
greater for "unnatural" transforms than for "natural" basic forms was
supported in Sedlak's fixed-order languages by ratios of 10-to-4 (more
than 2-to-1) for transforms and 7-to-6 (about equal) for basics.

Two special predictions were tested and supported: Prediction #3 was
that if O is marked in unitransitive sentences but *not* in bitransitives,
then the *same* marker will be used for D in bitransitives, and this was
upheld in 13 languages cited by Blansitt, spread across all types—this
being a neat case where the "real" DO appears on the surface; Prediction
#4 was that O is more likely to be incorporated in verbs than D, and this
was strongly upheld in both American Indian data reported by Sapir
(1911) and data on Mandarin Chinese reported by Chao (1968).

Some Experimental Psycholinguistic Evidence

Three experiments were designed to test in various ways the hypothesis
that, in the processing of bitransitive sentences presented in *either* basic
SVOD or transform SVDO orders, *the O is more tightly bound to the V
than is the D:* In Experiment I, Chris Tanz tested the specific hypothesis
that, given the SNP as a cue *and given recall* of the V, the *conditional
probability* of also recalling the O will be greater than of also recalling
the D—the difference was as predicted and significant at the 0.003 level.

In Experiment II, Quin Schultze, giving *both* SNP and V as cues,
tested the specific hypothesis that with the basic SVOD form presented
there would be more correct recalls of the sentence as given and fewer
shifts in surface order than with the transform SVDO presented; these
predictions were supported at the 0.05 level of significance—of the 16
bitransitive sentences used (basic and transform versions being given to
different subjects, of course), perfect recalls *as given* were 10 for the
basics and only 4 for the transforms (with 2 equal), but correct recalls
with shifted order were only 3 for the basics yet 11 for the transforms
(again with 2 equal).

Experiment III, using a probe-association technique reported by
Weisberg (1971), yielded perhaps that most interesting results and is the
design we are "exporting" to four of our cross-cultural language communities. As Fig. V.2 illustrates, sets of four sentences were presented
for reading on each of a series of slides—one bitransitive in transform
(SVDO), one generic sentence from Weisberg as a filler, one prepositional

SLIDE 1:

(1)   (5)   (12)   (7)
The janitor gave his nephew a bath.

(6)   (9)   (14)   (2)
Cold bread is eaten by slow children.

(8)   (16)   (11)   (13)
The dancer put the flowers on the trunk.

(10)   (3)   (15)   (4)
The landlord showed an actress to the engineer.

SLIDE 2:

(14)   (6)   (2)   (12)
The detective chased the Martian with black spots.

(5)   (11)   (9)   (13)
The secretary showed the professor the dance.

(16)   (3)   (1)   (8)
The agency gave a nurse to the family.

(15)   (10)   (4)   (7)
Trained artists paint correct letters.

Fig. V.2. Sentential sets for testing predictions about bitransitives

sentence, also mainly as a filler here, and one bitransitive in basic form (SVOD)—and after a brief blank interval the subjects are given a randomized series of single-word probes (4 from each sentence as shown), with the instruction to write down for each the first *other* word in the *same* sentence that occurs to them.

The predictions of prime concern here, of course, are those relating to probes in the two types of bitransitive sentences, and we can take them up in relation to the American English data presented in Table V.2, from Osgood and Tanz: (1) *that Vs as probes* (called "cues" in the table) *will yield a higher percentage of Os as responses than Ds*—this is clearly the case for (A), both presented forms combined, and stronger for the basic SVOD form (B) than for the transform (C), as would be expected; (2) *that Os as probes will yield higher percentages of Vs as responses than will Ds as probes*—this is the case for both presented forms combined (again, about 2-to-1) and, most interestingly, it is even greater for the SVDO transform (thus, even when D directly follows V in the surface-form presented, V occurs as response only 5% of the time). These results were significant at beyond the 0.01 level in both cases.

Most recently Annette Zehler (Osgood and Zehler, 1980) has completed a study on the *acquisition* of bitransitive sentencing in children from 3 to 5 years of age, in which both *comprehension* (Simply Acting Out the experimenter's sentences with various "human", "nonhuman but animate", and "inanimate" dolls and toys) and *production* (Simply Describing various transfer events acted out by the experimenter with the same objects) were tested. The Naturalness predictions were strongly upheld: the 3-year-olds comprehended (Acted Out correctly) *only* the SVOD sentencings by the experimenter and produced (in Simply De-

Table V.2. Mean Percents of Types of Responses to Types of Cues

(A) For SVOD and SVDO forms combined

		RESPONSES			
	S	V	O	D	ER
CUES S	—	24	24.5	22	29.
V	19.5	—	35	16	29.
O	30	16.5	—	32	21
D	25	9.5	42.5	—	23

(B) For SVOD form given

		RESPONSES			
	S	V	O	D	ER
CUES S	—	26	22	20	31
V	18	—	38	14	30
O	26	18	—	38	17
D	25	14	38	—	23

(C) For SVDO form given

		RESPONSES			
	S	V	O	D	ER
S	—	22	27	24	27
V	21	—	32	18	29
CUES O	34	15	—	26	25
D	25	5	47	—	23

scribing) *only* SVOD forms; the 4- and 5-year-olds understood and used both bitransitive forms in the simpler and prototypic situations (Human doll transfers Inanimate object to another human doll), but "reverted" to the basic SVOD when the situations were nonprototypic (Nonhuman Animate transfers Animate (e.g., small kitten doll) to another Nonhuman toy) or got more complicated (e.g., A transfers X to B and then B transfers X to C).

Although research with very young Kannada- and Japanese-speaking children (by Sridhar in Bangalore and Zehler in Hiroshima, respectively)—using only simple *two-entity action cognitions* for both Acting Out (comprehension) and Describing (production)—indicated dominance already of the adult SOV surface ordering—contrary to our expectations — when Dr. Farideh Salili replicated the Osgood-Zehler experiment with Farsi-speaking (SOV) children in Iran with the more complex *three-entity bitransitive cognitions,* 90% of the sentencings of these children, even up to the age of 5, turned out to be SVO in ordering!

Naturalness of Word-Ordering within the Constituents of Simplexes (F V)

At the within-constituent level, we must look carefully at the structures and functions of the LEXICON and the OPERATOR in this APG and how these two "mechanisms" are assumed to interact in both comprehending and expressing simplexes. The basic distinction is that, whereas LEX functions on a "word-like" unit basis and therefore must reflect language-specific rules for word-ordering within constituents, OPR functions on a "whole-constituent" basis and therefore can reflect language universals in cognizing and sentencing. So the problems for APG theory become, in essence, these:

(1) In learning to *comprehend* simple sentences, (a) how does LAD's LEXICON come to segment the more-or-less continuous flows from the Sensory Integration Level into the "word-like" units for which it has acquired distinctive meanings (i.e., how does it *encode* wholistic *percepts* of word forms into strips of discrete semantic features, little r_m components) and transmit these "upward" to OPR, and (b) how does LADS OPERATOR come to segment *this* flow of semantic information from LEX and assign it to the "whole-constituents" on which *it* must "operate" [i.e., assign the flow of information into its $M_1, - - (M) - \rightarrow$ and M_2 components]?

(2) In learning to *express* simple sentences in its language, (a) how does LAD's OPERATOR transmit "whole-constituent" semantic information from its components "downward" into LEX for expression and (b) how does LAD's LEXICON now extract feature subsets corresponding to "word-like" units and order the transmission of these units to the Motor Integration Level (i.e., how does it *decode* patterns of discrete semantic features into wholistic *programs* for expression of word forms, ordered according to the rules of LAD's language)?

Words vs Morphemes as the Natural Units in Lexical Processing

Now, in this performance theory LEXICONS are assumed to operate in terms of *word-like rather than morpheme units*. There are several reasons for this: first, referring back to my last lecture, you will recall our strong evidence for the salience of *the word* in language perception as compared with units either smaller (e.g., morphemes) or larger (e.g., ordinary noun phrases); second, although there are many single-morpheme word forms (single-featured like *the* vs *a* and multifeatured like *bachelor* and *marry*), there are also many multimorpheme word forms (like *anti/abort/ion/ist/s* and *inter/sect/ed*)—and, in any case, morphemes represent clusters of *semantic* features, which are precisely what the LEXICON encodes for each linguistic form; third, we must say "wordlike" rather than "word" units in order to account for, e.g., the clearly wordlike performance characteristics of nominal compounds like *stumbling block* as compared with *copper block,* as also demonstrated by Osgood and Hoosain (1974). In sum, since it is wordlike units that are demonstrably related to both percept-integrations in comprehending and program-integrations in expressing, they would seem to be the "natural" input and output units for a language performance theory.

The three *functional* notions relating to the LEXICON offered in my last lecture—a "global" *sign-learning* principle (F I), an "emic" *feature-learning* principle (F II), and a principle (F III) specifying frequency and recency effects on sign-processing—specify for this APG how the form/meaning relations crucial to the functioning of the LEXICON are established in the experiential history of the organism. Several structural notions relating to the LEXICON were also offered: one stated a principle for *temporal ordering* of semantic features on the basis of their overall frequency of usage (S XII), another stated *the bipolar and continuously variable coding* characteristics of semantic features (S X), and yet another (S XI) suggested *the nonarbitrary signing* (Positive vs Negative) of the poles of semantic features (in the general case).

Naturalness in Within-Constituent Ordering

All of these notions relate to the naturalness of information-ordering within the constituents of simplex cognitions that must, for any language, result from LEXICON → OPERATOR transfers. Particularly relevant, however, is a notion based on prelinguistic cognizing which—although it concerns OPERATOR functions (and actually is part of our revised F VII, as will be seen)—does involve LEX/OPR interactions. It is assumed that, within each component $[M_1, - - (M) - \rightarrow, M_2]$, OPR "scans" features in the order of their *criticality* in determining adaptive behaviors to the states and actions being comprehended: (1) *affective E-P-A features* prior to denotative features by virtue of their primitive survival value, (2) for denotative information characterizing *entities* (later NPs) *substantive* (identifying) *features* prior to modulating (adjectival, quantifying, etc.) features, and (3) for denotative information characterizing *relations* (later VPs), similarly, *nature-specifying* (identifying) *features* prior to modulating (tense, adverbial, etc.) features.

Now this clearly implies that N-followed-by-As ordering in M_1 and M_2 components should be more rapidly processed by OPR than As-followed-by-N and that V-followed-by-AV ordering of $- - (M) - \rightarrow$ components should be more rapidly processed than AV-followed-by-V—i.e., having "identifying" information always prior to "modulating" information in transfers from LEX to OPR. And *this* implies, for human languages, that *the former within-constituent orderings should be more natural than the latter.*

Again donning the booties of childhood, it seems intuitively reasonable that the "inherent" features of entities (e.g., the Graspable, Throwable, Rollable features of BALLS) should be more critical for appropriate behaving than their "incidental" features (e.g., their Color, Cleanliness, or Sport-identification). Similarly, the "inherent" natures of states or actions (their Being, Having, Contacting, Burning, etc.) should be available prior to the ways they are modulated (their Temporal, etc., tenses and their Manner, etc., adverbial shiftings). Greenberg (1963) informs us, relevantly, that N-followed-by-As languages outnumber As-followed-by-N languages by about two to one, but he offers us little as far as ordering within VPs is concerned (apparently, this is very much dependent upon basic typology).

LEX/OPR Functions in Comprehending vs Expressing

In stating the functional notions governing LEXICON/OPERATOR interactions (F V) it was necessary to distinguish processing in comprehending from processing in expressing, since *in comprehending* LEX is dependent upon percept-inputs from the Sensory Integration Level [and hence is *given* the language-specific sequencing of wordlike forms by (usually) adult speakers] whereas *in expressing* LEX is dependent upon unsegmented, whole-constituent, code-strips of features from the OPERATOR.

> IN COMPREHENDING: (1) LEX encodes wordlike forms, entailing both free morphemes (e.g., as in *the* vs *a*) and complexly bound morphemes (e.g., as in superfically simple *sparrow* or complex *unintentionaly* and *stumbling block*), into their feature codes as their percepts are successively received from the Sensory Integration Level; (2) OPR, utilizing language-specific cues that signal the boundaries of NP and VP constituents, assigns this information-sequence "horizontally" to its three components $[M_1, - - (M) - \rightarrow, M_2]$ for simplexes [at this point, 'egardless of the Naturalness (appropriateness) of codings for SNP, VP, and ONP constituents—but see F VII later]; and (3) utilizing cues for the conjoining of simplexes into complexes (e.g., *and/but*s, adverbials like *after* and *because*), OPR assigns the clauses of complexes "vertically" to its successive levels (again, regardless of the Naturalness of the clause ordering—but see F VI).

Rule (2) here requires at least a bit of elaboration. To the best of my knowledge, all languages provide surface cues (not always unambiguous, of course) for at least the natures (NPs vs VPs) and the boundaries of constituents within simple sentences and also for the natures (coordinate, main vs subordinate, congruent vs incongruent) and the boundaries of clauses within complex sentences. Since these surface cues *are* language-specific, they must be learned by the developing OPERATORS of LADS acquiring different languages (and I must confess that I have not yet considered the nature of such learning).

The cues are usually *unambiguous*. Thus in English typical cues for constituent *initial* boundaries of NPs are often articles and quantifiers *(a, the, some, all, many),* adjectives followed by plural nouns *(ancient ruins . . .),* plural nouns alone *(skyscrapers in New York . . .),* and undoubtedly others. Cues for constituent *terminal* boundaries are most typically the heads of NPs themselves, but may also be cues for initiating relative clauses (. . . *the one that . . . , . . . the young who . . .),* verb phrases (. . . *the blind were . . .),* and even terminal sentence [. . . *easy* (?)] or initial sentence (. . . the victims / / He then . . .) intonation patterns. Obvious cues for VP boundaries are auxiliary verb forms (. . . *had been)* and less obviously adverbs, either VP initial [. . . steadily (hammered). . . .] or VP terminal [. . . (hammered) steadily . . .], and of course heads of VPs themselves, when followed by NP-initial cues, are obvious terminal cues (. . . *jumped over* / the high . . .).

However, the cues for constituent boundaries are sometimes *ambiguous.* As an example of this in English, take syntactically ambiguous *ship sails today* as contrasted with unambiguous *the ship sails today* vs *ship the sails today:* note that *ship sails today* may be disambiguated either by continuation of the same sentence (. . . *with the tide* vs . . . *in cartons)* or by subsequent context *(my luggage is all packed* vs *my customers are waiting for them).* In other words, OPR must sometimes process beyond a boundary into other constituents before being able to ''mark'' the now-prior boundary or boundaries.

> IN EXPRESSING: (1) OPR transmits to LEX semantic code-strips for whole constituents, with either natural or unnatural ordering of the constituents of simplexes or the clauses of complexes, LEX not processing any *subsequent* received constituent until all features of the *preceding* constituent have been decoding into ''wording'' programs at the Motor Integration Level (otherwise there would be utter confusion!) and LEX is momentarily ''featureless''; (2) on receiving code-strips of semantic features for a given constituent from OPR, LEX (a) extracts those subsets of semantic features *for which word-forms are available in its language* (or, strictly speaking, in the speaker's idiolect) such that, taken together, the word-forms so extracted *exhaustively express the semantic content of the whole constituent,* and (b) outputs these feature-sets *to the Motor Integration Level,* in the order established by the speaker's experience of the language (i.e., within-constituent structure)

in comprehending, where the related programs for expressing are activated successively.

Note that this statement accounts for variations (a) among speakers of a given language and (b) across languages in the matter of lexicalization. Thus, a medically "aware" person may express a given code-strip of semantic features as *carcenogenic* while another speaker may use the periphrasis, *cancer-causing* or *that which causes cancer,* and so on. Similarly, a given language may express a certain semantic content with a single lexical item, e.g., *bring* in English, while another language may resort to a serial verb construction expressing the same semantic content, e.g., *tegedu-kondu-ba* 'having taken—reflexive auxiliary—come' in Kannada.

Finally, note that the output order of words in a given constituent is explained as having its origin in the speaker's experience *with comprehension.* Once again, there is ample psycholinguistic evidence, for all levels and types of constituents, pointing to the developmental priority of comprehension over production. Considering the language-specific nature of the ordering of words within constituents (e.g., auxiliary → verb in English and verb → auxiliary in Japanese), it is clear that such ordering is acquired by the language-learning child on the basis of his exposure to the adult language in comprehension.

Naturalness in Ordering the Clauses of Complexes (F VI)

The basic assumption made here is that, in both comprehending and expressing complex sentences with conjoined clauses, *the natural order of processing by the* OPERATOR *is that which corresponds to the order in which the states and/or events referred to in the clauses are typically cognized in prelinguistic experience.* Given the orderly nature of the physical world, in perceptual experience (of the adult as well as the prelinguistic child) related events are almost always cognized in their natural order—thus, for the Sequence Mode, antecedent before subsequent events (MOMMY GET UNDRESSED and then MOMMY GET IN BED); for the Sequential Cause Mode, causal state or event before effect state or event (DADDY DROP GLASS and so then GLASS SHATTER IN PIECES). Of course, unnaturally ordered perceptual cognizing *can* occur: a child could see MOMMY GET IN BED and then MOMMY GET UNDRESSED (under the covers), but it is most unlikely! I recall in an old movie where A CREAM PIE HITTING (recipient) OLIVER HARDY'S FACE was followed by a shot of STAN LAUREL (source) SLAPPING HIS KNEES AND (silently) LAUGHING!

Naturalness in expressing complexes will correspond to naturalness in comprehending them simply because this *is* the order required for original comprehension by potential speakers—whether derived from LEX in fresh cognizing or from MEM in re-cognizing. However, all known human languages provide means by which speakers can move clauses about in order to satisfy their momentary interests and motives—this being but one of many ways in which use of the linguistic channel frees humans from the chains that bind the nonlinguistic (perceptual) channel to reality.

But, given our prelinguistically based structures for cognizing, it follows that *even sentential complexes must be naturally ordered if they are to be comprehended by listeners, although they may be disordered in expression by speakers* (to satisfy their salience needs—see F VIII). Since all disordering of complexes requires BUFfing of whole clauses on the part of *both* speakers and listeners, this implies that *unnatural clause ordering in complexes will produce increased processing time*—we will take up some of the details of this in later lectures.

Naturalness of Clause Ordering in English

It is possible to order a variety of modes of conjoining simultaneously in terms of increasing *semantic complexity* of their codings and in terms of increasing *syntactic complexity* of their ordering (see Fig. V.3, taken from Gordana Opačić's 1973 thesis).

Complexity of semantic coding (top-to-bottom in the figure): Simple Junction is coded only +Congruent (*and* with its adverbial derivatives like *while*) or ⁻Congruent (*but* with its adverbial derivatives like *although*), and either clause order is natural; Simple Sequence adds a ±Sequence feature to ±Congruence [*and* (then) vs *but* (then) and adverbials like *before, after, yet,* and *although*], and clause orders can be either natural or unnatural (e.g., *Mary got undressed before she went to bed* vs *before Mary went to bed she got undressed*); similarly, for Simple Cause I a ±Cause feature is added to ±Congruence [*and* (so) vs *but* (still) and adverbials like *because, so, however, although*], and again orders can be natural or unnatural (e.g., *because it was raining John got wet* vs *John got wet because it was raining*); still more complexly coded, and also variable in order, are Sequential Cause II (both Sequence and Cause features added to Congruence) and Intention (Sequence and Intentionality added to Congruence).

Order of increasing syntactic complexity (from center outward in figure): It is interesting that the modes of conjoining that are acquired earliest, (1) underlying And/But conjoiners, are also the most constrained—they *must* be centered between clauses and (corresponding to perceived events) the clauses *must* be in natural order (witness the "mind-boggling-ness" of *!And Mary went to bed she got undressed* as

Fig. V.3. A hierarchy of modes of conjoining and associated forms

| | CONGRUENT | | | | | | INCONGRUENT | | | | |
MODES	Embedding (subordination) (5) Prepos., Cogs permuted	(4) Centered, Cogs permuted	(3) Prepositionable	(2) Substitutable	(1) Underlying (only centered)	AND_0	(1) Underlying (only centered)	(2) Substitutable	(3) Prepositionable	(4) Centered, Cogs permuted	(5) Prepos., Cogs permuted
Conversational carrier						AND_0					
Junction	WHILE	WHILE AND_1	WHILE	WHILE	AND_1		BUT_1	$ALTHOUGH_1$	$ALTHOUGH_1$	$ALTHOUGH_1$ BUT_1	$ALTHOUGH_1$
Sequence	$BEFORE_1$	$AFTER_1$	$AFTER_1$	$BEFORE_1$	AND_2 (THEN)		BUT_2 (THEN)	YET_1	$ALTHOUGH_2$	$ALTHOUGH_2$	—
Cause I	—	$BECAUSE_1$ $SINCE_1$	$BECAUSE_1$ $SINCE_1$	SO_1 $THEREFORE_1$	AND_3 (SO)		BUT_3 (STILL)	YET_2 $HOWEVER_1$	$ALTHOUGH_3$	$ALTHOUGH_3$	—
Cause II	—	$AFTER_2$ $BECAUSE_2$ $SINCE_2$	$AFTER_2$ $BECAUSE_2$ $SINCE_2$	SO_2 $THEREFORE_2$	AND_4 (SO THEN)		BUT_4 (STILL THEN)	YET_3 $HOWEVER_2$	$ALTHOUGH_4$	$ALTHOUGH_4$	—
Intention	(IN ORDER) TO $BEFORE_2$ SO_3	$AFTER_3$	$AFTER_3$	(IN ORDER) TO $BEFORE_2$ SO_3	AND_5 (SO THEN COULD)		$(BUT)_5$ (STILL THEN COULDN'T / DIDN'T)	YET_4 $HOWEVER_3$	$ALTHOUGH_5$	$ALTHOUGH_5$	—

well as *!Mary went to bed and got undressed*).[4] With subordinating adverbials, (2) centered adverbials that maintain natural order *(before, so, yet, however)* should be somewhat less difficult than, (3) preposed adverbials that maintain natural order *(after, because, although);* for example, *the road was icy so the car skidded* is somewhat easier than *because the road was icy the car skidded.* Much more difficult should be (4) centered adverbials requiring unnatural order (e.g., *John put on his street clothes after he took a shower*), and most difficult should be (5) preposed adverbials requiring unnatural order (e.g., *before John put on his street clothes he took a shower*).

Note that, as indicated by the subscripts, both the basic *and*s and *but*s and many of their adverbial substitutes are polysemous, shifting in sense with the mode of conjoining. A "proof" that, for example, and_1 and and_4 have different senses is obtained simply by substituting their subordinating adverbials across modes: thus *she read the novel and_1* (= while) *she listened to quiet music* for the Junction Mode and *she took arsenic and_4* (= so then) *she became ill* for the Cause II Mode are natural, but when we cross the substitutes we get very strange sentences, *? she read the novel so then she listened to quiet music* and *? she took arsenic while she became ill.*

Considerable research on the processing of complexes by both adults and children is now available, and it is generally consistent with these predictions. Most of the earlier studies dealt only with *before* and *after* (i.e., our Congruent Simple Sequence mode): Clark and Clark (1968), working with recall of sentences by adult subjects, found that both *naturally* ordered preposed *(after she stuffed the turkey she roasted it)* and centered *(she stuffed the turkey before she roasted it)* complexes were recalled better than *unnaturally* ordered (with *before* preposed and *after* centered). E. Clark (1971) also reported that in a comprehension task (Simply Acting Out with toys), with child subjects ranging from 3;2 to 4;11 in age, *naturally* ordered sentences *(after* preposed and *before* centered) were acted out with only 8% errors as compared with 58% errors for *unnaturally* ordered sentences *(before* preposed and *after* centered). There were *no* differences between *after* preposed (hence subordinate-to-main clause ordering) and *before* centered (hence main-to-subordinate ordering)—which is consistent with the Naturalness Principle but not with the linguistic notion that main clause followed by subordinate should be easier. I will report on two theses, by Hoosain and Opačić (both in 1973), later in connection with APG predictions about the processing of Unnatural (transform) vs Natural complexes.

---

[4] I use the symbol ! to indicate *unacceptableness* ("mind-boggling-ness") rather than *ungrammaticalness* (*); as far as I am aware, there is nothing ungrammatical about *Mary went to bed and got undressed,* although the preposed *and* in *And Mary went to bed she got undressed* may render it *both* ungrammatical and unacceptable.

Unambiguous Signaling of Naturalness in Clause Ordering for English

Referring back to Fig. V.3, the following can be noted: (1) Basic conjoiners *and* and *but* can only be centered between clauses and the clauses must be in natural order—therefore centered *and* or *but* (regardless of their mode-dependent senses) are unambiguous cues for naturalness. (2) In the Simple Junction mode (with adverbials *while* for congruent and *although* for incongruent complexes) either clause order or adverb location is natural *(while John played Mary sang; Mary sang while John played; although Many sang John wouldn't play; John wouldn't play although Mary sang)*—so there is no unnaturalness to *be* signaled. (3) For other modes of conjoining, adverbial substitutes for basic *and*s or *but*s that can *only be centered* between clauses (congruence-indicating *so* and *therefore;* incongruence-indicating *yet* and *however*) must also signal natural order unambiguously, (4) For all other adverbials, however—ones that can be *either* centered or preposed, in Sequence, Cause, Sequential Cause, and Intention modes—*the combined cues of the form of the adverbial (after, before, because, since, in order to,* and ubiquitous *although) along with its location* (centered or preposed) *provide completely unambiguous indicators of naturalness vs unnaturalness of clause ordering.*

This last category (4) needs some elaboration. We have already seen that, for Sequence, clauses must be naturally ordered if *before* is centered *(John cashed his check before he went shopping)* but must be unnaturally ordered if preposed *(before John went shopping he cashed his check),* and conversely for *after (after John cashed his check he went shopping / John went shopping after he cashed his check).* Similarly, for both Cause and Sequential Cause, note that congruent *because* (and *since*) signals naturalness when preposed *(because Mary fell in love with John she went on a diet; !because Mary went on a diet she fell in love with John)* and unnaturalness when centered *(John was executed because he poisoned his mother-in-law; !John poisoned his mother-in-law because he was executed).* Conversely, centering the *in order to* (and *before* and *so*) of the Intention mode signals naturalness (Execution before inferred Intention) and preposing signals unnaturalness (thus natural *John drilled a hole in the coconut in order to drink its milk* and unnatural *in order to drink its milk John drilled a hole in the coconut);* but note the "mind-boggling-ness" of *!John drank its milk in order to drill a hole in the coconut* or of *!in order to drill a hole in the coconut John drank its milk.*

All senses of the ubiquitous *although* (except that for Simple Junction), used with incongruent conjoinings, display the same unambiguous signaling function, in this case signaling naturalness if prepositioned and unnaturalness if centered. In the case of Simple Cause, for example, we have natural *although it was stifling hot he wore his heavy sweater* and unnatural *he wore his heavy sweater although it was stifling hot;* similarly, for the Intention mode, we have natural *although he searched through all his pockets he couldn't find the wedding ring* and unnatural *he couldn't find the wedding ring although he searched through all his pockets.* But note the utter unacceptability of reversing these relations: *!it was stifling hot although he wore his heavy sweater* and *!although he wore his heavy sweater it was stifling hot* for Simple Cause and, for Intention, of *!he searched through all his pockets although he couldn't find the wedding ring* and *!although he couldn't find the wedding ring he searched through all his pockets.*

The critical thing here is that what is signaled unambiguously in the surface structures—by adverbial *forms,* by their *locations,* or by *both combined—is not grammaticality but rather naturalness* (or unnaturalness) *of the ordering of meaningful information in the conjoined clauses.* Although the !-marked sentences above are mind-boggling, we know of nothing in contemporary transformational generative grammar that would tag them as ungrammatical. Nor is there anything ungrammatical about *!John poisoned his mother-in-law because he was executed* or about *!although he wore his heavy sweater it was stifling hot*—they are, simply, unacceptably mind-boggling.

Unambiguous Signaling of Naturalness in Other Languages

Is such unambiguous signaling of naturalness vs unnaturalness of clause ordering somehow unique to English? This is precisely what we have been checking with at least a small sample of other languages—Kannada in detail and some five others somewhat more superficially (Osgood and Sridhar, 1979)—and the evidence strongly suggests that such signaling is, indeed, a language universal. Since what is signaled is not grammaticality but naturalness, and since neither speakers or listeners are at all aware of such signaling—yet this is surely a part of their language *competence*—this would seem to have serious implications for the explanatory adequacy of Chomskyan TGG or any other purely linguistic competence theory.

Naturalness in Memory Functioning

In cognitive psychology generally (and psycholinguistics more particularly) the topic of memory has, over the past half-decade or so, been one of the most extensively studied, so in the final APG book there will be much data to check theory against. The *structural* notions already postulated for the MEMORY place constraints on the possible form of *functional* notions. You'll recall that MEM is organized "vertically" by Topics (M_1s) from maximum Positiveness to maximum Negativeness in their semantic codings and "horizontally" within Topics (as well as Commentary constituents, $- - (M) - \rightarrow$ s and M_2s) from most to least frequently differentiating features. This MEM is quite literally a "semantic memory" [in this respect like the Smith, Shoben, and Rips (1974) "set-theoretic" model] but, given its topic-commentary structure, it is also a knowledge-of-the-world "propositional memory" [in this respect like the Anderson and Bower (1973) "network" model].

Memory Search and Storage in Comprehending

Following the Naturalness Principle, Topics in MEM are usually the Figures of Stative Relations and the Sources of Action Relations (thus the M_1s), and therefore they must have +Substantivity and +Directionality basic codings. Given transfer of a processed cognition from OPR to MEM for either search or storage, the following functional notion F IX is proposed:[5]

> (A) Each nonzero feature of the probe Topic code-strip is compared from "top-to-bottom" with the Topic code-strips stored in MEM: (1) a $+/+$ match is followed by a shift "rightward" to the next nonzero feature in the probe and a $-/+$ mismatch is followed by a shift "downward" to minus codings on that feature, where a $-/-$ match will also produce a "rightward" shift; (2) if no probe/topic match is found, MEM search is terminated, but, if a match is found, that MEM topic is held "reverberating" as a topic-locus indicator.

Given the structural assumptions of "vertical" ordering of Topics in terms of Positiveness-to-Negativeness and "horizontal" ordering of features within Topics in terms of usage-frequency, this would seem to be the most efficient way to search the MEMORY.

> (B) The associated Commentary is similarly tested: (1) first the Relation $[- - (M) - \rightarrow]$ of the probe is compared against all relations *associated with this topic* and then (2) the Object (M_2) code-strip against all remaining entries for which *both* M_1 and the relation match; (3) if a complete match is found, (a) that "old" cognition is strengthened (a kind of "rehearsal") and (b) a copy is returned to the OPERATOR; but

---

[5] Although these functional notions relating to the MEMORY belong with the other Naturalness notions, and hence in this lecture, they were elaborated *after* the notions relating to Unnaturalness in sentencing had been "finalized", hence the (Roman) F #'s will be changed in the expanded APG book.

(4) if no complete match is found, the "new" cognition as a whole is entered in the appropriate locus for its topic-coding.

At this point, I have no idea as to what the "copying" process would be like, but it must be postulated to preserve information in the MEMORY. However, a number of testable predictions flow from this functional notion: for one thing, Topic probes should be more effective for whole-cog retrieval than Commentary probes; for another, the more Positive the feature codings of probes the quicker should be whole-cog recalls; and for yet another, the less elaborately constituent probes are coded (i.e., the more O-codings there are) the more rapidly they should be searched.

Question-Answering

What are functionally "questions" come in a wide variety of forms, as do expected "answers", and they vary in *modality:* linguistic Q / linguistic A ("How old are you, sonny?" / "I'm six, Grampa!"); linguistic Q / nonlinguistic A (as in the many sentence-verification studies where, e.g., after reading *the star is below the circle,* the subject sees a picture of STAR ABOVE CIRCLE and then pushes the "false" button); nonlinguistic Q / linguistic A (as in my Simply Describing demonstrations where, e.g., a perceptual event like seeing ONE BLACK BALL ROLL AND HIT ANOTHER "asks" and the observer's Simple Describing "answers"); and even nonlinguistic Q / nonlinguistic A (in other experiments, following instructions, two complex forms are flashed simultaneously and the subject simply pushes either a SAME or a DIFFERENT button). Linguistic Qs also vary widely in form—from the most direct WH-Qs (the *who, what, where, when,* and *why* of things), through verb-auxiliary-fronting Qs *(Is he . . . ?, Didn't you . . . ?, Have they . . . ?)* and assertions often implying Qs (as in responding "true" or "false" to *a squirrel is not a bird*), to very indirect Qs (like saying "It's hot in here" as a way of asking someone to open the window).

There are two possible sources of answers to questions: either direct, via dynamic feature-comparing within the OPERATOR itself, or indirect, via search of the MEMORY. It must also be kept in mind that, in this APG, inputs via the perceptual channel and the linguistic channel share the same cognitive system and the same semantic-feature code. We may now propose the following functional notion, F X:

(A) Since direct LEX → OPR → LEX transfers for encoding Qs and decoding As must require much less processing time than indirect LEX → OPR → MEM → OPR → LEX encoding and decoding (which also involves comparison in OPR of LEX-initiated with MEM-relayed cognitions before answering), if in (1), *a single-cog Q*, the features of the Topic (M_1) are semantically entailed in the total code-strip of the Object (M_2), which is automatically checked in OPR processing, then the A will be positive *(yes, true, same, right,* etc.) if the Relation [$- - -$ (M) $-\rightarrow$] is associative, but will be negative *(no, false, different, wrong,* etc.) if the Relation is dissociative; if, in (2), *a double-cog Q*, the two cogs, [$M_1 - -$ (M) $-\rightarrow M_2$] and [$M_1' - -$ (M) $-\rightarrow' M_2'$], have the same meanings for the Q-relevant components, which is checked "vertically" in OPR, then the A will be positive, but, if they have different meanings, then the A will be negative.

Examples of single-cog Qs involving entailment would be: for associative relations, e.g., X is a kind of Y *(is a penguin/bat a bird?,* with positive vs negative As) or X is the same as Y *(is a widow/widower a man whose wife has died,* with negative vs positive As); for dissociative relations, e.g., X is not a kind of Y or X is not the same as Y, the conditions for positive vs negative answers reverse, of course. Examples of double-cog Qs requiring OPR comparisons across cognitions "in parallel" are many and varied: in comparing the commentaries for pairs of topics (e.g., given the Q *Does Mary look like Susan?* and comparing from MEM [Mary / is / blond] and [Susan / is / brunette], etc., the A might be *Not much*); in comparing across linguistic and perceptual channels (e.g., hearing his friend say *Our waitress is topless,* John turns and confirms OUR WAITRESS IS TOPLESS, *Yeeeaaah!);* syllogistic reasoning would illustrate complex cases of multiple-cog Qs and their As.

(B) if none of the conditions under (A) are satisfied, then for verification Qs (1) the Q information in Cog$_1$ is held in OPR until (2) the information resulting from MEM search is transferred to OPR as Cog$_2$, and (3) the A will be positive if the relevant components of the two cognitions have the same meaning (again, checked "vertically") or negative if they have different meanings; (C) for information-seeking Qs (which always require MEM search), the Q-form as a cue (rising intonation, WH-form, preposed V-auxiliary, etc.) causes OPR (1) to transform the Q into a simplex Cog$_1$ plus Q-tag, in which the M_1 is the Topic, and transfer it to MEM, then (2) to accept from MEM as Cog$_2$s successively (a) ones having completely matching components (confirmatory, if such are stored in MEM), (b) ones having matching M_1 and $- -$ (M) $- \rightarrow$ components but different M_2s (either informative or irrelevant), and (3) to transfer either confirmatory or contradicting information (or "Don't" know!) to LEX for expressions as As.

Just a couple of examples must suffice: when I asked my wife "Is Jimmie Carter's wife a blonde?", she was silent for a moment (while her OPR consulted with her MEM) before she replied "Neither, she's a brown-haired gal, just like I used to be!" There are also information-seeking Qs (typically WH-Qs) which transform into *incomplete* cognitions in the

OPR, e.g., "Where did the cook put the paprika?" becomes [the cook / put (WH?) / the paprika]; if the listener's MEM is searched with both *the cook* and *the paprika* as code-strips (ideally in parallel, but probably in close succession), it may come up with a completion of the missing information [the cook / put *on the top shelf* / the paprika] (in which case the *new* information becomes the A) or it may not (in which case "I dunno" is the likely A).

Complexity in Memory Search

Although for overall efficiency MEM is structured so as to minimize search-time *for Topics,* given probes with basic initial semantic codings *for Relations* ($^-$Substantivity) or *for Objects* ($^+$Substantivity but $^-$Directionality), these "columns" in MEM *will be searched* (again, "left-to-right" by frequency-ordered features). But, since "vertical" ordering for Relations and Objects is *not* "top-to-bottom" in terms of max-Positiveness to max-Negativeness, there can be no saving of search time by automatically "dropping" to negative codings on each ^-f_i encountered as is the case for Topic search.

The greater *the number of Commentaries for a given Topic* in MEM, the greater will be the average search time; similarly, the greater *the number of Objects* (M_2s) for a given Topic/Relation pair, the greater will be the average search time. This aspect of APG_0 is similar to the Anderson and Bower (1973) "matching" model (" . . . match time is linearly related . . . to the number of associations searched during the attempted match . . . any associative fanning . . . will increase the mean MATCH time" (p. 239, also cf their Chap. 12).

The greater *the number of nonzero-coded features* in a Topic code-strip (i.e., the more "richly" it is coded, e.g., *the three little bearded old bachelors* vs *the old bachelor*), the greater will be the search time, *but* conversely (and typically compensatingly) the smaller should be the number of Commentaries.

The Cog_1s of *conjoined complexes* (always transferred from OPR to MEM in their Natural ordering in the comprehending process, see F VI earlier) *must carry an "address"* to their associated Cog_2s, this including the semantic characterizations of both the mode of conjoining (e.g., for Incongruent Sequential Cause, *but still then,* $^-$Congruence, $^+$Cause, and $^+$Sequence) and the Topic of the Cog_2. Just *how* this "address" information would be stored in MEM remains to be thought out; the obvious fact that people *do* link such conjoined complexes, in recollecting behavioral experiences, past listenings and readings, and the like, requires such postulation. The predicted ordering for speed of retrieving whole complexes from MEM should be easiest for complexes whose conjoined cogs have the same Topic, harder for complexes having different Topics but shared Relations and/or Objects, and hardest for complexes having no shared constituents.

The Memory as a Source in Expressing

In this APG the essence of *thinking* (reasoning, recalling, planning, etc., as well as day- and night-dreaming) lies in interactions between MEM and OPR (only the latter, by the way, involving *consciousness,* "awareness" of the meanings of cognitions). The direction of information "flow" is MEM → OPR (thus *re-cognizing*) as contrasted with LEX → OPR *(fresh cognizing);* the sets of cogs (propositions, ideas, recollections, etc.)—usually related by topics, commentaries, or linkages of complexes—received from MEM are processed in OPR via the same within-cog ("horizontal") and between-cog ("vertical") dynamics that apply in fresh cognizing.

Given the opportunity (situational) and urge (motivational) to talk, such *MEM-initiated cognitions may be expressed* via the usual OPR → LEX transfers (as reasoned arguments, explanations, justifications, proposals, recollections, etc.), subject to Salience, Congruence and Efficiency/Complexity dynamics and therefore to possible involvement of the BUFFER.

Given long-loop (articulatory/auditory) feedback, there is continuous *self-monitoring* by speakers, yielding "back-tracking" corrections (often on a full-constituent basis, cf, Maclay and Osgood, 1959). Processing-time delays (due to complexity of MEM → OPR, OPR <—> BUF, and OPR → LEX transfers) give rise to *pausal phenomena* (shorter, unfilled pauses and, longer, pauses filled with "conversational-ball-holding" *um*'s and *ah*'s).

Some Implications of the Semantic Nature of this Memory

Given that features are ordered "left-to-right" in all MEM components on the basis of overall frequency of usage and the necessary implication that higher-ordered features in the taxonomic sense must be more frequently entailed and hence be more "leftward" in code-strips, it follows (1) that *Topics having the same higher-order entailments* (e.g., *dog, wolf, fox,* etc., all entailing +Animate, ⁻Human, +Canine) *will be clustered close together* in the "vertical" ordering of cognitions in MEM and (2) that the higher (more "leftward") the order of a feature which

differentiates Topics (with + vs − codings), *the more remote* in MEM
will be the topics and *the larger will be the conceptual classes* thus
distinguished (e.g., Abstract vs Concrete conceptual classes larger than,
say, Male vs Female Human conceptual classes). Meyer (1973) gives
evidence that determining whether a word is a member of either of two
conceptual categories is faster when the categories are close than when
they are remote.

The fact that the MEM in this APG receives from OPR and stores the
semantic code-strips *for whole constituents* of perception-based and
linguistic-based cognitions, rather than being a "dictionary-like" store
of meanings of word forms (which here is a LEX function), implies the
following:

(1) In search and source functions of MEM, a range of *paraphrastic*
Topics, Relations and Objects will have *the same code-strips* in MEM
(the distinctions in their surface forms thus disappearing at the Representational Level); such distinctions in form *are* retained at the Sensory
and Motor Integration Levels (as *percepts* and *programs,* respectively),
but rapidly fading over time—see Sachs (1967) for one of the earliest
studies indicating that memory for surface structure is very short-lived
as compared with memory for meaning.

(2) As probes for MEM search, *paraphrases* of original constituents
will be *as effective* as the originals, and probes which, while different in
surface form than the original constituents, *convey the senses* of these
constituents—as determined by OPR cognizing dynamics across the
whole cogs ("horizontally") in original comprehending—will be *more
effective* than the originals. A recent paper (1975) by Anderson and
Ortony, titled "On Putting Apples into Bottles: A Problem of Polysemy",
is particularly relevant here: given, e.g., either *the container held the
apples* or *the container held the cola,* and then being given both *basket*
and *bottle* (among many others, of course, for other test sentence-pairs),
basket was a better probe for the former sentence and *bottle* a better
probe for the latter—i.e., the "instantiation" of the feature strip for the
general Topic, *container,* was differentially modified in OPR by the
Objects, *apples* vs *cola,* of the same cognitions in comprehending.

Since the constituents of cogs transferred from MEM to OPR for
expressing do have the paraphrastic character indicated in (2) above, the
actual *programs for talking* at the Motor Integration Level mediated via
LEX (semantic decoding) will also be *potentially paraphrastic expressions,* with efficiency for the Speaker (smallest N of word forms for a
constituent allowed by his vocabulary) competing with his concern about
complexity demands on the Listener (expanded paraphrases) in the
determination of the particular expression used.

Pollyanna and Congruence Dynamics: From Yang and Yin to *and* or *but*

Orientation

In this lecture we will begin at the beginning—the ancient Chinese metaphysics of *Yang and Yin*—where some of the most basic principles of human thinking were first (I believe) described. Then we will explore the simplest expressions of Yang and Yin in human thinking and talking—the dynamics of primitive affective Positiveness vs Negativeness, or what I will call *Pollyannaism*. We will then move on to more complex expressions of Yang and Yin in cognizing and sentencing—the dynamics of Congruence vs Incongruence, or what I will call *Psycho-logic*. And in both of these explorations we will, of course, be primarily interested in how these dynamics function in psycholinguistic theory and are tested in research. Finally we will inquire into the finer semantic details of cognitive congruence/incongruence relations as they are postulated to operate in this APG within the constituents of simplexes and between the clauses of complexes.

In *I Ching*

According to ancient Chinese metaphysics, as recorded some 4000 years ago in *I Ching* or the *Book of Changes* (Wilhelm translation, 1967), when the undifferentiated universe (symbolized by an empty circle) moved, light or *Yang* was produced, and when movement ceased, dark or *Yin* appeared. The continuous interplay between these primal bipolar forces of Yang and Yin (symbolized by a circle of interwound white and black segments) creates stress, change, and harmony in the universe as humans know it. The underlying polarity of Yang and Yin begins with light vs dark and extends not only into high vs low, creative vs receptive, firm vs yielding, moving vs resting, and masculine vs feminine but also into many other areas of human concern. This polarity is not simply evaluative; it is rather, as Wilhelm (p.297) concludes, a polarity between two global forces which can only be termed *the positive and the negative.*

This is the most ancient expression of certain basic characteristics of human cognitive processes, including language, I have been able to find. The first characteristic is the *bipolar organization* of cognitions (meanings are differentiated in terms of polar oppositions); the second is the *attribution of positiveness* to one of the poles of each dimension of qualification (*strong* and *active,* as well as *good,* are somehow psychologically positive as compared with their opposites); and the third characteristic is the tendency toward *parallel polarity* (poles of diverse dimensions being related in parallel, positives with positives and negatives with negatives, rather than in contrary directions).

In Linguistics

Linguistic theorizing is replete with bipolar structures, and Greenberg (1966) has brought together evidence from many languages to show that usually positives are unmarked and negatives are marked (thus *happy* vs *unhappy* but not *sad* vs *unsad*), positives are used to represent the entire dimension or category (we say *how tall is John now,* not **how short is John now*), and positives tend to be more frequent in usage. There is also ample linguistic evidence for parallel polarity, appearing as *congruence* rules governing the use of positives and negatives (see Klima, "Negation in English", 1964, for much evidence): thus, in my English it is natural to say *he was stupid to eat any purple mushrooms* but strange to say *he was stupid to eat some purple mushrooms* (*some* being positive and *any* negative linguistically), and it is natural to say *he was wise to take some medicine afterward* but impossible to say *he was wise to take any medicine afterward;* the same pattern holds for congruent/incongruent relations with *seldom* (negative) vs *often* (positive), as witness the naturalness of *he seldom has any money* and *he often has some money* as against the awkwardness of *he seldom has some money* and *he often has any money.* Note that *wise/stupid* refer to intellectual ability and *often/seldom* to rate of repetition over time, yet they both follow the same congruence rules when combined with *some/any,* which refer to quantity.

In Psychology

Yang and Yin are also prevalent in psychological theorizing, and they appear most clearly in models of *cognitive dynamics*—like Fritz Heider's (1958) *balance/imbalance,* theory (applied particularly to interpersonal perceptions and relations), Leon Festinger's (1957) *consonance/dissonance* theory (applied mainly to relations between cognitions and behaviors), and my own (Osgood, 1960) *congruity/incongruity* theory (applied primarily to semantic interactions and attitude change). The characteristics which these theories of cognizing share are clearly consistent with the implications of Yang and Yin: bipolar organization of the cognitive system, assignment of positive and negative valences to bipolar elements and their relations, and the assumption of parallel polarity among diverse, but positively and negatively signed, elements and relations.

Although differing in many other respects, these theories also agreed (1) *that cognitive elements only interact when brought into some relation with one another* (in language, syntactic relations like predicating, modifying, and conjoining), (2) *that cognitive inconsistencies create psychological stress, this stress varying with the magnitude of the inconsistency* (thus a cognitive *drive* of a negative sort), and (3) *that the resolution of such psychological stress is always toward consistency*—balance, consonance, or congruity, depending on which theory (thus drive *reduction* toward the kind of consistency that Ralph Waldo Emerson claimed to be "the hobgoblin of little minds", which can be found in high places as well as low, of course).

I do not introduce a lecture on Pollyanna and Congruence Principles with this hopelessly inadequate characterization of Yang and Yin because I am a mystic or because such great thinkers as Confucius and Lao-tse were inspired by it—and I might note that *I Ching* has served as much as a book of prophesy and magic as a book of wisdom. Rather it is because, against this background of ancient Chinese lore and its contemporary manifestations in linguistic and psychological theorizing, that I can best highlight some very primitive universals in human thinking that pervade all levels of language, from wording to sentencing, and yet have found very little explicit expression in linguistic or psycholinguistic theorizing. So let's try to fill in this gap a bit.

Affective Polarity Dynamics: Pollyannaism

The *American College Dictionary* defines *Pollyanna* as "a blindly optimistic person (from the name of the heroine in a novel by Eleanor Porter, 1868–1920)". I have generalized this heroine's name to a general principle, *Pollyannaism,* underlying massive evidence that humans are, *indeed,* "optimistic" in their processing of information—as well as quite "blind" to the fact that they *are* this way! In a very readable paper in *Psychology Today* (September, 1974), titled "The Power of Positive Speaking", Herb Clark reviews many of the studies done by himself and his colleagues at Stanford. He leads off with the sentence, "it is not the case that negative sentences are not harder to comprehend than affirmative'' and later advises the reader that "the lesson for writers, editors, teachers and talkers is to avoid getting tied up in too many nots'' (!).

Three Ways of Being Negative

At about the same time as the Clark et al. research was going on, my then research assistant, Rumjahn Hoosain, published a paper titled "The Processing of Negation'' (1973) in which—using conjoined predicative sentences (X is ADJ$_1$____ ADJ$_2$) and measuring the latencies for simply inserting either "and" or "but''—he was able to demonstrate three, independently variable, types of negativity:

(1) *Explicitly marked negation.* The use of *not*s in perfectly congruent sentences [comparing, e.g., *Tom is honest (and) brave, Tom is honest (and) not afraid,* and *Tom is not honest (and) not brave*] markedly increased processing times, by about 500 ms per *not*.

(2) *Affective negativity.* This is the inherent semantic negation reflected so universally in the minus poles of E, P, and A factors. In comparing conjoined negatives [like *Tom is short (and) weak* or *Tom is stupid (and) dull*] with conjoined positives [like *Tom is tall (and) strong* or *Tom is wise (and) bright*], where *both* types are perfectly congruent, Hoosain found that sentences with affectively negative adjectives took significantly longer to process than those with affective positive adjectives by about 340 ms on the average.

(3) *Cognitive incongruence.* As evidenced by conjoining with unmarked *and* vs marked *but* (covertly, of course, in English), incongruence is itself a kind of negativity, and this shows up clearly in processing times. Comparing congruents that elicit *and*s [e.g., *Tom is tall (and) strong, Tom is cruel (and) rough,* and even *Tom is not kind (and) not fair*] with incongruents that elicit *but*s [*Tom is tall (but) weak, Tom is kind (but) rough,* and even *Tom is not kind (but) not unfair*], the incongruents were found to increase processing time by about 400 ms on the average.

Polly I: Productivity and Marking of Positives vs Negatives

Elaborating a bit now on the first two "ways of being negative'', it should be noted that linguistically, as detailed by Greenberg (1966) at all levels of units, positiveness is highly correlated with both *productivity* (in usage frequency and diversity) and *marking* (of positive forms to create negatives but rarely the reverse). As already implied, marking can be either overt (*nots*, *uns*, etc.) or covert (as in pairs like *good/bad, tall/short, high/low*, etc.). In the latter (covert) case, there are a variety of linguistic tests that can be applied: (a) unmarked positives can be used for *neutralizing* polarity (thus *how good was the play?* invites either positive or negative reply, whereas *how bad was the play?* already implies an expected negative answer); (b) unmarked positives can be *nominalized* (thus what's the *height, length, and width of it?* but not *what's the 'lowth', 'shorth', and 'narrowth' of it?*); and (c) unmarked positives can be used in *quantified comparisons* (thus *X is half/twice as tall/old as Y* but not *X is half/twice as short/young as Y*).

Why do I call this aspect "Polly I"? In 1969 Jerry Boucher and I published a paper titled simply "The Pollyanna Hypothesis", and it reported data on productivity and marking based on the "tool-making" phase of our cross-cultural project for the 13 languages available at the time of writing; also reported were some parallel data collected by Frank DiVesta (1966) across *age-levels* of American children from 7 through 11 (using the "phase I" procedures for eliciting, etc., as in our cross-*language* research).

As shown on Table VI. 1 (from Boucher and Osgood, 1969), for our early cross-cultural data the *H-ranks* in column 1 (combining frequency

Table VI.1. Numbers of Qualifier Pairs for which the E+ Member is Higher or Lower than the E− Member in H-Rank, Frequency and Diversity

	H-Rank		Frequency		Diversity	
Language	E+ Higher	E+ Lower	E+ Higher	E+ Lower	E+ Higher	E+ Lower
Afghan Farsi	18	6[a]	19	6[a]	19	6[a]
American English	21	18	24	15	21	18
Belgian Flemish	18	11	18	11	18	11
Cantonese Chinese	28	5[a]	26	5[a]	28	5[a]
Finnish	18	15	20	21	23	20
French	24	12[a]	23	13[a]	23	13[a]
Iranian Farsi	18	10	17	13	19	12
Italian	23	11[a]	24	11[a]	32	16[a]
Mexican Spanish	24	10[a]	25	11[a]	25	12[a]
Netherlands Dutch	18	10	20	10[a]	20	10[a]
Swedish	19	10	18	11	19	11[a]
Turkish	23	7[a]	24	7[a]	24	7[a]
Yugoslav Serbo-Croatian	17	13	15	14	16	15
Totals	269	138[b]	273	148[b]	287	156[b]

[a] $p < 0.05$.
[b] $p < 0.001$.

of elicited qualifier responses with their diversity of usage across the 100 stimulus nouns) are higher for E^+ adjectives than for E^- for all 13 languages, this holding for both included *diversity* (all 13) in column 3 and frequency measures in column 2 (with one slight exception, Finnish). Clearly, positives are more productive in usage than negatives, and this conclusion holds across all our (now) 30 communities. Table VI. 2 shows that, for *marking,* all 11 languages apply affixes to positives in creating negatives rather than the reverse, with very few exceptions in the data (Finnish and Hong Kong Chinese being omitted since they rarely employ marking devices). This, again, clearly fits expectations.

Turning now to the DiVesta data, Table VI. 3 shows that, across all age levels and without exception for the five oppositional pairs illustrated, the affectively positive terms have higher H-*ranks* (i.e., have higher combined frequencies and diversities) than the affectively negative terms—the blanks indicating that the qualifier in question simply didn't occur at that age-level. When DiVesta simply plotted the mean H-*scores* for his data, E^+ terms began at the youngest age-level displaying much higher productivity and, through age 11, maintained their advantage.

Polly II: Ease of Processing Affectively Positive vs Negative Words

While there has been little theoretical debate over the validity and significance of explicit (overtly marked) negation, there has been, and still is, lively debate over whether the second "way of being negative"

Table VI.2. Frequencies of Applying Negative Affixes to the E+ vs E− Members of Qualifier-Opposite Pairs

Language	Affix on E+	Affix on E−
Afghan Farsi	4	0
American English	4	1
Begian Flemish	5	0[a]
French	5	0[a]
Iranian Farsi	8	1[a]
Italian	9	0[a]
Mexican Spanish	5	1
Netherland Dutch	6	0[a]
Swedish	5	2
Turkish	2	0
Yugoslav Serbo-Croatian	10	0[a]
Totals	63	5[b]

[a]$p < 0.05$ level.
[b]$p < 0.001$ level.

Table VI.3. H-Ranks of Paired E+ and E− Qualifiers Defining the Five Highest Loading E Scales as a Function of Age Level (DiVesta, 1966)

Scales	Chronological age									
	7		8		9		10		11	
	E+	E−	E+	E−	E+	E−	E+	E−	E+	E−
Good-bad	1	2	1	3	1	3	1	3	1	3
Pretty-ugly	5	98	6	79	9	48	9	74	14	78
Right-wrong	55	—	29	61	59	68	41	68	72	—
Sweet-sour	68	—	—	—	63	—	82	—	—	—
Funny-sad	27	61	16	38	19	35	29	60	36	57

is to be attributed to (covert) *linguistic marking* (a quasi-logical principle) or to *affective negativity* (a primitive psycho-logical principle). Both H. Clark (e.g., 1970) and E. Clark (e.g., 1972), among many others, have attributed the slower processing and later acquisition of such negative forms to their greater semantic complexity, due to marking (recall the types of linguistic tests for covert marking illustrated above).

The problem is that there are very high correlations for linguistic marking (overt *and* covert) with affective negativity (see Hamilton and Deese, 1971, for English evidence and Boucher and Osgood, 1969, for cross-linguistic evidence) and for both unmarkedness *and* positive affect with productivity in languages (see Greenberg, 1966, and Osgood, May, and Miron, 1975). However, not only is affective polarity general across signs in all channels, whereas marking is a strictly linguistic phenomenon, but affectivity is obviously prior to language in both species and individual development. So one might reasonably expect the former to be a determinant of the latter rather than the reverse.

In 1974-75 Osgood and Hoosain planned and executed an experiment— under what they thought would be the simplest conceivable conditions— to demonstrate conclusively the viability of affective negativity as a factor increasing processing time. It turned out to be inconclusive. Told before each item (randomly) to "look for positive" or to "look for negative", subjects were shown single words on a slide-projector (starting a timer) and all the subject had to do was to press a MATCH or a MISMATCH button (stopping the timer), depending on whether the affect of a word matched what he was told to expect; the single words were drawn from 67 oppositional pairs (again randomly chosen with respect to Positiveness/Negativeness and widely separated from their opposites in the ordering), nouns (*angel/devil, joy/pain*), adjectives (*tall/short, innocent/guilty*), verbs (*reward/punish, hire/fire*), etc., these pairs being put back together *by the experimenters* for analysis.

The prediction—*that matching responses would be faster for positive*

than for negative members of pairs—was confirmed over-whelmingly at
the 0.001 level, with latency differences ranging from 322 to 551 ms (1/3
to over 1/2 a second). What should also have been predicted from the
Congruity Principle (but wasn't) was *that mismatch responses would be
significantly* SLOWER *than match responses for positive words* BUT NOT
FOR NEGATIVE WORDS. Why? As the very word "mismatch" implies,
pressing the MISMATCH button is a "negative" response *and hence is
congruent with the meaning of any negative word*—effects of affective
negativity thus being neatly cancelled out by those of cognitive congruence: Unfortunately, the Clarks and I agree pretty much on congruence
dynamics!

The problem set for the "real" Polly II experiment was therefore this:
what type of differential responding would be equally congruent with
both positive and negative affective meanings? It was Rumjahn Hoosain's
insight that we could—even *more* "simply"—have the subjects identify
the affect of the projected words by just saying "positive" to positive
words (congruent) or saying "negative" to negative words (also congruent), measuring processing times with a voice-key on the subject's
throat. Exactly the same 67 oppositional pairs were used in this experiment, again with the single words from pairs being randomly ordered in
polarity sequence and widely separated from each other.[1] There was
thus only one major hypothesis to be tested here—*that correctly saying
"positive" to affectively positive words will be faster than saying
"negative" to affectively negative words*—in other words, to quote the
planned title for our article on this, "Pollyanna II: It Is Easier to 'Simply
Get the Meaning' of Affectively Positive than of Affectively Negative
Words" (in preparation, with Hong Kong Chinese data).

We can, with the aid of a few tables, run through the results on Polly
II—she was, true to her name, an optimist! For ease of presentation and
comprehension, I'll present each of the lexical types (noun pairs, adjective pairs, etc.) pointing out the occasional counterprediction cases—but
keep in mind that the members of pairs were presented *singly* to
subjects—and then give the summarizing statistics.

Table VI.4 gives the data for *noun pairs (victory* vs *defeat, angel* vs
devil, etc.): The "error" columns indicate the frequency (across the 18
subjects) with which a word the experimenters considered "positive"
was called "negative" by a subject, or vice versa (and you'll see that
this was gratifyingly rare!); the times are, as usual, in ms. Here the mean
difference was 29 ms and there were three contrary pairs (*hell* faster

---

[1] I should point out that, in selecting pairs of all types, we tried to maximize the proportion
in which the negative member actually has *higher* usage-frequency, e.g., *tall* (55/million) vs
short (212/million), ending up with 24 of the 67 pairs for which this was the case—and they
"behaved" just like the other pairs.

Table VI.4. "Errors" and Mean Response Times (in ms) for Noun Pairs

Positive	"Error"[a]	Time	Negative	"Error"	Time
victory	0	848	defeat	2	922
angel	0	893	devil	0	903
success	0	896	failure	0	918
kindness	0	909	cruelty	0	932
heaven	0	928	hell	0	888
happiness	0	854	misery	0	972
joy	0	795	pain	0	908
carefulness	2	1310	carelessness	0	1296
gain	0	1033	loss	0	987
pride	1	1002	shame	1	1027
Grand mean		947			976

[a] "Error" means that a subject called an item "positive" when the experimenters had coded it "negative", or vice versa; inspection will show that, with a few exceptions (e.g., *short* on Table VI.5.; *there, any,* and *after* on Table VI.9), this was rare.

than *heaven, carelessness* faster than *carefulness,* and *loss* faster than *gain*).

Table VI.5 gives results for *adjective pairs:* Note that there were 9 subjects who called *short* "positive" (when presented singly, of course) and 4 for whom *odious* was "positive" (maybe an unfamiliar word for them?)—I should point out that such "miscalls" were *not* counted in the

Table VI.5. "Errors" and Mean Response Times (in ms) for Adjective Pairs

Positive	"Error"	Time	Negative	"Error"	Time
tall	1	1061	short	9	1186
fertile	1	1047	barren	0	1102
clever	0	871	stupid	0	877
innocent	2	1084	guilty	0	985
merciful	1	1182	merciless	0	1296
fragrant	1	1131	odious	4	1255
tidy	0	943	messy	0	944
positive	0	892	negative	0	980
rich	0	1142	poor	1	909
wonderful	0	852	terrible	0	945
Grand mean		1021			1048

statistics. However, there were only two counter-Pollyannas (*guilty* faster than *innocent* and *poor* faster than *rich*) and the mean difference was 27 ms.

Table VI.6 presents the *verb-pair* data: Note that, to avoid confusion with nouns, the infinitive *to* was presented with each verb. Here there were very few "miscalls", the mean difference was a whopping 170 ms, and there were *no* counterprediction cases. Just *why*—other than sampling error—verbs should behave better than nouns, I have no idea.

Now on Table VI.7 (Type A) we report data comparing ordinary nonprefixed *positive* forms (Set 1) with both *negatively prefixed* forms, thus making them *negative* (Set 2), and quasi-synonymous *non-prefixed negative* forms. Thus here we have *to agree* vs *to disagree* vs *to argue*, *correct* vs *incorrect* vs *wrong*, and so forth. Note, first, that the prefixed (marked) negatives take longer than the nonprefixed negatives 'to get the meaning of' (by 74 ms); note, second, that as predicted from the Pollyanna Hypothesis, the positives are processed faster than either the nonprefixed (by 125 ms) or the prefixed (by 199 ms) negatives—and there was only one contrary case (*lacking* faster than *adequate*).

Looking now at the Type B comparisons on Table VI.8, we compare *negative* nonprefixed forms (Set 1) with prefixed forms, thus making them *positive* (Set 2) and both of these against *nonprefixed* positive forms (Set 3). Thus we have *biased* vs *unbiased* vs *fair*, *dispensible* vs *indispensible* vs *essential*, and so forth. Note that here the *nonprefixed negatives* (Set 1) are processed more quickly (by 140 ms) than the *prefixed positives* (Set 2)—*despite* the positive affect of the latter—and note further that the *nonprefixed positives* (Set 3) are processed much more quickly (by 391 ms!) than the neg-prefixed *positives* (Set 2), a much

Table VI.6. "Errors" and Mean Response Times (in ms) for Verb Pairs

Positive	"Error"	Time	Negative	"Error"	Time
to enjoy	0	844	to suffer	1	951
to reward	0	933	to punish	0	1020
to win	0	891	to lose	1	965
to praise	0	914	to blame	0	1042
to advance	0	980	to retreat	2	1250
to encourage	0	1012	to discourage	2	1481
to hire	0	1061	to fire	0	1125
to admire	0	940	to despise	0	1143
to trust	1	920	to doubt	1	1042
to rejoice	0	911	to regret	2	1091
Grand mean		941			1111

Table VI.7. "Errors" and Mean Response Times (in ms) for Nonprefixed and Prefixed Item Sets (Type A)

Positive	"Error"	Time	Negative	"Error"	Time	Negative	"Error"	Time
to agree	0	918	to disagree	2	1236	to argue	2	1164
correct	0	888	incorrect	1	1055	wrong	0	948
able	0	926	unable	0	1114	can't	0	1002
friendly	0	906	unfriendly	0	1001	hostile	0	970
impressive	0	1094	unimpressive	0	1299	mediocre	0	1297
adequate	0	1080	inadequate	0	1125	lacking	0	1058
consistant	0	1014	inconsistent	0	1295	contradictory	1	1321
efficient	1	983	inefficient	0	1153	wasteful	0	991
advantage	0	925	disadvantage	0	1246	handicap	0	1103
Grand mean		970			1169			1095

Table VI.8. "Errors" and Mean Response Times (in ms) for Nonprefixed and Prefixed Item Sets (Type B)

Negative	"Error"	Time	Positive	"Error"	Time	Positive	"Error"	Time
biased	0	1115	unbiased	3	1395	fair	0	926
dispensable	2	1699	indispensable	2	1466	essential	0	1018
blemished	1	1173	unblemished	2	1325	perfect	0	871
disputed	1	1333	undisputed	4	1425	authentic	0	1176
hurt	0	928	unhurt	2	1154	safe	0	873
troubled	1	1139	untroubled	1	1268	peaceful	0	885
prejudiced	0	1086	unprejudiced	0	1371	open-minded	0	990
destructible	0	1333	indestructible	1	1495	everlasting	0	1053
ambiguous	2	1310	unambiguous	5	1480	definite	0	1068
Grand mean		1235			1375			984

larger difference than between these nonprefixed positives (Set 3) and the nonprefixed *negatives* (Set 1), where the difference is only 251 ms — all of which would be strong evidence for the effects of overt marking, except that it is also the case that the prefixed forms are typically longer than nonprefixed forms. There are no exceptions in these data, however.

The last type shown on Table VI.9 consisted of 19 miscellaneous pairs. Many of these happen to be either the "responses" used (like *right/wrong, true/false,* and *yes/no*) or the "stimulus differences" tested (like *above/below, many/few,* and *more/less*) in psycholinguistic experiments—so researchers beware! Here there are a few high-frequency "miscalls" (e.g., *outside, there, any,* and *after* being called "positive" when presented singly); however, as you can see, there is a considerable difference in processing time (132 ms) for the positives vs the negatives, with only two contra-Polly exceptions (*without* faster than *with* and *nothing* faster than *something,* for reasons I can't fathom).

Table VI.10 gives the means for positives vs negatives of the various types we've been reviewing *for each of the 18 subjects.* The only column with which we need concern ourselves is the last—that giving the *grand means* for subjects across all types of oppositional pairs. I call to your

Table VI.9. "Errors" and Mean Response Times (in ms) for Responses to Miscellaneous Item Pairs

Positive	"Error"	Time	Negative	"Error"	Time
right	0	928	wrong	0	948
true	0	922	false	0	992
yes	0	915	no	0	917
and	0	1267	but	1	1408
over	3	1074	under	1	1268
inside	2	1203	outside	5	1450
above	1	1015	below	2	1228
with	1	1029	without	0	996
toward	0	1046	away from	0	1258
here	0	1014	there	14	1377
on	1	1141	off	1	1330
many	1	964	few	3	1251
much	2	974	little	3	1171
more	1	1025	less	0	1058
something	1	1117	nothing	0	926
some	2	1232	any	10	1382
often	0	1032	seldom	0	1174
always	3	969	never	0	1046
before	2	1572	after	11	1775
Grand mean		1076			1208

Table VI.10. Subject Means for Positive and Negative Item Pairs of Various Types

Subjects	Nouns (10)[a]		Verbs (10)		Adjectives (10)		From Neg. prefix Set A (9)		From Neg. prefix Set B		Miscellaneous (19)		M̄ All item Types (67)	
	+	−	+	−	+	−	+	−	+	−	+	−	+	−
1	0.875	0.843	0.844	0.953	0.920	0.930	1.083	1.064	1.023	1.142	0.927	0.970	0.939	0.978
2	0.940	0.982	0.926	1.030	0.971	1.026	0.993	0.984	0.974	1.125	1.086	1.055	0.995	1.035
3	1.298	1.291	1.019	1.341	1.301	1.563	1.166	1.420	1.368	1.487	1.869	1.580	1.410	1.464
4	1.025	1.037	1.033	1.344	1.116	1.114	1.022	1.311	1.061	1.267	1.070	1.263	1.056	1.226
5	0.924	0.773	0.934	1.070	1.113	1.080	0.970	1.109	1.000	1.280	1.054	1.115	1.006	1.063
6	0.943	1.003	0.973	1.209	0.980	1.122	0.993	1.037	0.908	1.140	1.032	0.962	0.980	1.062
7	0.875	0.713	0.880	0.864	0.963	0.983	0.949	0.936	0.996	1.002	0.910	0.900	0.925	0.897
8	1.174	1.122	1.024	1.265	1.122	1.242	1.200	1.263	1.096	1.254	1.369	1.618	1.192	1.338
9	0.968	0.951	1.008	1.031	1.009	1.039	0.961	1.023	0.998	1.064	1.021	0.998	0.998	1.104
10	0.929	1.241	0.972	1.632	1.186	0.929	1.129	1.350	0.927	1.772	1.284	1.516	1.101	1.416
11	1.013	0.980	0.970	1.007	1.018	1.039	0.945	1.192	1.028	1.371	1.139	1.234	1.035	1.145
12	0.936	0.878	0.923	1.050	1.008	0.916	0.890	1.059	0.926	1.224	1.080	1.152	0.978	1.057
13	0.827	0.874	0.872	0.970	0.908	0.856	0.770	0.843	0.831	1.099	0.807	0.960	0.939	1.036
14	0.740	0.820	0.783	0.889	0.804	0.961	0.722	0.823	0.768	0.893	0.698	0.789	0.745	0.852
15	0.838	0.892	0.877	1.101	0.899	0.933	0.758	0.821	0.874	0.911	0.709	0.788	0.810	0.892
16	0.760	0.817	0.946	1.025	0.958	0.990	0.992	1.048	0.941	1.230	1.045	0.974	0.953	1.004
17	1.012	0.913	1.001	0.956	1.058	0.956	1.060	1.028	1.007	1.267	1.287	1.218	1.100	1.075
18	0.841	0.922	0.837	0.956	1.030	0.983	0.887	1.265	0.983	1.465	0.870	1.798	0.902	1.303

[a]Ns of item pairs are in parentheses.

attention the fact that there are *only two subjects* who displayed shorter processing times overall for negative than for positive members of pairs—subjects #7 and #17 (I assure you this has nothing to do with the lucky#7!)—and you'll note that the actual differences are very small, only 28 ms for #7 and 25 ms for #17.

And last Table VI.11 provides a wrap-up on Polly II in terms of *sign tests*—actually for both Experiment I (with 28 subjects) and Experiment II (with 18 subjects). I should point out that, although Experiment I was confounded *interpretation*-wise by the congruence of MISMATCH responding with Negative Affect, this could *not* influence the Positive vs Negative differences within oppositional pairs (since MATCH/MISMATCH assignments were *randomly* related to Affect Polarity). Looking first, then, at *item pairs across subjects* (N = 67 items): for Experiment I (with 28 subjects), 53 items were as predicted from the Pollyanna Hypothesis and 12 were contradictory, with 2 items being equal (no differences); for Experiment II (with 18 subjects), 55 items were as predicted and 7 were contradictory, with 5 items equal. Looking now at *subjects across item pairs:* for Experiment I, 27 of the 28 subjects performed as predicted and only 1 contrariwise; for Experiment II, 16 of the 18 subjects behaved Pollyannawise and only 2 contrariwise. We applied the very tough min-F (H. Clark, 1973) statistical test to these sign-test differences, and in all cases the differences were significant at the 0.001 level or beyond. Q.E.D.!

Rumjahn Hoosain returned to his home and a job at the University of Hong Kong several years ago, and he has recently sent me a replication of Polly II on twenty native speakers of Mandarin Chinese (also college student subjects). Since there are no Thorndike–Lorge usage frequency counts available for Chinese, he obtained *subjective* usage estimates from 26 native speakers, using a procedure suggested by J. B. Carroll in 1971. Only an essence of Hoosain's findings can be given here. However, as will be seen, his data for Chinese Pollyannaism are highly significant and entirely consistent with our American English results.

As shown on Table VI-12—and paying particular attention to columns 4 (the response time in milliseconds)—for 8 Chinese *noun* items (like *victory/defeat, heaven/hell,* etc.) the mean times for saying "positive" vs. "negative" (in Chinese, of course!) were 765 for affectively positive and 839 milliseconds for affectively negative members of these pairs (again shown separately and randomly), with 6 of the 8 pairs going as predicted—only *angel/devil* and *gain/loss* slightly reversing the trend.

The next table (VI-13) gives the results for 25 *adjective* word-pairs — many more than for the American English experiment (most of the words used in the English study for the *prefixing* conditions turned out to be adjectival in Chinese thus *perfect/imperfect* turn out to be *perfect/blemished* in Chinese). As can be seen, the mean "saying" latencies here

Table VI.11 Summary of Sign Tests

For item pairs across subjects

		+	=	×	
EXPERIMENT I:	Nouns	7	1	2	
(N = 28	Adjectives	7	1	2	
subjects)	Verbs	10	0	0	
	Neg Sets	16	0	2	
	Miscellaneous	13	0	6	
	All types of items:	53	2	12	= 67
EXPERIMENT II[a]:	Nouns	7	0	3	
(N = 18	Adjectives	7	2	1	
subjects)	Verbs	10	0	0	
	Neg Sets	16	1	1	
	Miscellaneous	15	2	2	
	All types of items:	55	5	7	= 67

For subjects across item pairs

		+	=	×	
EXPERIMENT I:	Nouns (N = 10)	18	3	7	
(N = 28	Adjectives (N = 10)	16	2	10	
subjects)	Verbs (N = 10)	25	1	2	
	Neg Sets (N = 18)	25	2	1	
	Miscellaneous (N = 19)	17	6	5	
	Across all 67 items:	27	0	1	= 28
EXPERIMENT II[a]:	Nouns	8	3	7	
(N = 18	Adjectives	8	4	6	
subjects)	Verbs	16	1	1	
	Neg Sets	16	2	0	
	Miscellaneous	11	1	6	
	Across all 67 items:	16	0	2	= 28

[a]Means difference ≤0.020 ms.

were 831 milliseconds for positives and 875 for negatives, with 19 of the 25 pairs going as predicted; among the pairs going the "wrong way" were *rich/poor, careful/careless, consistent/contradictory* and *essential/ dispensible*.

There were 13 *verb* word-pairs (like *to enjoy/to suffer, to praise/to blame* and *to turn on/to turn off*), and as shown on the next table (VI-14) the mean "saying" times were 827 for positives and 1000 milliseconds for negatives—a whopping difference, and there were *no exceptions*.

Table VI.12. Translations (1), Mean Subjective Magnitude Estimates in Log Scores (2), Errors (3), and Response Times in Milliseconds (4) for Chinese Nouns

	1	2	3	4		1	2	3	4
勝利	victory	2.103	0	753	夬敗	defeat[a]	2.338	0	861
天使	angel	1.857	0	846	魔鬼	devil	2.000	0	782
成功	success	2.293	0	738	夬敗	failure[a]	2.338	0	861
天堂	heaven	1.844	0	719	地獄	hell	1.900	0	849
幸福	happiness	2.402	0	757	痛苦	misery[b]	2.273	0	839
快樂	joy	2.322	0	717	痛苦	pain[b]	2.273	0	839
收獲	gain	2.214	0	853	損失	loss	2.267	0	850
友善	friendliness	2.099	0	739	敵意	hostility	2.142	0	831
	Mean	2.142		765			2.191		839

8} Chinese translations of members of these pairs are identical.

You may recall that the American English data for verb pairs also displayed the same whopping difference for positive vs. negative verbs — but we haven't the foggiest idea as to just *why* Pollyanna effects should be particularly strong for verbs.

Finally, on Table VI-15 we have the Chinese results for a set of *miscellaneous* word-pairs (like *open-minded/prejudiced, yes/no, always/ never,* and *right/left*). Here the mean "saying" latencies were 951 milliseconds for positives and 999 for negatives, but there were two reversals—*before* took longer than *after* and *right* took longer than *wrong*. For American English, although the *before/after* pair went as predicted, most interestingly the *right/wrong* pair showed the same reversal as for the Chinese. In general, however, the English and Mandarin Chinese data display the same over-all trends. The Clark-type ANOVA remained to be done at the time of this writing.

Polly III: Ease of Processing Congruent vs Incongruent Sentences

Turning finally to the third "way of being negative", the two theses completed in 1973 by Rumjahn Hoosain and Gordana Opačić both utilized congruent and incongruent conjoined sentences. However, since

Table VI.13. Translations (1), Mean Subjective Magnitude Estimates in Log Scores (2), Errors (3), and Response Times in Milliseconds (4) for Chinese Adjectives

	1	2	3	4		1	2	3	4
高	tall[a]	2.318	0	795	矮	short	2.185	0	851
肥沃	fertile	1.895	0	960	貧瘠	barren	1.783	1	912
聰明	clever	2.310	0	750	愚蠢	stupid	2.196	0	842
慈悲	merciful	2.179	0	823	殘酷	merciless	2.121	1	868
芳香	fragrant	1.809	0	854	刺鼻	odious	1.545	1	1046
整齊	tidy	2.214	0	797	凌亂	messy	2.103	1	808
正	positive	2.327	0	715	負	negative	2.081	0	776
富貴	rich	2.156	1	860	貧窮	poor	2.296	1	852
極妙	wonderful	2.073	0	790	可怕	terrible	2.338	0	894
仁慈	kind	2.176	0	779	殘忍	cruel	1.853	0	771
小心	careful	2.324	0	918	粗心	careless	2.210	0	862
高	high[a]	2.318	0	795	低	low	2.245	0	881
好	good	-	1	822	壞	bad	-	1	919
大	big	-	0	839	小	small	-	0	817
真實	true	2.287	0	734	虛假	false	2.046	0	870
多	many	2.392	0	915	少	few	2.426	1	938
能幹	able	2.268	1	816	無能	can't	2.171	0	931
足夠	adequate	2.180	0	838	缺乏	lacking	2.296	0	844
一貫	consistent	1.990	1	992	矛盾	contradictory	2.196	4	828
有利	advantageous	2.217	1	807	不利	disadvantageous	2.277	0	865
公平	fair	2.226	0	748	偏袒	biased	2.113	0	887
必需	essential	2.386	1	1149	可無	dispensable	1.766	1	1034
完美	perfect	2.237	0	759	沾污	blemished	2.003	1	844
肯定	definite	2.241	2	799	含糊	ambiguous	2.105	0	851
正確	correct	2.159	0	732	錯誤	wrong	2.246	0	886
	Mean	2.204		831			2.113		875

[a]Chinese translations of members of this pair are identical.

- Not available.

the Opačić thesis was designed to test the Naturalness Principle as it relates to complexes (F VI), I will review its design and results in Lecture VIII—where we will be comparing the processing of theoretically basic (natural) vs transform (unnatural) sentences. The Hoosain thesis, however, was specifically designed to test the implications of APG theory for processing congruent vs incongruent complex cognitions. In three subexperiments, congruence dynamics for three types of conjoined cognitions were investigated: (1) sentential clauses with other sentential

Table VI.14. Translations (1), Mean Subjective Magnitude Estimates in Log Scores (2), Errors (3), and Response Times in Milliseconds (4) for Chinese Verbs

	1	2	3	4		1	2	3	4
享受	to enjoy	2.273	0	849	吃苦	to suffer	2.058	3	995
獎勵	to reward	2.135	0	763	懲罰	to punish	2.148	0	903
贏	to win	1.947	0	824	輸	to lose	2.058	2	956
讚賞	to praise	2.273	0	775	責備	to blame	2.078	0	1057
前進	to advance	2.193	0	749	退卻	to retreat	1.861	0	865
鼓勵	to encourage	2.288	0	793	勸阻	to discourage	2.061	11	1226
聘用	to hire	1.956	1	1007	開除	to fire	2.107	0	1029
仰慕	to admire	2.073	0	789	藐視	to despise	2.124	0	1046
信任	to trust	2.262	0	788	懷疑	to doubt	2.324	1	899
鼓舞	to rejoice	2.116	0	783	慌惜	to regret	2.072	0	1035
同意	to agree	2.323	0	791	爭論	to argue	2.265	2	999
開	to turn on	2.323	0	928	關	to turn off	1.988	3	1055
自豪	to be proud	2.017	2	914	羞愧	to be shameful	2.043	1	937
Mean		2.168		827			2.091		1000

clauses (i.e., the linguistic channel); (2) outline facial expressions with other facial expressions (i.e., the perceptual channel); and (3) sentential clauses with outline facial expressions (i.e., across linguistic and perceptual channels).

Conjoined clauses. In this experiment (Hoosain, 1974) three clauses were conjoined, the first two with an adverbial (*while, because, before, after*) and then this two-clause sentence as a whole had to be conjoined with a third clause with an *and* or a *but* inserted by the subject. Two latency measures were taken—the first for the subject to say "ready" as soon as he understood the first two-clause sentence, displayed on a SLIDE 1, and the second for the subject to say either "and" or "but" after he had comprehended the third clause, displayed on a SLIDE 2, *in relation to* the prior sentence. An example will help, I'm sure: ONSET OF SLIDE 1, *the shop was crowded while the sale lasted,* STARTS TIMER—/ PAUSE/—SUBJECT SAYING "ready" STOPS TIMER (latency #1) AND SHIFTS PROJECTOR TO SLIDE 2, *they sold much/little of the merchandise* (where *much* is congruent and *little* incongruent), RESTARTING TIMER—/PAUSE/ —SUBJECT SAYING "and" or "but" STOPS TIMER (latency #2).

Table VI.15. Translations (1), Mean Subjective Magnitude Estimates in Log Scores (2), Errors (3), and Response Times in Milliseconds (4) for Miscellaneous Items

	1	2	3	4		1	2	3	4
平靜	peaceful	2.303	1	856	擾亂	to trouble	2.074	0	930
開放	open-minded	2.322	0	804	偏見	prejudiced	2.197	0	888
是	yes	2.485	0	770	否	no	2.303	0	792
上面	above	2.229	0	871	下面	below	2.270	0	983
朝向	toward	1.888	0	1008	背向	away from	1.737	3	1112
時常	always	2.363	2	947	永不	never	2.155	6	1141
之前	before	2.410	2	1321	之後	after	2.251	4	1082
右	right	2.317	4	1179	左	left	2.341	6	1108
快	fast	-	1	806	慢	slow	-	1	956
	Mean	2.290		951			2.166		999

-Not available.

The purpose of the first latency measure was to test the prediction from Chomskyan TGG (and made by many psycholinguists) *that main-clause followed by subordinate-clause should be processed more easily than the reverse order* (in our example, *while* centered should be easier than *while* preposed); however, there was no significant difference here. As to the second latency measure, designed to test the congruity hypothesis—*that congruent "and" complexes should be processed faster than incongruent "but" complexes*—this effect was significantly confirmed (at the 0.02 level). At the end of the experiment and without forewarning, the subjects were given a recall test, with one key word as the cue (in our example, *shop*) for each complex sentence: most interestingly, the *incongruent* complexes were much better *recalled* (at the 0.001 level), which Hoosain attributes to motivational salience (the "surprise" effect) of incongruent sentences (another example from his materials, *the house was peaceful because the children were quiet*, BUT *the parents were worried*).

Conjoined facial expressions. In this experiment (Hoosain, 1977)—as illustrated in Fig. VI.1 under Roman I—subjects were shown pairs of outline facial expressions on slides, SLIDE-ONSET STARTING A TIMER, the subjects having been instructed to conjoin them by saying either "and" or "but", which STOPPED THE TIMER. (The full instructions were to the effect that "here are the faces of two hypothetical people as they react

I. CONGRUENCE/INCONGRUENCE AMONG FACIAL EXPRESSIONS

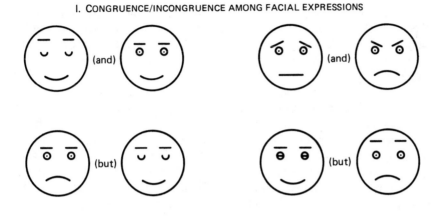

II. CONGRUENCE/INCONGRUENCE BETWEEN FACES AND SENTENCES

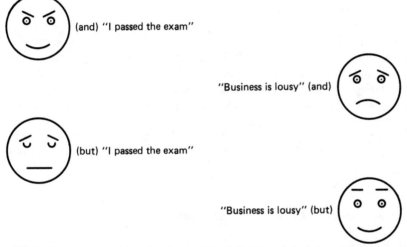

Fig. VI.1. Congruence dynamics in conjoined facial and facial-sentence expressions

to the same hypothetical event (examples given); Person A feels a certain way 'and' so does Person B or Person A feels a certain way 'but' Person B feels another''.) The top pairs under Roman I yielded *and*s and the bottom pairs *but*s significantly beyond chance. Harking back to the second "way of being negative", both this experiment and the next yielded significantly faster processing of affectively *positive* congruent pairs than of affectively *negative* congruent pairs.

Facial and sentential expressions conjoined. As shown by the examples under Roman II in this Figure, in this experiment (also reported in Hoosain, 1977) outline faces were paired with short sentences, which the subjects were told to assume as being simultaneously "uttered" by the faces; again subjects were instructed to conjoin the cognitions by simply saying either "and" or "but". For half of the subjects the outline face was on the left and the sentence on the right, while for the other half the same combination would have sentence to the left and face to the right. Again congruence predictions were upheld significantly, e.g., *and*s being produced by the upper pairs and *but*s by the lower pairs. Most interestingly, however, having sentences on the left (and hence, for English readers, presumably processed first) produced much faster response times for *both* congruent and incongruent pairings (although still with significant differences between them)—suggesting that the linguistic channel is more "finely tuned" than the facial-perceptual channel.

Congruence Dynamics: Psycho-Logic

We refer to our species as *homo sapiens*, but *homo loquens* would be more accurate. Other animals have been shown to symbolize the not-here and not-how to some degree, but no other animal uses a shared set of abstract rules for making assertions about the world. This is at once our great advantage as a species and, potentially, our downfall. When humans are exposed to assertions made by others that are cognitively inconsistent with their own Yang and Yin, what I call *Psycho-logic* enters the picture. This is an entirely non-logical, but very potent psychological, process.

A Mini-Theory of Cognitive Psycho-Logic

The predictions made in a variety of experiments I will report derive from a set of eight postulates about the cognitive system and its dynamics. They are all part of the general performance theory I'm working on. My characterizations of these postulates must be very brief—which is easy for Numbers 1, 2, 3, and 5, with which you should be very familiar by now—and I refer you to Osgood and Richards (1973, "From Yang and Yin to *And* or *But*") for more detailed elaboration.

(1) *All complex cognitions are reducible to interlocking sets of irreducible simplex cognitions.* Thus, for just one example, the cognitive correlate of the complex sentence, *Nixon was conservative but clever,* would be two conjoined simplex cognitions, [Nixon / was / conser-

vative] but [Nixon / was / clever], interlocked in a relation of incongruence, hence *but*—which reveals how *this* speaker feels about conservatives, of course! (Since people have little control over the "natural" use of their *and*s or *but*s, I think we may have the seeds of a very subtle attitude test here.)

(2) *A simple cognition is a signed, directed relation* ($\overset{\pm}{\rightarrow}$) *between two meaning elements* (M$_1$ *and* M$_2$). The directions of relations are presumably of a limited number of basic types, e.g., Being (A *is* B), Causing (A *makes* B), Possessing (A *has* B), Valuing (A *likes* B), and so on, along with their negatives (A *is not* B, etc.). The meaning elements, M$_1$ and M$_2$, also have their own positive and negative affective valences—as will be seen.

(3) *Meaning elements are analyzable into simultaneous sets of bipolar semantic features* (f$_{1-n}$), *these features being variable in sign and* (in the general case) *in magnitude*. The features of affective meaning, Evaluation, Potency, and Activity (E, P, and A), found to be universals in our cross-cultural research with the semantic differential technique, are continuously variable from positive to negative poles through zero, and this will show up clearly in our data on the usage of *and* vs *but*. This postulated bipolarity of semantic features is the first characteristic of Yang and Yin, of course.

(4) *Each feature of a meaning element can have only one sign and one value at any one moment*. Just as one *cannot* simultaneously clench and open his hand (reciprocally antagonistic reaction systems à la Sherrington), so in theory the *same* meaning element cannot be both +f$_i$ and −f$_i$ at the same time (*Mary* cannot be simultaneously coded *married* and *unmarried*). On the other hand, just as one *can* both smile and clench his fist simultaneously (different reaction systems), so in theory we can have independent variation in the signing of *different* semantic features (*Mary* can be both *married* and *quite short*). To the extent that the semantic features comprising the meaning of a component are driven in opposed directions (e.g., in trying to interpret phrases like *sudden eternity* or *gradual surprise*), anomaly will be experienced and there will be pressure toward *compromise reactions* in the semantic system. This is *within-constituent congruity*.

(5) *Each semantic feature has a nonarbitrary polarity, one pole being cognitively positive* (+) *and the other negative* (−). This, of course, is the second characteristic of Yang and Yin. But by what criteria does one assign positive and negative polarities to features? One criterion is purely intuitive—the feeling that Living is somehow positive with respect to Nonliving, for example. Overt linguistic marking (e.g., is *not*, *un*happy, steward*ess*, widow*er*, etc.) is another.

Probably the best criterion of polarity is congruence with clearly contrastive forms like *some* vs *any* (as I used earlier).

(6) *For any given feature, a cognition is perfectly congruent only if the absolute values of* M_1 *and* M_2 *are the same and the algebraic product of the signs of the meaning elements and their relation is positive.* Note that here we are dealing with *between-constituent congruity* as contrasted with within-constituent congruity. Since in simplex cognitions we have only three signed entities, M_1, M_2, and their relation ($\rightarrow$), we have only eight possible combinations of signs: the four congruent cases (upper half of Fig. VI.2) will have an *even* number of negatives, either two or none; the four incongruent cases (lower half) will have an *odd* number of negatives, either one or three.

Let us now consider a hypothetical member of the conservative "Silent Majority" in California (for whom Ronald Reagan was + and Berkeley Students were −) and see which types of assertions such a person would find congruent and which he would find incongruent. He should find *Ronald Reagan admired Richard Nixon, Ronald Reagan distrusted radicals on campuses, Berkeley Students hated Ronald Reagan,* and *Berkeley Students are radicals* to be entirely credible assertions. On the other hand, he should find *in*credible the assertions that *Ronald Reagan despised Richard Nixon, Ronald Reagan is a radical at heart, Berkeley Students supported Governor Reagan,* and *Berkeley Students are not radicals.*

Now those of you who consider yourselves liberal—or even a bit radical—may be startled to find that assertions assumed to be

CONGRUENT COGNITIONS

$M_1(+)$	$\overset{+}{\rightarrow}$	$M_2(+)$	RONALD REAGAN ADMIRED RICHARD NIXON.
$M_1(+)$	$\overset{-}{\rightarrow}$	$M_2(-)$	RONALD REAGAN DISTRUSTED RADICALS ON CAMPUSES.
$M_1(-)$	$\overset{-}{\rightarrow}$	$M_2(+)$	BERKELEY STUDENTS HATED RONALD REAGAN.
$M_1(-)$	$\overset{+}{\rightarrow}$	$M_2(-)$	BERKELEY STUDENTS ARE RADICALS.

INCONGRUENT COGNITIONS

$M_1(+)$	$\overset{-}{\rightarrow}$	$M_2(+)$	RONALD REAGAN DESPISED RICHARD NIXON.
$M_1(+)$	$\overset{+}{\rightarrow}$	$M_2(-)$	RONALD REAGAN IS A RADICAL AT HEART.
$M_1(-)$	$\overset{+}{\rightarrow}$	$M_2(+)$	BERKELEY STUDENTS SUPPORTED RONALD REAGAN.
$M_1(-)$	$\overset{-}{\rightarrow}$	$M_2(-)$	BERKELEY STUDENTS ARE NOT RADICALS.

Fig. VI.2. Congruent cognitions illustrated

congruent for this hypothetical member of the Silent Majority are *also* congruent for you, and similarly for the incongruent ones. But note that the assertions would fit in *different* cognition-types for you, e.g., congruent *Ronald Reagan admired Richard Nixon* would be $M_1 (-) \xrightarrow{+} M_2 (-)$, an instance of "birds of a feather flock together"!

(7) *Given the values and signs of any two components of a cognition on any feature, the congruent value and sign of the third component on that feature are implied.* Knowing that ex-Secretary of State Henry Kissinger was negatively evaluated by someone and knowing that the relation A *favors* B is signed + (associative) in ordinary English, one could expect this someone to have had a negative feeling about "retaliative economic strikes" (without having the foggiest idea of what this phrase meant) when he read that *Secretary Kissinger favors* retaliative economic strikes. It is important to keep in mind that the "implications" here are not matters of *logic* but of *psychologic*.

This becomes clear if we substitute meaningless elements in the four *incongruent* assertions in this figure and apply Postulate 7: For example, if we insert nonsense syllable LEEM for the M_1 in the third incongruent, yielding LEEMS SUPPORTED RONALD REAGAN, then LEEMS *should be* $^+$Yang for our hypothetical conservative—but the *message* reads BERKELEY STUDENTS! In other words, *in incongruent assertions* (according to Postulate 6) *each pair of constituents implies* (according to Postulate 7) *a sign for each third constituent which is incompatible with the actual sign of that constituent* (according to Postulate 4). It therefore follows that *between*-element incongruity for cognitions as wholes reduces to *within*-element incongruity for all their components. Jangling stress is thus created simultaneously across all constituents.

(8) *Both within and between meaning components related in a cognition, semantic features having the same polarity* (+ or −) *will summate to yield an overall ratio on an underlying Positiveness/Negativeness dimension.* This, of course, is the third characteristic of Yang and Yin. Using affective Evaluation, Potency, and Activity features— and in that order—where we have data, we can illustrate such summation: *within-constituent* Positiveness should be greater for *champion* (+, +, +) than for *friend* (+, +, 0) than for *author* (+, 0, 0), than for *person* (0, 0, 0); moving into Negativeness, *old people* (0, 0, −) should be less negative than *fat people* (−, 0, −) and these in turn less than *beggers* (−, −, −); *between-constituent* summation of Positiveness would be illustrated by *progress was dynamic* being more Yang than *progress was steady,* and summation of Negativeness by *that man is sickly* being less Yin than *that beggar is sickly.*

Predictions for Use of *and* vs *but* in Conjoined Cognitions

We are now in position to consider the determinants of using conjunctive *and* vs disjunctive *but*. The negative affinity of *but* (Yin) as against the positive affinity of *and* (Yang) is clearly shown by using coordination with our old friends *some* (Yang) and *any* (Yin). *John reached for the deck* AND *took* SOME *cards* is entirely acceptable, but *John reached for the deck* AND *took* ANY *cards* is impossible; on the other hand, while *John reached for the deck* BUT *took* SOME *cards* is strange at best, *John reached for the deck* BUT *didn't take* ANY *cards* is just fine—and note that here the *double* Neg (BUT and ANY) renders the whole positive.

But what are the cognitive determinants for *selecting* negative *but*? According to linguist Robin Lakoff (1971), there seem to be two major, convergent ones, and both are forms of cognitive incongruity—*semantic opposition* (or "contrast") and *denial of expectation* (or "surprise"). Compare the following sentences:

John is tall but Bill is short;
John hates ice cream but I like it;
John is tall but he is no good at basketball;
John hates ice cream but so do I;
John loves ice cream but so do I.

In the first there is only "contrast" (*tall/short*), and one can also use *and;* the same thing holds for the second sentence (*hates/likes*); in the third (*tall but not basketball*) sentence there is only "surprise" and only *but* seems acceptable; in *John hates ice cream but so do I* there is again only "surprise" (that anyone should hate ice cream), and *but* is preferred; and the only condition under which *but* could be preferred in the last sentence (where there is *neither* "contrast" nor "surprise") would be the presupposition that *anything* John loves I will hate! It would seem that where *only* semantic opposition ("contrast") is involved, either *and* or *but* are possible, but where denial of expectation ("surprise") is involved (or both), *but* is either preferred or required.

In the research to be described momentarily our experimental materials were of the form *X is ADJ____ADJ* and therefore represent a special case in which M_1 (the common topic, X) is deliberately "empty" (meaningless and unsigned), the relations are always positive (*is*), and the M_2s are different adjectives which vary in both the sign and the degree of their polarity on some *n* features. Our postulates lead to the following general prediction: *to the extent that the two cognitions being conjoined yield the same predicted signs for X ("empty" M_1), they are congruent and* AND *will be preferred; to the extent that the two cognitions yield opposed predicted signs for X, they are incongruent and* BUT *will be preferred.* Now, there are two very special conditions under which the above prediction does *not* hold, and they are particularly informative as to the cognitive dynamics operating here.

The first (A) is a terminal constraint on the use of *and—the case in which the M₂s are synonymous.* To say *Rockefeller is rich and rich* is simply redundant, of course, but there is a range of *near*-synonymy through which this prohibition spreads. As shown on the left of Fig. VI.3, *Rockefeller is rich* AND *wealthy* is also ruled out, but *Rockefeller is rich* AND *prosperous* is barely acceptable (he's not only made it but he's making more); *Rockefeller is rich* AND *healthy* is clearly OK, and even *Rockefeller is rich* BUT *healthy* passes if one wants to imply that there's something incompatible about being rich and being healthy!

The second condition (B) is a terminal constraint on *but—the case in which the M₂s are psychological opposites.* Neither *and* nor *but* can be used in *Rockefeller is rich_____poor.* On the face of it, this is puzzling: here we have maximally polar and incongruent cognitions, and yet *but* is prohibited. It is true that the terminal constraint on *but* displays the

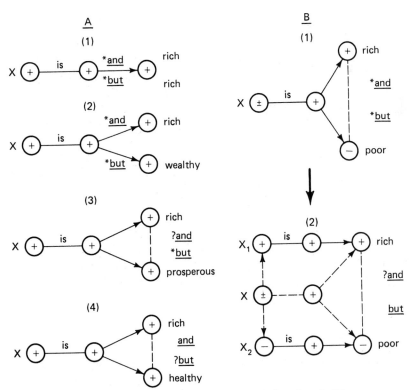

Fig. VI.3. Terminal constraints on use of *and* and of *but*

same graded character as *and*—as witness *Rockefeller is rich* BUT *impoverished* (impossible), *Rockefeller is rich* BUT *not prosperous* (possible), and *Rockefeller is rich* BUT *unhealthy* (definitely OK)—but the solution to the puzzle lies elsewhere: *in the implied disintegration of the common topic* (M_1), signalled by the use of *but*.

As illustrated on the top right of this figure, the cognition [X is rich] implies in psycho-logic that X has *positive* polarity, whereas the cognition [X is poor] implies that X has *negative* polarity; their conjunction would therefore force (X) to assume antagonistic values on certain semantic features, and this runs contrary to our Postulate 4. As shown on the bottom right, *the solution is cognitive differentiation of X into two elements*—it is X_1 who is rich and X_2 who is poor. In this way, cognitive congruity or balance is restored, and it is the negative *but* that accom-
plishes this algebraic balancing act (thus $\overset{+}{rich}$ $\overset{-}{but}$ $\overset{-}{poor}$). This disintegration of the common topic is often expressed in one way or another in conjoined sentences involving *but* and intense incongruity, e.g., *as a* BUSINESS MAN *John is very rich but as a* HUMAN BEING *John is very poor* or *John is rich* IN GOLD *but poor* IN WOMEN.

Presumably, the fewer the features driven in antagonistic directions, the less intense will be the incongruity and the more *and* will be preferred to *but*. This is our Postulate 8, and it predicts that the shift in preference for *and* vs *but* will be a *continuous* function of the semantic similarities among the pairs of conjoined adjectives (M_2s). Thus, as illustrated in the left-hand column of Fig. VI.4 (and substituting *Mary* for X), for our experimental situation: (1) for *Mary is sweet_____kind*, predict only *and*, since a dominant $^+$Evaluation feature is shared by both adjectives; (2) for *Mary is sweet_____brave*, predict *and* preferred, since *same*-polarity on different features, $^+$Evaluation and $^+$Potency, is being combined; (3) for *Mary is sweet_____cowardly*, predict *but* preferred, since *opposed*-polarity on different features, $^+$Evaluation and $^-$Potency, is being combined; and (4) for *Mary is sweet_____cruel*, predict only *but*, since adjectives are opposed on the same dominant feature, $^+$Evaluation and $^-$Evaluation.

The right-hand column merely shows that the same rules hold for affectively negative initial cognitions—thus from *Mary is ugly* AND *cruel*, though *ugly and cowardly* and *ugly but brave* to *Mary is ugly* BUT *kind*.

A Cross-Language Test of Theory

The original experiment was done with American English-speaking subjects and is reported in Osgood and Richards (1973). However, it is the conviction of the staff of our Center for Comparative Psycholinguis-

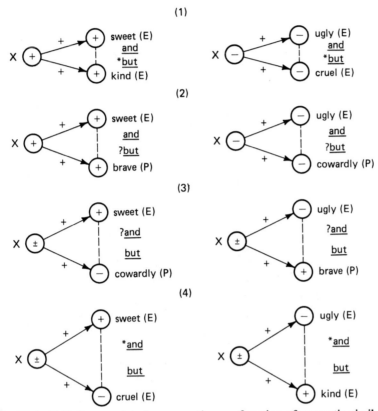

Fig. VI.4. Shift from *and* to *but* as continuous function of semantic similarity

tics that *the only way to extract what is universal in human communi-cative behavior from what is unique to particular languages and cultures is via cross-linguistic, cross-cultural research utilizing demonstrably comparable methods.* In this lecture, therefore, I will summarize repli-cations of the basic experimental design across (now) 12 of the 30 communities that have been involved in our 20-year project.

You will recall that, in the "tool-making" phase in each community, qualifiers (adjectives) were elicited from 100 teen-age boys as their first associations to 100 culture-common nominal concepts. The qualifier types were ordered in terms of their *productivities* (frequency and diversity of usage) and the 50 most productive were made into 7-step bipolar scales. Then another set of 100 boys rated the same 100 concepts against these scales, and the indigenous cubes of data generated were factor-analyzed. Table VI.16 presents the American English results, with scales organized in terms of their dominant factor loadings on the

Table VI.16. Loadings of Semantic Differential Scales on Evaluation (E), Potency (P), and Activity (A)[a]

Scale	E	P	A	Scale	E	P	A
Dominantly E				straight-crooked	0.76	0.30	0.08
nice-awful	0.96	-0.02	-0.09	true-false	0.72	0.36	0.04
sweet-sour	0.94	0.02	-0.04	full-empty	0.69	0.32	0.04
good-bad	0.93	0.03	-0.05	unbroken-broken	0.66	-0.06	-0.08
heavenly-unheavenly	0.93	0.00	-0.21	soft-hard	0.66	-0.45	0.07
mild-harsh	0.92	-0.20	-0.06	round-square	0.43	-0.14	-0.14
beautiful-ugly	0.91	0.00	-0.07	*Dominantly P*			
happy-sad	0.91	0.04	-0.13	big-little	-0.15	0.81	-0.24
helpful-unhelpful	0.90	0.02	-0.02	powerful-powerless	0.16	0.75	0.18
clean-dirty	0.90	-0.06	-0.04	deep-shallow	-0.11	0.69	-0.32
faithful-unfaithful	0.89	0.17	0.04	strong-weak	0.04	0.68	0.13
useful-useless	0.89	0.09	-0.02	long-short	0.02	0.64	-0.23
needed-unneeded	0.89	0.02	-0.04	high-low	0.29	0.64	-0.23
sane-mad	0.88	0.19	0.08	heavy-light[b]	-0.45	0.57	-0.18
fine-coarse	0.87	-0.20	0.00	serious-funny	-0.31	0.49	-0.29
honest-dishonest	0.86	0.16	0.01	sharp-dull[b]	0.39	0.47	0.29
safe-dangerous	0.85	-0.16	0.06	hot-cold	0.06	0.45	0.36
white-black	0.82	-0.09	-0.12	many-few[c]	0.03	0.12	0.12
fresh-stale	0.81	0.05	0.10	*Dominantly A*			
rich-poor	0.81	0.22	-0.09	fast-slow	-0.14	0.22	0.64
shiny-dull[b]	0.79	0.21	-0.04	young-old	0.39	-0.42	0.56
smart-dumb	0.79	0.30	0.24	noisy-quiet	-0.39	0.25	0.56
smooth-rough	0.78	-0.43	0.02	alive-dead	0.52	0.13	0.55
light[b]-dark	0.78	0.05	-0.06	known-unknown	0.16	0.10	0.48
tender-tough	0.77	-0.36	0.01	dry-wet	0.03	0.11	0.12

[a] American English semantic differential loadings reported in Osgood, 1964. Loadings shown are for the first listed adjective of each pair. "Good", "Potent", and "Active" are represented by the positive poles of E, P, and A.
[b] Duplicate adjectives appearing in two different scales.

universal E, P, and A factors. *Exactly equivalent data were available for each of our collaborating communities.*

Method. Following explicit rules for random sampling from their indigenous versions of this table, our colleagues selected pairs of adjectives to insert in 200 "sentence" frames—X is ADJ$_1$_____ ADJ$_2$—for this experiment. Our SD data make possible three different characterizations of semantic similarity: (1) *Global similarity.* As illustrated under Roman I on Fig. VI.5, the overall correlations between scales reflect the simultaneous influence of *all* operative semantic features, not just affective E, P, and A; thus *true* (from a *true-false* scale) and *useful* (from a *useful-useless* scale) are quite similar in global meaning (r = 0.65), whereas *true* and *old* (from a *young-old* scale) are essentially unrelated in meaning (reversing signs, r = −0.08). (2) *Affective similarity.* As illustrated under Roman II, from the loadings of scales on E, P, and A factors we can obtain the absolute algebraic differences in affective

I. GLOBAL SEMANTIC SIMILARITY

Unfactored Correlation Matrix

		1	2	3	etc.
true-false	1	—			
useful-useless	2	0.65	—		
young-old	3	0.08	0.29	—	
	etc.				

Global Similarity Index

X is true ___ useful = 0.65
X is true ___ old   = −0.08

II. AFFECTIVE SIMILARITY

Factor Loadings

	E	P	A
true-false	0.72	0.36	0.04
useful-useless	0.89	0.09	−0.02
young-old	0.39	−0.42	0.56
etc.			

Absolute Differences

	E	P	A
X is true ___ useful	0.17	0.27	0.06
X is true ___ old	1.11	0.06	0.60

III. AFFECTIVE DOMINANCE SIMILARITY

Factor Loadings

				Dominance Types	
true-false	0.72	0.36	0.04	X is true ___ useful	= E − E
useful-useless	0.89	0.09	−0.02	X is true ___ old	= E − A
young-old	0.39	−0.42	0.56	X is useless ___ strong	= E − P
strong-weak	0.04	0.68	0.13	X is weak ___ young	= P − A

Fig. VI.5. Three indices of semantic similarity of adjectives

meaning; thus again *true* and *useful* are very similar affectively, but *true* and *old* (reversing signs for *old,* since it is the right-hand term) are very dissimilar for our American English teen-agers. (3) *Affective dominance similarity.* As shown under Roman III, the factor on which a scale has its largest loading (regardless of sign) is its dominant affective feature; thus adjective pairs in the experimental sentences can be characterized as to dominance type (E-E for *true/useful,* E-A for *true/old,* and so forth). Adjectives sharing the same dominant feature are, in that sense, more similar than adjectives dominant on different features.

Approximately 50 native-speaking subjects (nearly always college students) in each location were instructed (for American English) simply that "certain pairs of words seem more acceptable to a speaker of English if they are joined by the conjunction *and,* and some seem better if joined by the conjunction *but*" (obvious examples, e.g., *X is big* AND *heavy* and *X is poor* BUT *honest,* were given), and they were to complete each of the 200 experimental sentences with whichever conjunction seemed best. The instructions for other cultures were adapted from those for English. Half of the subjects had the "sentences" in one order (e.g., *X is true_____useful*) and the other half in the other (*X is useful_____true*). Now let's look at the *results.*

Global semantic similarity. Figure VI.6 presents the scatter-plot for American English (AE) of the correlations between *global similarity* (horizontal dimension, *r*s ranging from near -1.00 on the left to near $+1.00$ on the right) and percent frequency of inserting *and* in the sentences (vertical dimension, %s ranging from near 100% at the top to near 0% at the bottom). Each little x represents a particular "sentence", and the higher the overall correlation the better the prediction of *and/but* usage from global semantic similarity—the correlation for AE being 0.76, a value significant at well beyond the 0.001 level.

The parallel *horizontal* lines mark the 0.001 confidence levels around the overall mean frequency of *and* (which, for AE, was 62.5%); for all sentences falling *outside* this interval, one conjunction was chosen significantly more often than the other at the 0.001 level of confidence, the upper level for significant *and* being 67% and the lower level for significant *but* being 58% (confidence interval only 9%). The fine *vertical* lines mark the magnitudes of positive correlation (for *and*) and negative correlation (for *but*) at which five or fewer significant "wrong" predictions occur—thus an indicator of the *sensitivity* with which the congruence vs incongruence judgments are made; for AE, there are only five cases where *but* is significantly preferred (move *but*s than *and*s) for "sentences" correlating equal to or greater than r = $+0.20$ and only four cases where *and* is significantly preferred for correlations less than or equal to r = -0.20—a fine sensitivity, indeed, since rs of 0.20 account for only 4% of the variance. Note, finally, that this is a *continuous*

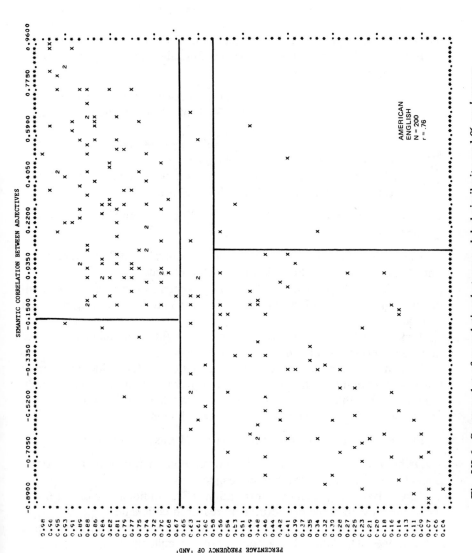

Fig. VI.6. Scatter-plot of correlation between global similarity and % *and* usage for American English

function—there is no discrete correlation level at which an abrupt shift from *and*s to *but*s occurs.

Now, before presenting *comparative* cross-linguistic data, and to convince you of the overwhelming universality of these phenomena, let me spin around our little world quickly, displaying identical scatter-plots for American English *and* for 11 other language-culture communities.

Figure VI.7 repeats the American English plot, along with three Western European groups:

Belgian Flemish, 64% *and,* correlation between global similarity and % *and* 0.53, confidence interval 8%—Prof. J. Costermans, research colleague;

Swedish, 70% *and,* predictive correlation 0.58, confidence interval 8%—Ms. Maud Jonson, research colleague;

Finnish, 61% *and,* predictive correlation 0.59, confidence interval 11%—Prof. Jorma Kuusinen, research colleague.

Figure VI.8 presents plots for two East European and two West Asian groups:

Hungarian Magyar, 66% *and,* predictive correlation 0.78, confidence interval 8%—Dr. Jenö Putnoky, research colleague;

Yugoslav Serbo-Croatian, 62% *and,* predictive correlation 0.74, confidence interval 8%—Drs. Gordana Opačić and Vid Pečjak, research colleagues;

Turkish, 67% *and,* predictive correlation 0.69, confidence interval 6%—Dr. Doğan Cuceloğlu, research colleague;

Iranian Farsi, 55% *and,* predictive correlation 0.48, confidence interval 6% (I should point out that the generally lower reliability here is probably due to the fact that this was the only location where *high-school* subjects were used)—Dr. Rumjahn Hoosain, research colleague.

Figure VI.9 gives plots for four South and East Asian groups:

Delhi Hindi, 56% *and,* predictive correlation 0.65, confidence interval 5%—Dr. Ladli Singh, research colleague;

Thai, 51% *and,* predictive correlation 0.71, confidence interval 6%—Dr. Jantorn Buranabanpote-Rufener, research colleague;

Malaysian Malay, 56% *and,* predictive correlation 0.70, confidence interval 9%—Dr. Wong Fong Tong, research colleague;

Japanese, 50% *and,* predictive correlation 0.84, confidence interval 6%—Dr. Yasumasa Tanaka, research colleague.

I rather confidently expect that you are duly impressed by the consistency of these cross-language data! There are several theoretical questions we can ask of these data on the effects of global similarity, some of which we have already noted in scanning the scatter-plots.

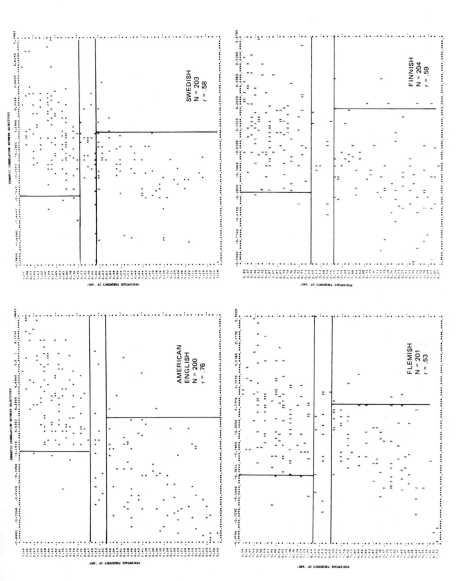

Fig. VI.7. Scatter-plots for American English and three Western European communities

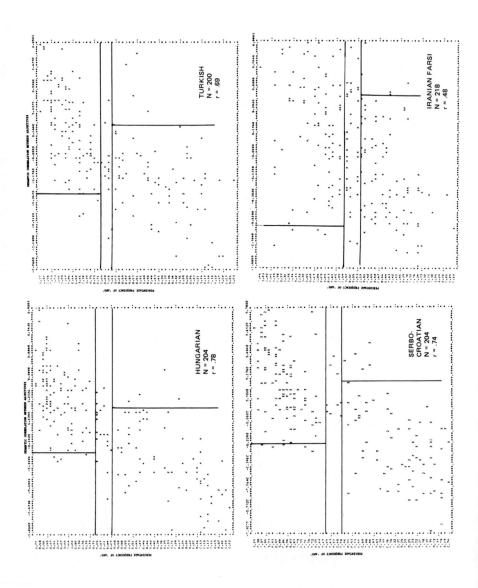

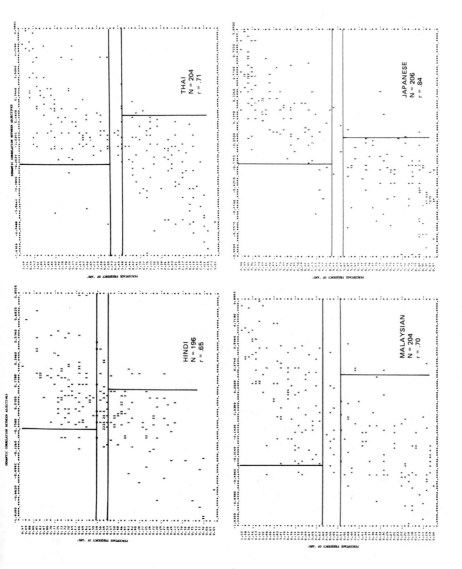

Fig. VI.9. Scatter-plots for four South and East Asian communities

Evidence for linguistic marking? The hypothesis here is that affectively unmarked (positive) *and* will be used more frequently overall than affectively marked (negative) *but.* As can be seen in column (1) of Table VI.17, for all of our communities % *and*s is greater than 50% (upper values), as predicted; however, all Asian groups [except the Turks (TK), data collected in Ankara] show only slight overall preference for unmarked *and,* and I have no idea, linguistic or cultural, as to why this should be so. Is it possible that the preponderance of *and*s merely reflects a bias in sampling toward adjective pairs that happen to be positively correlated? Inspection of the % items with positive rs [lower values in column (1)] indicates that % *and*s is consistently higher than % +rs—although again the difference is smaller for Asian groups.

Reliability of the data? It will be recalled that in each location, two forms, A and B, were given on which the orders of the adjectives were reversed [e.g., (A) *X is soft_____black*; (B) *X is black_____soft*]; the correlations of the % *and* responses across the two forms provide a *minimal* estimate of reliability for this task. With the exception of Iranian Farsi (high-school subjects), and possibly Delhi Hindi, all reliability estimates [column (2)] are very satisfactory. All of the *predictive correlations* of % *and* from the global semantic similarity index [column (3) here] are significant at beyond the 0.001 level.

Sensitivities to congruence/incongruence? The last two columns in this table indicate upper and lower 0.001 confidence limits for significant *and*s and *but*s, along with the interval between them, for each community [column (4)], and cut-off correlation values for *and*s and *but*s, with five or less significant exceptions [column (5)]. Although the *confidence intervals* are fairly constant (ranging from 0.09 to 0.05), our Asians display less bias toward higher *and* %s (consistent with their apparently reduced linguistic marking effect). Except for the Iranian Farsi high-schoolers (and perhaps the Malaysians), *sensitivities* to congruence/incongruence effects are very high, correlations of only ±0.20 or so being sufficient to throw judgments toward clear-cut *and* or *but* judgments.

Global vs affective similarity and same vs different feature dominance? How well do affective E-P-A features alone (Similarity Index 2) predict discriminative usage of *and* vs *but,* as compared with global semantic similarity (Similarity Index 1)? The answer, for the American English data, was "nearly as well": the multiple R for prediction from E-P-A factor-score differences was 0.68 (as compared with 0.76 for global similarity) for *all* sentence types and was 0.82 and 0.88 for *E-E* and *P-P* shared-dominant types (as compared with 0.87 for both combined on global similarity). Also for American English, predictive correlations from global similarity to % *and*s were much higher for sentences with adjectives having the *same* dominants (both E-dominant and P-

Table VI.17. Summary of Results for Global Similarity Measure

	(1) % items *and* (upper values); % items positive r (lower values)	(2) Reliability ($r_{A,B\ forms}$)	(3) Predictive correlation ($r\{^{freq.\ and,}_{global\ sim.}\}$)	(4) 0.001 confidence limits for *and* (upper) and *but* (lower); interval width (in parens)		(5) r-values for *but* (upper) and *and* (lower) cutoffs (≤5 sig. wrong predictions)
AE[a]	62.5 54.0	0.89	0.76	66.7 58.2	(9)	−0.15 but +0.13 and
BF	63.7 48.3	0.88	0.53	67.5 59.9	(8)	−0.37 but +0.21 and
SW	70.1 50.7	0.82	0.58	73.9 66.3	(8)	−0.31 but +0.12 and
FF	60.9 46.6	—[c]	0.59	66.6 55.2	(11)	−0.26 but +0.25 and
HM	66.2 54.9	0.87	0.76	70.4 62.0	(8)	−0.21 but +0.14 and
YS	61.8 53.9	0.90	0.73	65.5 57.9	(8)	−0.23 but +0.22 and
TK	66.9 49.0	0.91	0.69	69.7 64.2	(6)	−0.29 but +0.23 and
IF	55.2 50.9	0.53	0.48	57.9 52.4	(6)	−0.56 but +0.48 and

Table VI.17 (*continued*)

	(1) % items *and* (upper values); % items positive r (lower values)	(2) Reliability (r_{A,B} forms)	(3) Predictive correlation (r{freq. *and*, global sim.})	(4) 0.001 confidence limits for *and* (upper) and *but* (lower); interval width (in parens)		(5) r-values for *but* (upper) and *and* (lower) cutoffs (≤5 sig. wrong predictions)
DH	55.6 52.0	0.67	0.65	58.2 53.1	(5)	−0.16 but +0.14 and
TH	51.3 49.0	0.90	0.71	54.4 48.1	(6)	−0.20 but +0.20 and
MM	56.2 45.1	0.88	0.70	60.7 51.7	(9)	−0.38 but +0.32 and
JP	50.0 45.1	0.98	0.84	53.0 46.9	(6)	−0.24 but +0.09 and
cc mean	60.03 49.95	0.84	0.67	63.7 56.3	(7)	−0.25 but[b] +0.19 and[b]

[a]Identifications: AE (American English); BF (Belgian Flemish); SW (Swedish); FF (Finnish); HM (Hungarian Magyar); YS (Yugoslavian Serbo-croatian); TK (Turkish); IF (Iranian Farsi); DH (Delhi Hindi); TH (Thai); MM (Malaysian Malay); JP (Japanese).

[b]Cross-cultural means computed without IF data (N = 11).

[c]FF data not available.

dominant—there were too few A-A types for analysis) than those with adjectives having *different* dominants (E-P, E-A, and P-A types)—multiple Rs being 0.82 and 0.88 for the former and only 0.42, 0.58, and 0.46 for the latter.

Table VI.18. Summary of Results for Affective Similarity and Feature Dominance

	(1) Predictive correlations for same (upper) vs different (lower) dominant features; global similarity	(2) Predictive correlations for same (upper) vs different (lower) dominant features; affective similarity	(3) % *and* for same dominant: congruent (++,−−) upper vs incongruent (+−,−+) lower	(4) % *and* for mixed dominant: congruent (++,−−) upper vs incongruent (+−,−+) lower
AE	0.87	0.85	82	74
	0.59	0.49	39	62
BF	0.68	0.72	84	72
	0.27	0.41	52	64
SW	0.73	0.73	83	71
	0.36	0.47	54	65
FF	0.66	0.71	78	68
	0.50	0.57	37	66
HM	0.87	0.90	92	74
	0.53	0.52	35	53
YS	0.84	0.88	84	76
	0.51	0.56	34	40
TK	0.82	0.87	90	64
	0.50	0.76	52	70
IF	0.56	0.62	63	57
	0.26	0.28	47	54
DH	0.58	0.66	65	53
	0.61	0.46	46	54
TH	0.84	0.90	84	54
	0.47	0.39	23	51
MM	0.73	0.78	80	69
	0.63	0.63	37	43
JP	0.90	0.91	87	71
	0.71	0.74	22	40
cc	0.76 ⎤ 0.63	0.79 ⎤ 0.66	81	67
mean	0.50 ⎦	0.52 ⎦	40	55

What about cross-language evidence on these matters? As shown in Column (1) of Table VI.18, with only a single exception (DH, Delhi Hindi) the predictive correlations from *global similarity* to frequency of *and* are always higher for adjective pairs sharing the *same* dominant affective feature (upper values) than for pairs having *different* dominants (lower values)—and the CC means are 0.76 for same-dominant vs 0.50 for different-dominant with a mean of 0.63. The predictions from *affective similarity* alone, as shown in column (2), are actually even more impressive: there are *no* exceptions, the predictive correlations always being higher for *same*-dominants than for *different*-dominants—and the CC means are 0.79 vs 0.52 for same- and different-dominant items, with a mean of 0.66.

Columns (3) and (4) in the table compare *congruent* (+ +; − −) with *incongruent* (+ −; − +) adjective pairings in terms of % *and*s given as responses—thus testing the major hypothesis of our research, namely *that congruent cognitions will be conjoined with* ANDs *and incongruent ones with* BUTs. This is strikingly the case for sentences whose adjective pairs shared the *same* dominant affective feature [column (3)], where the % *and*s for congruent items are always far above (mean 81%) those for incongruent items (mean 40%). Although the same trend also holds for sentences whose adjectives had *different* dominant affective features [column (4)], it is much weaker (means 67% vs 55%) and, in fact, is slightly reversed for two of our languages (TK, Turkish, and DH, Delhi Hindi). However, this evidence for more *and*s with same-polarity vs different-polarity adjectives *across different affective features* is in the direction predicted from the third (parallel-polarity) characteristic of Yang and Yin.

The Finer Semantics of Congruity Interactions

Two "molecular" structural notions (S X and S XI) stated the bipolar, reciprocally antagonistic nature of semantic features (mediator components in this APG) and the nonarbitrary Positive/Negative signings of the poles of these features (nonarbitrary in principle, if not always in practice). Given their reciprocally inhibitory nature, it must follow that, functionally, *within* any component of a simplex cognition, each semantic feature (componential r_m) can have only one sign and one value (polarity direction, if nonzero, and intensity level) at any one moment. You will recall that in this APG, since mediator components derive from reciprocally antagonistic overt reactions, behaviorally speaking it is just as impossible to have a $^{\pm}r_m$ mediation process as it is to simultaneously open and clench one's hand.

Within-Constituent Congruence Dynamics

Given cues for the natures (SNP, VP, ONP) and boundaries of constituents, OPR accepts from LEX the semantic code-strips for the word-forms included in each constituent (cf, F V), necessarily fusing the features of word-forms in complex constituents (e.g., in comprehending perceived A TREMBLING SKINNY KITTEN or heard *the three little bearded old men*). The rules for semantic fusing are: (1) that *same sign* polarity fusions (+/+ or −/−) yield *intensification* of a feature (e.g., *violent rage; plead with humbly*); (2) that fusions of *signed with unsigned* (zero) codings (+/0 or −/0) yield *modification* of meaning, the whole constituent assuming the polarity and intensity of the signed term (thus *lively hope* making the hopefulness more Active and *plead with sincerely* making the pleading more Moral); and (3) that fusions of *opposed signs* on the same feature (+/−) yield semantic anomalies (e.g., *violent contemplation; plead with tolerantly*). Using the Semantic Interaction Technique, these rules of semantic fusion have been studied with both emotion adjective/noun (Osgood and Wilkins, 1969 unpublished) and interpersonal verb/adverb (Osgood, 1970) materials, with clearly supportive results—and it might be noted in passing that this technique could be used to *determine* the polarities of *non*-obvious semantic features.

Within-constituent Pollyanna and Congruence dynamics have been reported by Meredith Richards in a recently published study (1977) on adjective ordering in English: (a) that in attributive adjective sets (the A_1 A_2 N) the affectively more positive As are usually preferred prior in ordering (e.g., *the cute clever girl* preferred over *the clever cute girl*); (b) that congruent adjectives in attributive sets display more stable ordering patterns across speakers than incongruent adjectives (e.g., *expensive new clothes* OR *cheap old clothes* more stable than either *expensive old clothes* OR *cheap new clothes*); (c) that there is an "overwhelming" preference for affectively positive adjectives to be prior in *incongruent* sets (e.g., *a safe flimsy bridge* OR *a dangerous sturdy bridge* rather than the reverse orderings) as compared with *congruent* sets (e.g., either ordering reasonably acceptable for *a safe sturdy bridge* OR *a flimsy dangerous bridge*); and (d) that attributive sets (the A A N) display more stable ordering than predicative (the N is A and A). Richards plans to make similar tests cross-linguistically. With regard to rule (3) above, it should be noted that semantic anomalies yield cancellations of intensity *toward* zero if they are nonpolar (e.g., +1 fusing with −2) and the true sense of anomaly only when they are polar (+3 and −3). And there is the question, with polar anomalies, whether the OPERATOR must reject the cognitions *or* allow the feature in question to simply reduce *to* zero— we do use such anomalies most effectively (as in *he's sure a youthful old duffer!*).

Between-Constituent Congruence Dynamics

Again given the reciprocally inhibitory nature of semantic features, (1) it must also follow that simplex cognitions as wholes will be *perfectly congruent* semantically only when, for each feature, the *product* of the signs is positive across the three components and the *absolute values* (intensities) of the codings are the same; and, as we've already seen, *this* implies that, given the signs and intensities of any two components of a simplex cognition, *the congruent sign and intensity of the third component is predicted* via psycho-logic. (2) To the extent that simplex cognitions are internally *incongruent*—i.e., the signs and intensities of constituent features inputted from LEX differing from those predicted in the OPERATOR—(a) cognitive stress is produced simultaneously across all three components, (b) resolutions of such cognitive stress are always in the direction of congruence, and, (c) if the cognitions are credible, produce immediate shifts in the meanings of constituents, but, if the cognitions are incredible (intense polar antagonisms), there may be interactions with MEM which may serve to "bolster" or "weaken" the meanings of certain constituents in the interest of overall congruence (cf, Abelson and Rosenberg's (1958) notion of *Symbolic Psycho-logic*).

"Leftward" Fusion of Semantic Information in Simplex Stative Cognitions

Unless blocked by polar antagonisms on features, information in the M_2s of stative cogs will tend to be carried by the Relation (typically, perhaps exclusively, the pure stative verb *to be*) into the M_1s (the topics), the signs of M_2 features being maintained in the case of Associative Relations (X *is* Y, e.g., *Tom is happy* becoming semantically *happy Tom*) and being reversed in the case of Dissociative Relations (X *is not* Y, e.g., *Tom is not happy* becoming semantically *sad Tom*). I think that, at this point, it would be debatable whether such M_2-into-M_1 fusions are limited to the relation of Being (*Tom is happy*) or extend to certain other stative relations like Having (*Tom has curly hair* → *curly-haired Tom*) or perhaps even to stable stative relations generally (*golf bags hold the clubs* → *the golf-club-holding bags*?). Such fusions also raise problems about storage in the MEMORY—can we have "commentary-less" cogs [M_1 / $\emptyset$ / $\emptyset$]?

The same three fusion rules as given above would apply here as well, yielding (1) intensification of certain features of the topic, (2) addition of certain features to the meaning of the topic, and (3) reduction of the intensities of certain features toward 0 codings in the case of nonpolar antagonisms. It is here that *simile* and *metaphor* would be handled in this APG: in *apposite* similes and metaphors (e.g., *billboards are (like) warts on the face of the country side*) a low-salience affective feature of the topic (*billboards*) is amplified or even shifted in polarity by a high-salience feature of the commentary (*warts*). Production of similes and metaphors involves semantic "rule-breaking" by the speaker—but he must follow "rules for breaking rules" if his productions are to *be* apposite. Thus, for example, I find *the thunder shouted down the mountainside* (where the +Potent *thunder* is "humanized" by the +Potent and + Human *shouted*) entirely apposite and poetic, *my brakes shouted at me* at least borderline in acceptability, and *the summer breeze shouted down the mountainside* absolutely inapposite; similarly, *the daisies smiled at me* is just fine, but *the stones smiled at me* is impossible. Clearly, a sufficient degree of semantic *overlap* is essential.

Semantic interactions of this sort across all three components of simple cognitions also function to select among alternative *senses* of word-forms. Take for example the VPs in physicalist "dead metaphors" like *you haven't given me any idea of what you mean,* where the sense of *give* must be coded Abstract rather than Concrete. And just imagine the "boggling" of the mind of one who says "I'm just *buying* time" and someone asks him "how much are you *paying* for it?"! The same sense-selection rules apply to NPs, of course; you will recall that *basket* and *bottle* were actually *better* cues for recalling *the container was full of apples* and *the container was full of cola,* respectively, than was the word *container* itself in an experiment by Anderson and Ontony (1975).

"Upward" Fusion of the Commentaries of Complexes Having a Common Topic

Unless blocked by polar antagonisms on features, (1) the Relations and Objects $[--(M)-\rightarrow$ and $M_2s]$ of the Cog_2s of *congruent complexes* will fuse "upward" semantically into those of their Cog_1s (again, following the same three rules given above), and only the modified Cog_1s will be transferred to MEM (e.g., *Tom respects his philosophy professor* AND *he* (Tom) *admires his* (professor's) *lecturing style* becoming a fused cognition "translating" roughly as [Tom / is very favorably impressed by / his philosophy professor's lectures]). Processing of this sort would seem to be required by the evidence supporting "A Constructive vs Interpretive Approach" to human memory (cf, Bransford, Barclay, and Franks, 1972). (2) *Incongruent complexes* (conjoined by *but*s and their adverbial derivatives) cannot be fused in this manner, and therefore require more processing time (as well as more "space" in MEM), which has been amply demonstrated experimentally by Hoosain (as reported earlier in this lecture) and is right now being tested with children by Linda Hunter.

Here again you might note how the common topic of conjoined complexes *selects* among the senses of M_2s of commentaries—how $^+$Human *Tom* selects among the senses of *sweet* in *Tom is sweet and kind*. But what about fusions of M_2s that do *not* have parallel polarities across features? This, of course, brings us back full circle to Yang and Yin (the third, parallel polarity, characteristic). While the M_2s in *Tom is kind and lively* (the adjectives $^+$ on E and A, respectively) can fuse nicely, this is *not* the case for *Tom is kind but dull* where the *but* signals incongruence—and, as the ancient Chinese intuited, conjoined incongruent cognitions are harder to comprehend and must increase the load on one's memory.

Salience Dynamics and Unnaturalness in Sentence Production

Orientation

In Lecture IV we took up Naturalness as it relates to the functional notions of this APG governing the LEXICON (F I - F III) and in Lecture V as it applies to the functional notions relating to the OPERATOR in the processing of simplexes and complexes via interactions with the LEXICON (F IV - F VI). In the next two lectures we will review these notions and add notions F VII and F VIII, under two major topics: in *this* lecture, we take up *Salience Dynamics in Cognizing* (where a brief review of F IV - VI is most relevant) and how such dynamics produce *Unnaturalness in Sentence Production* by speakers; here, in a detailed review of F VII and F VIII, we finally come to interactions between OPERATOR and BUFFER—*and* come to grips with (probably) the most complicated aspects of language, Man's most complex cognitive achievement. In my *last* lecture, we will see how (in this APG) *Unnaturalness in Sentencing is Processed in Comprehending* by listeners; and we will come finally to detailed APG predictions of processing difficulty and a proposal for systematic research on sentence comprehending.

Salience Dynamics in Cognizing

Here it will be necessary to distinguish between *"Natural" Salience* (with which F IV through F VI are concerned) and *"Unnatural" Salience* (with which F VII and F VIII are concerned). Thus I have put both the "Natural" and the "Unnatural" above in quotes, since, although both types of salience are natural in the sense of reflecting underlying performance principles, the former is "natural" in reflecting the structures developed *in prelinguistic perceptual cognizing* while the latter is "unnatural" in reflecting disorderings of prelinguistic cognizing structures, due to the motivations of human language users *in linguistic sentencing*— and the two, perfectly natural (without quotes!) performance principles can either cooperate or compete with each other, as will be seen.

We must also distinguish between Speakers (in producing) and Listeners (in comprehending), since Speakers may "cooperate" with Listeners by producing naturally ordered sentences or may not by producing unnaturally ordered sentences that better express their own momentary motivations. Since Functional Notion IV (the basic Naturalness notion for simplexes) was not explicitly stated in Lecture V, we will do so here.

"Natural" Salience

Relating to the OPERATOR, Processing of Simplexes

> F IV. (A) Postulation of three, primitive, perception-based distinctions yields a semantic characterization of the constituent structure of simplex cognitions: (1) *Substantivity,* distinguishing +Substantive Entities from ⁻Substantive Relations; (2) *Directionality,* distinguishing +Salient (directionally prior) Figures and Sources from ⁻Salient (directionally subsequent) Grounds and Recipients; (3) *Stativity*, distinguishing +Static (stable, spatial) Stative Relations from ⁻Static (unstable temporal) Action Relations.

This, you will recall, was what I suggested as *a semantic characterization* of the most fundamental syntactic distinctions made by linguists in defining the constituent structures of simple sentences—and I pointed out that such a "translation" from syntax into semantics is essential for an APG that, beyond the LEXICON, operates entirely on patterns of semantic information. This is something about which I imagine the little linguists in you would like to hotly debate:

> F IV. (B) This semantic characterization implies that simplex prelinguistic cognitions will be naturally (1) *tripartite in structure,* thus [$M_1 -$ $- (M) \rightarrow M_2$] (where the Ms refer to meanings, the subscripts to Entities, and the dashed arrows to Relations), (2) *salience-ordered* (with M_1s representing Figures of states and Sources of actions and the M_2s the Grounds of states and the Recipients of actions), and (3), depending on the Relation, *of two basic types,*
> (a) *Stative Cognitions* [FIGURE (M_1) $--$ (STATE) $\rightarrow$ GROUND (M_2)] and
> (b) *Action Cognitions* [SOURCE (M_1) $--$ (ACTION) $\rightarrow$ RECIPIENT (M_2)],
> both implying necessarily an underlying SVO structure for natural sentencing of simplexes.

Now *this* part of F IV, with its strong claim about SVO being the prelinguistically natural ordering of components in cognizing, has already come in for some rather warm, if not hot, debate. But I would point out again that the claim is *only* that SVO languages do most closely match the postulated *prelinguistic* cognizing structures for Stative and Action Relations—*not* that SOV, or even VSO, are in any sense "abnormal". Nevertheless, one does have to account, I think, for (a) the fact that nearly ⅔ of the known human languages *are* SVO, (b) that there are many historical instances of *shifts from SOV into SVO* and apparently none in the reverse direction, and (c) the cross-language linguistic and experimental psycholinguistic *evidence* that I cited for F IV in Lecture V (particularly with respect to bitransitive sentences).

Relating to LEXICON/OPERATOR Interactions

In Lecture V a formal statement of Functional Notion V was given, so here we need only review the essentials as they relate to the issue of salience dynamics in sentence production. The crucial difference between LEXICON and OPERATOR functions is that the former operates on a "wordlike" unit basis and the latter on a "whole-constituent" basis. Thus LEX is the "transducer" in this APG, coding wholistic linguistic or perceptual signs into *code-strips of semantic features in comprehending* and decoding such feature patterns into *programs for behaving,* either linguistically or otherwise, *in expressing*. And to reemphasize a crucial point, *everything that transpires in cognizing*—all OPR, BUF, and MEM interactions—*is semantic in nature*.

As I pointed out in Lecture V, whereas the fact that the LEXICON operates on a "wordlike" basis—because of the perceptual salience of wordlike units, as compared with units either smaller (morphemes) or larger (whole NPs or VPs)—ties it to *language-specific* within-constituent word-ordering rules, the fact that the OPERATOR fuses the semantic information of words-within-constituents frees it to reflect *language universals*. Most significantly, this also means that differences between information in linguistic and perceptual channels is eliminated in the OPERATOR.

However, since OPR is assumed to universally "scan" the semantic information in its constituents in the order of their *criticality* in determining adaptive behavior, languages which order "identifying" features (i.e., those carried by the head nouns of NPs and the main verbs of VPs) prior to "modulating" features (e.g., those carried by adjectives in NPs and adverbials in VPs) should be somewhat easier to process by their (human) OPERATORS—and therefore languages with N-followed-by-As or V-followed-by-ADVs, or both, should be more "natural" than those with "unnatural" reverse orderings, like English. Although all languages appear to provide cues for the natures and boundaries of constituents, they are again *language-specific* and must be "learned" by the OPERA-TORS using each language—but the "how" of such learning is not obvious to me at this point.

Now, as to F V (B), IN EXPRESSING—which is most relevant here—OPR transmits "down" to LEX semantic code-strips for whole constituents, *which may be in either natural or unnatural ordering,* and LEX "faithfully" transforms this semantic information into programs for talking or acting at the Motor Integration Level of the "Little Black Egg". In other words, *salience dynamics are assumed to typically determine the ordering of whole constituents in OPR, not the ordering of word-forms within constituents.* However, this is only "typically": as we will see, high salience of certain features *within constituents* may cause OPR to "highlight" certain word-forms (e.g., moving forward the NEG feature carried by *never* to produce *néver have I been to the White House*); in such cases, LEX is, in effect, given the semantic feature set for some particular word-form and—again, "faithfully"—delivers the set to the Motor Integration Level for the appropriate program.

As indicated in F V (B) (1), *in expressing* Speakers may produce either naturally ordered or (following Salience Dynamics) unnaturally ordered constituents, hence the OPR → LEX transfers of constituents must shift. And, under (2), that, both for different individuals within the same language and across different languages, semantically equivalent "paraphrases" of constituent information is not only possible but likely (examples were given), but all expressing from the OPERATOR the same within-component total meaning. And note, finally, that ordering via the LEXICON to wording *programs* in expressing is dependent upon the word-ordering rules acquired *in comprehending*—reflecting the consistent priority of comprehension over production in language development.

Relating to the OPERATOR, Processing of Complexes

Since F VI was not formally stated in Lecture V, I do so here.

> F VI: (A) In both comprehending and expressing complexes (conjoined clauses in sentencing), the natural order of processing is that which corresponds to the order in which the states or events (referred to in the clauses) *are typically cognized in prelinguistic experience*; (B) complexes MUST be so ordered if they are to be comprehended, but they MAY be disordered in expressing (to satisfy efficiency and salience needs of the speaker—see F VIII); (C) all reordering, for both comprehending and expressing, *involves temporary transfers of whole clauses between OPERATOR and BUFFER,* and hence increased processing difficulty (see F VIII); (D) *congruent cognitions* are conjoined by ANDs (and their adverbial semantic equivalents) and *incongruent cognitions* are

conjoined by BUTS (and their adverbial semantic equivalents), with the features of the conjoiner being entered in the tag-slot for Cog_1.

This notion extends the Naturalness Principle to the ordering of simplexes (clauses) within complexes (conjoined sentences), again in terms of natural ordering of cognitions in prelinguistic experience. I pointed out that, while unnatural ordering of complexes *in perceptual experience* is very rare, it is characteristic of all *languages* that considerable freedom of clause ordering is provided by the use of adverbials. What I think is really significant here—for linguistic as well as psycholinguistic theorizing—is that, *apparently* in all languages, as in English and Kannada, *the combination of form and locus of conjoiners provides unambiguous cues for Naturalness vs Unnaturalness of clause ordering for the Listener.* Gordana Opačić's thesis provided us with a way of ordering modes of conjoining simultaneously in terms of *semantic complexity* and in terms of *syntactic complexity*—more on which anon.

Evidence Relevant to "Natural" Salience

As for F IV (naturalness of constituent-ordering), in an earlier lecture I reported some *cross-language linguistic data* bearing on "natural" salience: (1) that for bitransitive sentences, the proportions of languages having the unnatural form (the dative recipient closest to the transfer verb) was greatest for SVO, less for SOV, and least for VSO, this fitting expectations that the greater the predicted increase in processing time, the less likely the transform; (2) that the dative recipient (the "real" DO) would be more frequently marked than the verb-embedded entity being transferred (the "so-called" DO), particularly in "unnatural" transforms, and (3) that (a) when O is marked in unitransitive sentences (which is rare, of course) the *same* marker will be used for D in bitransitives and (b) that O is more likely to be incorporated in verbs than D (the theoretically separate component, M_2). As to *experimental psycholinguistic evidence*, a series of experiments by Tanz and Schultze (see Osgood and Tanz, 1977), utilizing a variety of methods, indicated that the so-called DO is more tightly bound to the verb than the so-called IO.

As for F V (naturalness of word-ordering within constituents), the prediction that words "identifying" Entities should be prior to those "modulating" these Entities was supported by Greenberg's (1963) evidence that N → As languages outnumber As → N languages by about 2-to-1, but no consistent data was reported for V - AV ordering. And, as for F VI (naturalness of clause-ordering in complexes), some confirmatory evidence will be offered near the end of Lecture VIII.

Just a bit of additional evidence on F IV can be added (*see* Osgood and Bock, 1977): (1) As to *language development in children,* Bates (1976) has argued that a "salience" principle accounts for word-order in early stages—that names of Entities having gestaltlike *figural* properties will be ordered prior to Entities having *ground* properties—and Bates also cites data indicating that, at the one-word stage, children tend to express that component of cognitions which is undergoing greatest *change or emphasis,* e.g., if a series of different objects is being put in a bucket by the child, the changing Entities (ONPs) will be expressed. Also relevant, Bloom (1970) reports that children rather rigidly follow a rule to place *animate* nouns in subject position and *inanimate* nouns in object position.

(2) As to *language performance in adults,* Bever (1970), as later elaborated in Fodor, Bever, and Garrett (1974), reports that listeners follow the general strategy to " . . . segment together any sequence X . . . Y in which the members could be related by primary internal structural relations, actor action object" (Bever, p. 290), and that, using the "click displacement" paradigm, the evidence strongly implies the cognitive unitariness of "sentoids", my $M_1 - - (M) - \rightarrow M_2$ cognitions (see Fodor, Bever, and Garrett, 1974, pp. 328–339). More recently, Carroll and Tannenhaus (1975) have demonstrated that the magnitudes of "click" location-shifts are much greater toward the boundaries of complete clauses (full cogs) than toward the boundaries of incomplete clauses (e.g., greater for *I felt sorry for the bum / so I gave him a dime* than for *the old painted wooden pipe / was on display at the local museum*).

"Unnatural" Salience

What (in quotes) I call "unnatural" salience is that imposed by Speakers upon the (necessarily) natural ordering of their own cognitions in order to *express* their momentary motivational states. Needless to say, such shenanigans on the part of Speakers apply pressures on Listeners if they are to *comprehend.* You might note that, while the "natural" (in quotes!) salience of ordering constituents within simplexes (F IV), of ordering word-forms within constituents (F V) and of ordering clauses within complexes (F VI) applies equivalently in both comprehending (by Listeners) and expressing (by Speakers), this equivalence does *not* hold for the "unnatural" (in quotes) salience to which functional notions F VII and F VIII are addressed: when, given his own motivational states (on which I'll elaborate momentarily), the Speaker produces a transform sentence (*dis*ordering of the natural order of information), the OPERATOR of the Listener, in order to comprehend, (1) must check for Naturalness and detect the loci and natures of the disordering (F VII) and, (2), must interact with the BUFFER (F VIII-II) in order to restore *real* Naturalness. Of course, the Speaker also pays a price to satisfy his motivations—in order to produce unnaturally ordered transforms, his OPERATOR, too, must usually resort to interactions with his BUFFER (F VIII-I)—all of which we'll see momentarily. But now let's take a deeper look at the dynamics of "Unnatural" (in quotes) Salience in sentencing.

Salience Dynamics

It has been intriguing to me that, until rather recently, linguists have rarely asked themselves just *why* Speakers ever produce unnaturally ordered utterances (i.e., transforms from the assumed forms in Deep Structure). Perhaps the reason is that the question itself is really relevant only to *performance*—and the fact that the Young Turks in linguistics *are* now asking this question would therefore seem to imply that they are moving toward a "predictive" performance theory and beyond a purely "descriptive-explanatory" theory. In any case, this question does have a long history. In 1900, for example, we find psychologist Wundt formulating a "principle of placing emphasized concepts first":

> Where word positioning is free, not bound by a hard and fast traditional rule, etc., the words follow each other according to the degree of emphasis on the concepts. The strongest emphasis is naturally on the concept that forms the main content of the statement. It is also the first in the sentence (Blumenthal, 1970, p. 29).

Descriptivist Bloomfield in 1914 noted that:

> The emotional relations of the elements . . . affect the sentence in various ways in different languages. A method in English, for instance, is to place the emotionally dominant element in some way out of its usual position, preferably first or last (pp. 113–114).

And many other early expressions of the same notion could be cited.

Three Salience Variables

One factor affecting salience is *Vivedness*—a type of salience *intrinsic* to the semantic codings (particularly affective Evaluation, Potency, and Activity) of the constituents to be expressed in sentencing. The underlying cognizing notion here is that components with more intense (polarized) feature-codings will tend both to be processed more quickly and therefore to be earlier in expression. I might also emphasize that there is *an intimate relation between stress and forward* (or backward) *move-*

ment (and note that STRESS itself is a sure-fire indicator of behavioral drive): if naturalness of ordering is maintained, then a subsequent component having high salience will tend to be stressed (*the maid dusting the hall saw a vámpire*). If salience is even stronger, and wins out over naturalness, then the stress is typically carried along with the forward movement (*a vámpire was seen by the maid dusting the hall*). But note that *non*salient elements are not likely to be moved forward unnaturally—*dusting the háll, a vampire was seen by the maid* is strange indeed, unless it is assumed that it was *the vámpire* who was *dusting the hall*!

Another competitor with Naturalness is *Motivation-of-speaker*—a type of salience *extrinsic* to the normal semantics of constituents that is *attributed* by the speaker as a result of his *focus* (personal interest, involvement, etc.) on naturally subsequent constituents in expressing. Here, of course, we expect considerable individual differences in tendencies to pre-pose (or post-pose) constituents—one man's concern with the object of a naturally active construction (like *somebody took the key*) may be such as to lead him along the path to passivization (*the kéy was taken by somebody*).

And yet another competitor with Naturalness is *Topicality*—also an *extrinsic* type of salience, due to the relatively greater availability of the feature-sets representing (usually) Entities (NPs) recently cognized in perceptual or linguistic processing (cf, F III). If I have just seen MY PIERRE RUSHES TOWARD THE WINDOW GROWLING AT A BIG BROWN-AND-BLACK DOG ON THE LAWN, I am more likely to produce *that ugly mutt belongs to the Smiths down the street* in commenting to my house-guest than *the Smiths down the street own that ugly mutt*. Topicality relates to notions like Theme/Rheme, Given/New, and, of course, Topic/Comment. A bit later we will have the opportunity to observe all of these Salience Dynamics in operation producing transformations—and I should point out that, although Vividness, Motivation-of-Speaker, and Topicality are independently variable, they often *converge* in their effects.

Competition of "Unnatural" with "Natural" Salience Principles

Although what I have called "unnatural" salience dynamics may happen to reinforce orderings dictated by "natural" dynamics, they often serve to produce disordering and hence must *compete*—which is one of many reasons why predictions from any APG must be probablistic in nature. However, in my original study of Simply Describing by adult English speakers ("Where Do Sentences Come From?", 1971)—in which, you'll recall, a series of perceptual demonstrations with everyday Entities in diverse Stative and Action Relations were described with simplex or complex sentences as the events seemed to require—what was impressive was how *improbable* unnaturally ordered sentencings were. For one example: when in D-1 subjects saw THE MAN IS HOLDING A SMALL BLACK BALL (where "the man" was yours truly!), it was not surprising that nearly all describers produced the active form (+Animate Human vs ⁻Animate Object); but it *was* surprising when—after having seen a whole series of events involving small black balls—in D-9 they saw THE MAN IS HOLDING A BIG BRIGHT BLUE BALL, the describings were only 5-of-20 passives, *a big blue ball is being held by the man*, despite the novel color and size of the ball. In a nutshell, simply describing in this situation was overwhelmingly Natural, despite several deliberate attempts like this to create Unnatural sentencings.

Kay Bock's thesis (1975, summarized in Osgood and Bock, 1977) was focussed on the effects of *inherent semantic Vividness* upon sentencing. The total design was extraordinarily complicated, and I can here give you only the essence of it. Working with a set of optional transformations—Dative, Equative, Genitive, Passive, and Phrasal Conjunct Inversions—the Vividness of the relevant NPs was manipulated.

Here's an illustrative sentence-set from the Dative Inversion group, where the dative recipient can be either +Vivid *the St. Bernard* or ⁻Vivid *the dog* and the transfer object can be either +Vivid *the frisbee* or ⁻Vivid *the ball*; the eight possible sentences (given to different subsets of subjects, of course) were the following:

(1) $^{+\ +}$Vivid: Natural—the boy tossed the FRISBEE to the ST. BERNARD
(2)   Unnatural—the boy tossed the ST. BERNARD the FRISBEE
(3) $^{+\ -}$Vivid: Natural—the boy tossed the FRISBEE to the dog
(4)   Unnatural—the boy tossed the dog the FRISBEE
(5) $^{-\ +}$Vivid: Natural—the boy tossed the ball to the ST. BERNARD
(6)   Unnatural—the boy tossed the ST. BERNARD the ball
(7) $^{-\ -}$Vivid: Natural—the boy tossed the ball to the dog
(8)   Unnatural—the boy tossed the dog the ball

The predictions would be as follows: (A) For both $^{+\ +}$Vivid sentences (1 and 2) and $^{-\ -}$Vivid sentences (7 and 8), the Natural orderings (1 and 7) would be produced more correctly (as originally presented), and with fewer shifts in constituent order, than the Unnatural orderings; in other words, in these cases *only* Naturalness can be an effective factor.

The more interesting predictions involve either mutual reinforcement or mutual competition between Naturalness and Vividness principles. (B) For the two $^{+\ -}$Vivid sentences (3 and 4) we have *reinforcement*—in (3), *the boy tossed the* FRISBEE *to the dog,* of maintaining the Natural ordering, and, in (4), *the boy tossed the dog the* FRISBEE, of shifting *to* the Natural ordering; here the prediction must be maximizing of correct recall as given in (3) and shifting ordering in (4). (C) For the two $^{-\ +}$Vivid sentences (5 and 6), on the other hand, we have *competition*—in (5), *the boy tossed the ball to the* ST. BERNARD, for Naturalness to maintain the given order and for Vividness to transform it, and, in (6), *the boy tossed the* ST. BERNARD *the ball,* for Naturalness to shift the order and for Vividness to maintain it; here we expect reduction *toward* chance ordering in recall, but probably with the more basic Naturalness "winning out".

Because of the complexity of design (number of interacting variables) and the subjective nature of assigning Vividness to NPs by the experimenters (Kay Bock also had other subjects give *vividness* and *preference ratings* to all the constituents and whole sentences respectively—see the full paper), the statistical variance was rather high; nevertheless, the overall pattern of the results was consistent with the predictions made here. Again, in a nutshell, both Naturalness and Vividness have independent effects that combine to produce the expected trends, but Naturalness appears to have the greater weight.

Supporting Evidence

And there is supporting evidence elsewhere. In the same 1977 volume on *Sentence Production* as the Osgood/Bock paper, Suitbert Ertel (our West German colleague in cross-cultural research, by the way) reports several relevant experiments, all designed to test the hypothesis that in sentencing the speaker focusses on that nominal constituent that is *closest to his ego* (an aspect of our *Motivation-of-speaker* variable).

In one experiment subjects were shown cartoonlike drawings with several girls and boys, with names, in various positions in relation to a fence, and a "speaker" [with the usual balloon (but "empty") coming out of his mouth]. Given hypothetical sentences like *Hans is watching the girl in front of the fence,* and asked to name the girl in question, subjects tended to adopt the perspective of the cartoon "speaker", *regardless* of orientation of the picture with respect to themselves.

In another experiment on kinship reasoning, male and female subjects were given statements like *my sister is your daughter* or *my nephew is your brother*—or, to reverse the ego-closeness from sentence subject to sentence object, the synonymous sentences *your daughter is my sister* or *your brother is my nephew*—and then asked "who can say this to whom?" Not only were sentences with the *ego*-related concept as subject (*My X is . . .*) processed faster than those with the *alter*-related concept as subject (*Your X is . . .*), but—most significantly—male subjects selected *male* speakers and listeners in their answers while female subjects selected *female*!

A third experiment was actually a content analysis—of sports writers' reports of *identical* soccer games—and, with only sentences in which players of *both* teams were mentioned, the prediction that home-team players were more likely to appear as sentence-subjects was upheld at a high level of significance.

What Cooper and Ross (in their "World Order", 1975, paper) refer to as the "Me first" principle is very much like Ertel's Ego-closeness or our Speaker-motivation: spatial deixis (*they hunted here and there/*there and here; they talked about this and that/*that and this*); temporal deixis (*I think of him now and then/*then and now; sooner or later/*later or sooner they'll arrive*); generational closeness (*my son and grandson/ *grandson and son take after me*); WASPness (!) (*they played cowboys and Indians/*Indians and cowboys*); humanness (*'taint a fit night out for man nor beast/*beast nor man*).

Unnaturalness in Sentence Production (F VII)

In detailing Functional notions VII and VIII of my developing *Toward an Abstract Performance Grammar*—which are by all odds the most complicated—I will make more "stops-in-course" for giving illustrative sentences than has been the case so far—illustrative, that is, of how the OPERATOR and the BUFFER interact in the processing of unnaturally ordered sentences, in both their production (this lecture) and their comprehension (next lecture)[1]. In some aspects—particularly for F VII— there will be overlaps with anticipations made in earlier lectures; however, this is not only inevitable but, I think, useful.

There is an interesting, and significant, difference between F VII and F VIII, however, which I must note at the outset: whereas F VII is strictly concerned with OPR/BUF interactions involved in *comprehension* (for the Listener), F VIII falls naturally into *expression* (Speaker) vs *comprehension* (Listener) processing dynamics—and I take them up in that order, under F VIII-I (here) and F VIII-II (Lecture VIII), because, as you will see, not only are the OPR/BUF interactions rather different in expressing and comprehending, but it is the *Speaker* who, in effect, sets problems for the *Listener*.

Detection of Unnaturalness in Sentencing by Listeners

General Function of F VII

Utilizing both cues for Naturalness derived from prelinguistic perceptual cognizing and language-specific cues for acceptability/grammaticality derived from early linguistic experience (see F IV - F VI), *the* OPERATOR

---

[1] These functional notions and illustrative analyses were developed jointly by C.E.O. and his linguist research assistant, S. N. Sridhar.

scans semantic information received from the LEXICON, *and assigned* ["left-to-right" to its M_1, – – (M) – →, *and* M_2 *components, see* F V], *for compatibility with the rules it has developed.* (Details of this scanning process are then detailed as follows.)

> F VII (A). Within each component, OPR scans features *in the order of their criticality* in determining adaptive behaviors to the states and actions being comprehended: (1) *affective features* (Evaluation, Potency, and Activity) prior to denotative features, by virtue of their primitive survival value; (2) *for denotative information characterizing entities* (later NPs), *substantive* (identifying) features prior to *modulating* (adjectival modifying, etc.) features; and, (3) *for denotative information characterizing relations* (later VPs) similarly, *nature-specifying* (identifying) features prior to *modulating* (adverbial, tense modifying, etc.) features.

Since we have already considered this operation in an earlier lecture, detailed elaboration of the process will not be necessary. You will recall that it is the Graspable, Throwable, Rollable, etc., "identifying" features of BALL-object Entities that are more critical for adaptive behaviors than their Color, Size, Cleanliness, etc., "modulating" features; and similarly, it is the "identifying" features of Relations that are more critical than their "modulations" (thus ROLLED → SLOWLY, SPOKE → SOFTLY, and so forth). (I should add that Salience dynamics will often result from such scanning—see F VIII-I.)

You will also recall that this notion led to a Naturalness principle governing the transfer of word-order information from LEX to OPR in our F V. I might also note something here that seems potentially relevant to *translating* across languages and language *learning*: since, regardless of the language, OPERATORS fuse the semantic information of word-forms within constituents, *within-constituent* wording disorders should cause less disturbance in cross-language comprehending and expressing than *between-constituent* disorderings—*but* learning the cues for *the natures and boundaries* of constituents should pose problems. Although I have no evidence on this at hand, it should be readily obtainable from experts in bilingualism and second language learning.

Checking for Naturalness within and Compatibility between Constituents

> F VII (B). *In comprehending simplexes,* OPR (1) checks component code-strips for Naturalness within and Compatibility between constituents of the codings on basic Substantivity, Directionality, and Stativity features (*see* F IV), (2) the code-strips for constituents that are unnaturally disordered are transferred cyclically to the BUFFER, being stored in "push-down" fashion, and then, (3) as "leftward" movement of the remaining information within the simplex occurs [*see* F VIII-II (C)

below for details], the temporarily stored constituent information is returned to the cog components left open.

F VII (C). *Whole cognitions having incompatible codings* are either processed and sent to the MEMORY *as acceptable "metaphors"* or rejected *as semantically anomalous*, dependent upon the degrees of featural incongruity (see notions relating to fine, cross-constituent, congruity dynamics in Lecture VI).

While (B, 2) and (B, 3) are really summary anticipations of what will be detailed in F VIII-II (C) in my next lecture, (B, 1) and (C) require some elaboration here. Referring back to what, in discussion of F IV, I called "A Semantic Characterization of the Constituent Structures of Simple Cognitions", the following should be noted: (a) that scanning by OPR of the $\pm$Substantivity and $\pm$Directionality features is required for detecting *Unnaturalness* of constituent ordering within simplexes; (b) that scanning the $\pm$Stativity feature is also required for detecting *Incompatibility*, primarily if not exclusively—possible exceptions being Relations (VPs) that are themselves ambiguous as to being $^+$ or $^-$Stative (Stative *or* Action Relations).

If a cognition—*either* Stative or Action—is to be *Natural*, then its M_1 must be both $^+$Substantive and $^+$Directional (signaling the Figure of a state or the Source of an action as the SNP), its $--$ (M) $\rightarrow$ must be $^-$Substantive and $^+$Directional (signaling a naturally directed VP), and its M_2 must be $^+$Substantive but $^-$Directional (signaling the Ground of a state or the Recipient of an action as the ONP). Note that it is the meaningful relations between the *entities* (M_1 and M_2) in simplex cognitions that determine Naturalness of constituent ordering; compare the natural stative sentence *a Mexican shawl is draped on the wall* with unnatural *the wall has draped on it a Mexican shawl* and compare the natural action sentence *the Great Dane burst the beach ball with a single bite* with unnatural *the beach ball was burst with a single bite by the Great Dane*. It is the shift in entity ordering that forces the changes in VP structures.

Conversely, it is the meaning of the *relation* [$--$ (M) $\rightarrow$] that determines whether the entities are involved in a $^+$Stative or $^-$Stative (= Action) cognition. Witness that the entities and their ordering are identical in stative *the neighbor's kid is sitting on our canvas lawn chair* and in action *the neighbor's kid is ripping up our canvas lawn chair*. It is the shift from $^+$ to $^-$Stativity of the *relation* (VP) that, in effect, "conveys" the stative vs action codings onto the entities.[2] Note that whereas the inherent semantics of entity-pairs entirely determines *Nat-*

---

[2] In our statement and adumbration of F IV earlier, we probably should have coded entities as ^{0}Stativity and, of course, relations as ^{0}Directionality, since in both cases the semantic codings are in no sense "inherent" in the semantics of the NPs and VPs, respectively.

uralness of simplexes, it is the inherent semantics of relations that entirely determines the *Compatibility* of simplexes. Thus one can say *the Mexican shawl caresses the wall* or say *the Great Dane is murdering the beach ball with a single bite* only metaphorically.

In Natural stative and action cognitions the relations are always +Directional (like *the cat is sitting on the pillow* and *the cat jumped on the pillow*); if we reverse the ordering of M_1 and M_2, we get ridiculously anomalous sentencings like *the pillow is sitting on the cat* (or *the ball is holding the man*) and *the pillow jumped on the cat* (or *the ball grabbed the man*), which could only be metaphorical at best. However, there are ⁻Directionality codings for Relations that yield compatible cognitions, but they are all Unnatural.

If M_1 is + − − (RECIPIENT) and M_2 is + + − (SOURCE), but the Relation is − − − (a *leftward-directed* action relation), then we have one of the conditions for producing an ordinary passive construction (e.g., *the vámpire was rented a house by the realtor*), in which the salience of the Recipient takes precedence over the natural SOURCE - ACTION - RECIPIENT relation. If M_1 is + + + (i.e., FIGURE) and M_2 is + − + (i.e., GROUND) and the Relation is − − + (i.e., *leftward* stative), then we have the conditions for expressing what might be called "Passive Statives" (for example, *the cow is surrounded by the cornfield*). If M_1 is + + − (SOURCE) and M_2 is + − − (RECIPIENT), but the relation is − − + (a leftward-directed *stative* relation), then perhaps we have the cognitive conditions for a *potential* action, instigated by a *potential* recipient (e.g., *the sailor was attracted by the flirtatious bar-girl*).[3]

Checking for Naturalness in Comprehending Complexes

F VII (D). *In comprehending complexes,* subsequent to processing of Cog_1 (naturally prior clause linguistically) according to (B) and (C) above, given the cue for *Unnatural clause ordering* (combined form and locus of conjoiner—*see* F VI), (1) the prior clause$_1$ is transferred constituent-by-constituent to BUF in the reverse order of that received (i.e., "right-to-left"), (2) the naturally prior cognition but subsequent clause$_2$ becomes Cog_1 (in effect, is "moved up" in OPR), and (3) the BUFfed constituents for the naturally subsequent cognition are returned to OPR, now as Cog_2 [*see* F VIII-II (D) for details].

Here, first, recall that certainly in English and Kannada, probably in the five or so other languages that S.N. Sridhar is presently studying, and possibly universally, the *combined* cues of form and locus (centered

---

[3] I've been unable to come up with any acceptable cases in which the NPs of Action and Stative relations are crossed (that is, SOURCE - RELATION - GROUND, or FIGURE - RELATION - RECIPIENT)—which doesn't mean that they are inconceivable, of course!

or preposed) of conjoiners (basic or adverbial) give *unambiguous cues* as to the Naturalness or Unnaturalness of the clause order. Second, again the steps (1) through (3) in this statement are really anticipations of the detailed analysis to be presented in F VIII. And, third, as will also become clearer in F VIII, the reason for the "left-to-right" transfer of constituents of simplexes to BUF, but "right-to-left" transfer of the clauses of complexes, is that this guarantees restoration of natural order in both cases—and, in the case of complexes, this makes obvious sense because the entire first clause *as well as the conjoiner* (often being centered) must be processed before naturalness of the clause ordering can be determined.

Expressing Unnaturally Ordered Sentences by Speakers (F VIII-I)

F VIII-I states the essence of the APG theory of cognitive processing in EXPRESSING sentences that are unnaturally ordered due to the effects of Salience Dynamics upon Speakers. Section (A) indicates that the Speaker always starts with simplex or complex cognitions that are *naturally ordered,* and, if "unnatural" salience motivation *is not* affecting him, that his ordering of constituents and word-forms within constituents of simplexes will be natural, as well as the sequencing of the clauses of complexes. (B) gives an overview of what is assumed to happen when salience *is* affecting the Speaker—with the earlier (or later) expression of constituents of simplexes or clauses of complexes from the OPERATOR either leaving the remainder of the information in natural order for expression or requiring use of the BUFFER. Section (C) details the interactions involved when use of the BUFFER *is* required for expressing *simplexes* of various sorts and section (D) details the interactions when its use is required for expressing *complexes* of several sorts.

> F VIII-I (A). For the Speaker, the ordering *in the* OPERATOR of cognized constituents within simplexes and of simplex clauses within complexes *is always natural*; when constituents are expressed *in natural order,* the ordering of word-forms *within* constituents always conforms to the surface rules of the particular language and always exhausts the semantic information in each constituent (*see* F V).

Why must the Speaker always begin with naturally ordered simplexes and complexes? As was implied in F IV - VI and will be detailed in F VIII-II, cognitions received must be either "naturally" natural in ordering or what is "unnaturally" ordered must be restored to natural ordering—*if the Listener is to comprehend.* It follows that what has been freshly processed by the OPERATOR and stored in the MEMORY—whether

simplexes or complexes and whether via perceptual or linguistic channels—*must already be in natural order*.

> F VIII-I (B). Salience dynamics operating on the Speaker may
> produce *displacements* of constituents (or parts thereof) of simplexes
> and whole clauses of complexes from their natural order, leaving
> semantically "empty" (ø) or reduced components: (1) if, for *simplexes*,
> the displacement via overt expression (movement "leftward" for earlier
> expression) or via transfer to the BUFFER (movement "rightward" for
> later expression) leaves the remaining constituents (or parts thereof) *in
> natural order* for expression, the remainder of the cognition is simply
> expressed, and no (further) use of BUF is required; (2) if, *for simplexes*,
> the displacement of constituents (or parts thereof) leaves the remainder
> *in an order unnatural for expression*, then (further) use of BUF is
> required (*see* C below); (3) *for complexes*, displacement of a naturally
> subsequent clause for earlier expression *always* requires BUFfing of the
> naturally prior clause or clauses (transferred to BUF from right-to-left
> by constituents).

Although movement "leftward" of salient material for earlier expression is typical for English ("tag-questions" being one obvious exception),
other languages may display considerable "rightward" movement for
later expression (e.g., Serbo-Croatian and Slovenian), and the latter
requires temporary BUFfing, as indicated. Now we may consider some
sentential examples where [B (1)] applies. I will always give, first, the
natural form from which the Speaker "takes off" and the unnatural form
which he expresses; then, second, I will offer a step-by-step APG
analysis of the processing.[4]

**Illustrative Analyses of Speaker Productions of Unnaturally Ordered
Sentences**

F VIII-I (B, 1) Examples

Topicalization: I will have a marfini ⟹ A marfini I will have
                          (1) Given SPKR MOT, EXP *A marfini* → [I /
                          will have / ø]
                          (2) EXP remainder, *I will have*

Adverb Preposing: I saw a róbin yesterday ⟹ Yésterday I saw a
                          robin
                          (1) Given SPKR MOT on the "when", EXP
                          Yésterday
                          (2) EXP remaining full cog, *I saw a robin*

---

[4]I also indicate what I think to be "natural" stress; the doubled arrows (⟹) always indicate
the shift from natural to transform ordering; the single arrows (→) always indicate the
shifts *in* OPR contents (or *to* BUF) occasioned by each step in the production process.

Subject-verb (aux)
Inversion:

John is a thérapist? ⇒ Ís John a thérapist?

(1) Given Q MOT, EXP *Ís* → [John / ø / a therapist] [?]

(2) EXP remainder, *John a therapist*

Ditto - partial express:

John saw the crime? ⇒ Díd John see the crime?

(1) Given Q MOT, EXP *Díd* → [John / ø see / the crime] [?]

(2) EXP remainder, *John see the crime?*

F VIII-I (C) When use of the BUFFER is required for expressing *simplexes* [B (2) above]: (1) if the salience-motivated constituent (or part thereof) *is shifted to utterance initial (or terminal) position,* (a) it is expressed (or transferred to BUF), leaving a constituent-holding ø, (b) unnaturally coded constituents (or parts) are transferred to BUF (left-to-right), (c) remaining constituents (or parts), if any, are expressed, and (d) code-strips from BUF are expressed as they are returned to OPR.

(C, 1) Examples

"Rightward" AV displacement:

The fat lady ate gréedily the pie ⇒ the fat lady ate the pie gréedily

(1) Given SPKR MOT for "manner", BUF *greedily* → [the fat lady / ate ø / the pie]

(2) EXP remainder, *the fat lady ate the pie*

(3) As returned from BUF, EXP *gréedily*

[NOTE: prior EXP of *greedily* for emphasis would require no buffing, hence [B (1)] above.]

Passivization:

Everyone admires Napóleon ⇒ Napóleon is admired by everyone

(1) EXP the SPKR-salient *Napóleon* → [everyone / admires / ø]

(2) Avoiding ungrammaticality (*everyone* in the Relation slot), BUF *everyone* → [ø / admires / ø]

(3) EXP unnaturally directed Relation, *is admired by*

(4) As returned from BUF, EXP *everyone*

[NOTE: here assume that, except for Directionality, *admires / is admired by* have identical semantic codings, thus from — (M) → to ← (M) —.]

PP-phrase prepos-
ing:
         The cat ran into the garden ⇒ Into the gárden ran the cat

         (1) Given focus on "where", EXP *Into the gárden* → [the cat / ran / ø]

         (2) Given "poetic" MOT (??), BUF *the cat* → [ø / ran / ø]

         (3) EXP *ran*

         (4) As returned from BUF, EXP *the cat*

[NOTE: if assume a secondary MOT for Action and (2) becomes EXP *ran,* then no BUFfing needed.]

Negative AV prepos-
ing:
         I have néver been to the White House ⇒ Néver have I been to the WH

         (1) Given salience of Neg, EXP *Néver* → [I / have ø been to / the WH]

         (2) Since not part of Relation, BUF *I* → [ø / have ø been to / the WH]

         (3) EXP *have* → [ø been to / the White House]

         (4) Given place-holding ø initially and features of SNP topmost in BUF, EXP from BUF, *I*

         (5) EXP remainder in OPR, *been to the White House*

F VIII-I (C) continued: (2) if the salience-motivated constituent (or part thereof) *is shifted to a noninitial (or nonterminal) utterance position,* (a) the constituents (or parts) cognitively *prior to* ("leftward" of) that position are expressed, (b) those *subsequent to ("rightward" of) that position are transferred to BUF (left-to-right),* (c) the salience-motivated constituent (or part) is expressed, and (d) code-strips remaining in BUF are expressed as they are returned to OPR.

(C, 2) Examples

Particle Movement:
         John looked up the topless wáitress ⇒ John looked the topless wáitress up

         (1) EXP *John looked* → [ø / ø up / the topless waitress]

         (2) BUF *up* → [ø / ø / the topless waitress]

         (3) EXP salient *the topless wáitress*

         (4) As returns from BUF, EXP *up*

Dative Movement:
         The art gallery sold a painting to Jackie Onássis ⇒ The art gallery sold Jackie Onássis a painting

         (1) EXP *the art gallery sold* → [ø / ø a painting to / Jackie Onassis]

(2) BUF *a painting* (to = ∅) → [∅ / ∅ / Jackie Onassis]

(3) EXP salient *Jackie Onássis*

(4) As returns from BUF, EXP *a painting* (∅)

[NOTE: it is assumed that the *to* in the basic bitransitive form is a semantically "empty" syntactic marker.]

Possessive Reversal: Then Custer entered Sitting Bull's wígwam ⇒ Then Custer entered the wígwam of Sitting Bull

(1) EXP *Then Custer entered* → [∅ / ∅ / ∅ / Sitting Bull's wigwam]

(2) BUF *Sitting Bull* (poss.) → [∅ / ∅ / ∅ / ∅ (def.) wigwam]

(3) EXP salient *the wígwam*

(4) As returns from BUF, EXP *of Sitting Bull*

[NOTE: it is assumed (a) that X's Y, *not* Y of X, is the natural structure (e.g., "Mommy shoe", *not* "Shoe Mommy" is order in child language), and (b) that the surface expressions of the possessive (SB's W and *the* W *of* SB) are semantic equivalents.]

> F VIII-I (D) When use of the BUFFER is required for processing *complexes [B (3) above]: (1) if the naturally subsequent cognition (Cog$_2$) in complexes* **conjoined by adverbials** *is more salient to the Speaker, (a) the naturally prior cognition (Cog$_1$) is transferred to BUF (right-to-left), (b) Cog$_2$ is expressed, either preceded or followed by expression of the conjoiner (coded in the tag-slot) depending on Naturalness signaling requirements, and (c) Cog$_1$ is expressed as its constituents are returned from BUF to OPR.*

Since the Speaker's OPERATOR *must,* in theory, start production with completely "naturalized" simplexes and complexes, it follows that—of the diverse modes of conjoining and expressing *full* complexes—only the use of *adverbials* permits permutation of whole clauses. Recall that *and*s and *but*s (in any of their varied senses) must be centered, with the clauses in natural order. As for D (1) in this statement, you will also recall that, according to F VI, in English the combined form and locus of any adverbial *unambiguously* signals (unintentionally, for the benefit of the Listener) whether or not the information in the clauses *is* naturally or unnaturally ordered. We may begin therefore, appropriately, with the conjoining of clauses representing whole cognitions via use of adverbials.

(D, 1) Examples

Simple Sequence Adverbials (I):   Mary sharpened her hunting knife [and then] Mary skinned the súckling píg ⇒ [Before] Mary skinned the súckling píg, she sharpened her hunting knife

(1) Given salience of *suckling pig* cognition, BUF naturally prior Cog_1 "right-to-left" → *her hunting knife* then *sharpened* then *Mary*—"push-down" fashion into BUFFER, thus top-to-bottom in BUF,

$$\left\{ \begin{array}{l} \text{Mary} \\ \text{sharpened} \\ \text{her hunting knife} \end{array} \right\}$$

(2) EXP semantically appropriate equivalent of basic conjoiner ([and then] in the tag-slot), *before*

(3) EXP naturally subsequent Cog_2, remaining in OPR, *Mary skinned the súckling píg*

(4) As returned from BUF, using redundancy-deleting PN, EXP *she sharpened her hunting knife*

[NOTE: that BUFfing whole cogs "right-to-left" guarantees natural order upon return—NOT *ad hoc* since, unlike simplexes, OPR must have checked *whole cog* for unnaturalness within, *plus* (and/but type or adverbial equivalent) conjoiner, before transfer.]

Simple Sequence Adverbials (II):

Starting from same underlying structure as above
⇒ Mary skinned the súckling píg [after] she sharpened her hunting knife

(1) Given salience of *pig* cognition, BUF Cog_1 → (top) Mary / sharpened / her hunting knife (bottom) in BUF

(2) EXP Cog_2 from OPR, *Mary skinned the súckling píg*

(3) EXP appropriate adverbial, *after*

(4) As returns from BUF, EXP (with PN), *she sharpened her hunting knife*

[NOTE that, while *before* (above) signals Unnaturalness when preposed, *after* (here) signals same when *centered;* note also that, in both examples, redundancy deletion via PN substitution usually is applied to second clause expressed—but not necessarily, of course.]

Simple Cause Adverbials:

Rain flooded the golf course [and so] John got soaked ⇒ John got sóaked [because₁] rain flooded the golf course (as expressed by John's newly wed wife!)

(1) Given MOT focus on John, BUF naturally
$Cog_1 \rightarrow$ (top) *rain / flooded / the golf course*
(bottom) in BUF

(2) EXP Cog_2 from OPR, *John got sóaked*

(3) EXP appropriate adverbial, *because*

(4) As returns from BUF, EXP Cog_1, *rain flooded the golf course*

Sequential Cause Ad-
verbials:

Grampa slipped on the ice [and so then] Grampa broke his leg $\Rightarrow$ Grámpa broke his lég [because$_2$] he slipped on the ice (as expressed by his little grandson!)

(1) Given salience of "leg-breaking", BUF naturally $Cog_1 \rightarrow$ (top) *Grampa / slipped on / the ice* (bottom)

(2) EXP Cog_2 from OPR, *Grámpa broke his lég*

(3) EXP appropriate adverbial, *because*

(4) As returns from BUF, and with PN substitution, EXP, *he slipped on the ice*

[NOTE: (a) that while *because* can be either preposed (signaling Naturalness) or centered (signaling Unnaturalness), substitute *so* can only be centered, signaling Naturalness (cf, Grampa slipped on the ice so he broke his leg / *so Grampa broke his leg he slipped on the ice); (b) that, whereas *because*$_1$ substitutes for *and so* (Simple Cause), *because*$_2$ substitutes for *and so then* (Sequential Cause)—thus *because* having multiple senses just like *and*s or *but*s.]

F VIII-I (D) continued: (2) if the naturally subsequent cognition (Cog_2), *embedding as a relative clause* a naturally prior cognition (Cog_1), is more salient to the Speaker, (a) the naturally prior Cog_1 is transferred to BUF (again, right-to-left), (b) the naturally subsequent Cog_2 (now remaining in OPR) is expressed up to and including the NP which Cog_1 will further characterize, (c) Cog_1 is expressed, initiated by the semantically appropriate relative PN replacing that NP[5], followed by the remaining constituents in BUF, and (d) the remainder of Cog_2 (if any) is expressed;

(D-2) Examples

Relativized SNP:

A man came to dinner [and] (that) man stole the silverware $\Rightarrow$ the man who came to dinner stole the sílverware

---

[5] If the relativized NP is part of a prepositional phrase (*see* Example below) then the preposition must accompany the relative PN.

(1) Given salience of "stealing silverware", BUF natural $Cog_1 \rightarrow$ *a man / came to / dinner* in BUF
(2) From salient Cog_2, as Definite NP, EXP, *the man*
(3) As returned from BUF, and with shift to appropriate REL NP, EXP Cog_1, *who* (= that man) *came to dinner*
(4) From remainder of Cog_2 in OPR, EXP, *stole the silverware*

[NOTE: (a) that embedded clauses must *always* (we think!) be psycholinguistically *prior* in cognizing; (b) that the (that) in underlying Cog_2, often substituted for more specific REL PNs, is syntactic, but semantically "empty"; and (c) that *if* the head noun *plus* the relative clause have already been stored in MEM as *a single Topic* and this is now being *re*-cognized by SPKR, the complex reduces to a simplex for him [the-man-who-came-to-dinner / stole / the silverware].]

Relativized ONP:　　　John hit a man [and] that man had a concussion
　　　⇒ the man (who) John hit had a concússion
(1) Given salience of "a concussion", BUF naturally $Cog_1 \rightarrow$ *John / hit / a man*
(2) From salient Cog_2, as Definite NP, EXP, *the man*
(3) As returned from BUF, with deletion of redundant *a man,* EXP *John hit*
(4) EXP remainder of Cog_2, *had a concússion*

[NOTE: in this case, if one were to express from BUF (following expression of Definite *the man* from Cog_2) the appropriate REL PN, then—since *a man* is in the ONP slot of BUFfed Cog_1—the M_1 (*John*) and the — (M) → (*hit*), both being "above" *the man,* would have to be returned to OPR as a "Cog_3" → [John / hit / ø], greatly complicating the processing; it is interesting that, in my English at least, while the PN in the RELATIVIZED SNP above is *not* deletable, **the man came to dinner stole the silverware,* it is not only deletable here but preferred that way (*the man John hit had a concussion* better than *the man whom John hit had a concussion*)—thus supporting the analysis offered here.]

Relativized PP-phrase:　　A knife was very sharp [and] John sliced with (that) knife the salami ⇒ The knife with which John sliced the salami was very sharp
(1) Given primary salience of "(very sharp) knife", EXP, with shift to Definite NP, *the knife* → [ø / was / very sharp] for Cog_1 in OPR

(2) Given secondary salience of the "knife function", BUF Cog_1 remainder $\rightarrow \phi$ / *very sharp*
in BUF

(3) From Cog_2 in OPR, with PP and appropriate
REl PN, EXP *with which* $\rightarrow$ [John / sliced ϕ
/ the salami] in OPR

(4) EXP remainder of Cog_2 from OPR, *John
sliced the salami*

(5) As Cog_1 remainder returned from BUF, EXP
was very sharp

F VIII-I (D) continued: (3) if the naturally subsequent cognition
(Cog_2) *has a "commentative" relation* to the necessarily prior "topical"
cognition (Cog_1) being commented on, but is more salient to the Speaker,
then (a) the "topical" Cog_1 is transferred to BUF (again, right-to-left),
(b) the "commentative" Cog_2 is expressed (with its redundant embedded
Cog_1 component deleted (ϕ) in anticipatory fashion), followed optionally
by a semantically "empty" syntactic marker (like *that*), and (c) "topical" Cog_1 is expressed as its constituents are returned from BUF to
OPR.

(D, 3) Examples

*Affirming Commen-
tative;*

Mary is pregnant [and] I am sure [Cog_1] $\Rightarrow$ I am
súre Mary is pregnant

(1) Given Ego salience of "comment", shift to
BUF necessarily $Cog_1 \rightarrow$ *Mary / is / pregnant*
to BUF ("right-to-left")

(2) EXP "commentative" Cog_2, *I am súre (that)*
ϕ [= *marker for Cog_1*] (3)

With generalized REL PN optional, EXP Cog_1
as returned from BUF, *(that) Mary is pregnant*

[NOTE: the phrase "Ego salience" must be interpreted broadly, to
include not only the salience of the comment made by the speaker, but
also that of anyone elese's comment, as long as the speaker, in reporting
it, finds it salient. Thus, not only is *I doubt* fronted, but also cases like
HARRY *doubts* . . . [Presumably, there are significant cultural differences
in expressing commentative cognitions by "fronting" the comment. For
example, the languages of the Indian Subcontinent, despite their typol-
ogical similarity (SOV), differ in whether or not they employ the
"comment-first" structure. The Indo-Aryan languages (e.g., Hindi, Bengali) employ it, while the Dravidian languages (e.g., Kannada, Tamil)
employ the topic-comment structure. It should be noted, however, that
even the latter group of languages normally has the English-type structure
as an alternative strategy, to express the salience of the comment.

Although we do expect to find significant *cultural* differences in expressing Ego-states by "fronting" of one's comments, we have no solid evidence. Sridhar plans to compare the E-P-A of Self concepts with this linguistic difference across our 30 language-culture communities.]

Negating Commentative:

Mary is pregnant [but] I doubt [Cog_1] $\Rightarrow$ I doúbt that Mary is pregnant

(1) Given Ego salience of "comment", shift to BUF the necessarily $Cog_1 \rightarrow$ *Mary / is / pregnant* BUF ("right-to-left")

(2) EXP "commentative" Cog_2, *I doúbt* (that) $\emptyset$ [= Cog_1]

(3) EXP Cog_1 as returned from BUF, (*that*) *Mary is pregnant*

[NOTE: in *my* English, retaining *that* seems more natural with Negating!]

Oblique Commentative:

Peter Pan was a fairy [and] [Cog_1] is obvious (to me) $\Rightarrow$ It is óbvious (that) Peter Pan was a fairy

(1) Given "oblique" Ego salience of "comment", BUF the necessarily $Cog_1 \rightarrow$ *Peter Pan / was / a fairy* in BUF

(2) EXP "commentative" Cog_2, with syntactic marker *it* representing BUFfed [Cog_1], *it is óbvious* (to me)

(3) EXP (*that* optional?) Cog_1 as returned from BUF, (*that*) *Peter Pan was a fairy*

[NOTE: the implicit *to me*, which would tie SPKR to the comment, is often deleted—but not necessarily, e.g., with stress, . . . *is obvious to me that* . . .]

Alter (by Ego) *Commentative:*

Mary found in the bar John [and] Mary was annoyed (that) [Cog_1] $\Rightarrow$ Mary was annóyed to find John in the bar

(1) Given salience of Alter's "comment" (to SPKR in reporting), BUF naturally prior $Cog_1 \rightarrow$ *Mary / found in the bar / John* in BUF

(2) EXP Alter-commentative Cog_2, *Mary was annóyed* (at) [Cog_1]

(3) Return of naturally prior Cog_1 to OPR $\rightarrow$ [*Mary / found in the bar / John*] in OPR

(4) Deleting redundant *Mary* and shifting past *found* to generalizing infinitive *to find*, EXP *to find*

(5) Given secondary salience of *John* (and/or language-specific "stylistic" rules for English), EXP *John*

(6) EXP remaining *in the bar* from OPR

[NOTE: (a) it is assumed that *John* is the "real" M_2 of Cog_1 and that *in the bar* is a PP-phrase embedded in its VP (try passivization test: *John was found in the bar by Mary* but **John in the bar was found by Mary*); (b) the shift in (4) from *that Mary found* to generalizing infinitive *to find* is a redundancy-avoiding device typically used by speakers; (c) and note particularly that, although holding EXP of *in the bar* while EXPing *John* does involve a slight increase in processing difficulty for the speaker, it is much less (as we will see) than that required for the listener in comprehending, since no BUFfing is involved.]

This last sentential example illustrates nicely the contrast in processing difficulties between speaker productions and listener comprehensions of unnaturally ordered transform sentences—*there is, generally, much less transfer from OPR to BUF* (and holding in BUF) *required in production by the speaker than in comprehension by the listener*. This is because the speaker, in overtly expressing constituents—and even parts of constituents (e.g., *to find* and then a bit later *in the bar*)—is able to "get rid of" semantic information-sets rather than having to "hold onto" them, as the listener must do. Note also that in all of the examples of *simplex* transform productions, no more than *a single OPR/BUF transfer* was ever required; similarly, in all examples of *complex* transform productions, only *a single OPR/BUF transfer* (always of the whole, naturally prior, Cog_1 clause, "right-to-left") was ever required. Since most of the sentential examples used here for EXPRESSING will also be used for COMPREHENDING, these rather gross differences in processing difficulty will become very clear in my last lecture.

Some Literature Relevant to Salience Dynamics and Sentence Production

A number of recent papers in both linguistics and psycholinguistics relate quite directly to what I have called Salience Principles (Vividness, Motivation-of-Speaker, and Topicality). Here I can only briefly mention them (more detailed treatment will be given in my *Toward an Abstract Performance Grammar*). Linguist Postal's book *On Raising: One Rule of English Grammar and Its Theoretical Implications* (1974) offers a wide variety of what are obviously salience-motivated "forward" shifts in sentencing, but it is (understandably) more concerned with "theoretical implications" for TGG than for an APG; Fillmore's "The Case for Case Reopened" (1977) also provides many similar illustrations and further indicates concern with performance dynamics—"scenes" being communicated in sentencing, "perspective"-shifting by speakers and listeners—and he even (p. 76) speaks of "the salience conditions favoring inclusion in perspective"; psycholinguist Brian McWhinney's "Starting Points" (1977) offers a Perspetive Hypothesis which is clearly related to the salience notions presented here, with "starting points" serving the functions of determining the attentional focus, the perspective, the agent, and the given (topicality), and he brings together a variety of research evidence; and linguist Evelyn Ransom, in an as-yet-unpublished paper titled "A Constraint on the Advancement and Demotion of NP's" (1977), also draws heavily on psychological (empathy, a type of Motivation-of-speaker) and semantic (Definiteness, Humanness, and Animacy, thus what has been called inherent Vividness here) notions in elaborating (note!) *"acceptability hierarchies"* of dative and passive transformations.

What I have called Topicality (as one of the salience notions in this APG) goes back *at least* to the idea of Functional Sentence Perspective as developed by the Prague School, but many Amerirican scholars seem to trace it back to Halliday (1967–1968). Clark and Haviland (1977), using both linguistic and psychological evidence, develop a psycholinguistic theory of the dynamics of the "Giver-New Contract" that is quite similar to that offered here. Morgan (1975) offers many and varied examples of how, in interpersoral communication, it is the "given" that (being redundant) is deleted—for examples, (Q) *What does Trick eat for breakfast? /* (A) *Bananas;* (Q) *Did Harry's talking to Martha annoy Harriet?* (A) *No, his talking to Thélma* (responding simply with *Thelma* would be ambiguous).

Putting the "given" prior to the "new", as noted earlier, must often run into conflict with the other salience dynamics operating on a speaker (both inherent Vividness and extrinsic Motivation-of-speaker). Schachter (1973) provides many examples of this (without explicitly referring to the conflict): he notes (p. 41) that "a cleft sentence presupposes the existence of some entity that is appropriately characterized by the out-of-focus clause contained in the sentence", but it is this "out-of-focus" clause that would, in terms of Topicality, be the "given"—borrowing one of his examples, instead of responding to *they carry you off in something* (the presupposition) with *they carry you off in a coffin,* the more motivated speaker says *it's a cóffin they carry you off in.* However, all of these salience-induced manipulations by speakers cause problems for Listeners, as we will see in Lecture VIII.

Processing of Unnaturally Ordered Sentences in Comprehending

Orientation

As I pointed out in Lecture VII, *in effect* the Listener's task is to "recover", via interactions between his OPERATOR and his BUFFER, the *naturally ordered* cognitive structures from which the Speaker necessarily started. F VIII-II gives the essence of this abstract performance theory as it applies to Listeners' COMPREHENDING sentences that have been unnaturally ordered to satisfy the salience motives of Speakers.

In this final lecture I will first give formal statements of the sections of F VIII-II—along with elaborations and sentential examples of the steps postulated by theory for processing, as before—and I will then offer some "adumbrations" on comprehending unnatural sentencings. These will include the following: *a predicted hierarchy of processing difficulty* for transforms of various types; *a proposal for systematic research on processing times in comprehending;* making a minor but interesting detour, *multiple center-embedding,* as perhaps transforms posing the greatest cognizing difficulty; *relations* (of lack thereof) *between this APG theory of processing and Yngve's "Depth Hypothesis";* and finally, some of the most *relevant linguistic and psycholinguistic evidence* on comprehension processing times.

Formal Statement of F VIII-II with Sentential Examples

By way of an "overview", a brief summary of the various sections of this complex functional notion would seem to be in order before launching into details.

Section (A) of F VIII-II indicates, in (1) and (2), that only when Speaker disordering *has* occurred is Listener re-ordering required—and in (3) that there is *no guarantee* that our Listener will be successful! Section (B) indicates in (1) and (2) that, when the Listener's OPR has detected cues for disordering *of simplexes,* as many as two *cycles* of OPR/BUF interactions may be required to achieve comprehension—and, most significantly in (3), that in the processing of *complexes,* any disordering of simplexes detected must be processed *prior to* continuing with the complex. As in F VIII-I for Expressing, Section (C) here *details* the interactions involved for Comprehending when use of the BUFFER *is* required in processing *simplexes* of the various sorts, and Section (D), similarly, when BUF is required for processing *complexes* of the various types.

> F VIII-II (A) and (B). For the Listener, in order to comprehend simplex and complex sentences, the OPERATOR *must* have the constituents of simplexes and the clauses of complexes *in their cognitively natural order:* (1) if the sentences received from a Speaker *are already in natural order* (see F IV, VI) then no use of the BUFFER is required; (2) if, due to salience dynamics operating on the Speaker, either the constituents of simplexes or the clauses of complexes *are in unnatural order,* as determined by OPR checks (see F VII), interactions between OPR and BUF must be initiated to restore natural ordering; (3) if, following its OPR/BUF interaction rules (see below), no natural ordering can be obtained, there is no transfer to MEM and the Listener typically displays the behavioral signs of comprehension failure.

Recalling discussion of Section (A) of VIII-I on EXPRESSING, if we think momentarily of the Listener as a potential Speaker at some later point in time, what VIII-II does is simply guarantee that any cognitions, simplex or complex, that *are* successfully comprehended will be stored in their natural order—and thus become what this Listener-becoming-*Speaker* must start with in Expressing.

> (B) Assuming that (a) salience dynamics have caused the Speaker to produce an unnaturally ordered sentence and (b) the Listener's OPERATOR has detected cues for the disordering: (1) if, *within simplexes,* following the rules for constituent transfers to the BUFFER (*see* C below), *a single OPR → BUF → OPR cycle* yields a natural ordering, Listener comprehends, OPR/BUF processing terminates and the cognition is transferred to MEM; (2) if a single cycle still yields unnatural ordering, *a second OPR → BUF → OPR cycle is* initiated (following the same rules), and if it yields natural ordering, Listener comprehends, OPR/BUF processing terminates and the cognition is transferred to MEM; (3) given cues for unnatural ordering of *the clauses of complexes,* (a) the naturally prior cognition *always* becomes Cog_1 in OPR, and then the naturally subsequent Cog_2 is completed, either via "leftward" shift of constituents into the components "emptied" by the "upward" shift of Cog_1 or via transfers to BUF (see D below), and (b), if any of the

clauses of complexes in the processing via (a) above have themselves, as simplexes, unnaturally ordered constituents, then rules governing (1) and (2) above are *immediately* applied, with further processing of the complex held up until the simplex is "naturalized".

The reason for specifying *only two cycles* (B-2) is simply that Sridhar and I were unable to find *any* simplex transformations for which more than two cycles were required to restore natural order—which, of course, doesn't mean that there aren't any such! This may be due simply to the fact that there are only *three* components in OPR for simplexes. Presumably the same processing strategy as postulated for two cycles *would* apply equivalently to more than two, if such seem required.

F VIII-II (C) When use of the BUFFER is required for comprehending *simplexes* [B (1) and B (2) above]: (1) if the constituent in which unnaturalness is detected *is itself initial* (i.e., in the M_1 component), (a) it is transferred from OPR to BUF, (b) remaining constituents *move "leftward"*, and (c) such OPR/BUF transfers continue (with "push-/down" storage in BUF) until a constituent natural in M_1 appears; (2) if the constituent in which unnaturalness is detected *is noninitial* [i.e., in the $- - (M) - - \rightarrow$, the M_2 or in information subsequent to a completed cognition], (a) the single constituent *immediately prior to* ("leftward" of) that providing the unnaturalness cue is transferred from OPR to BUF, (b) remaining constituents move "leftward", and (c) such OPR/BUF transfers continue until a constituent natural in M_1 [or in $- - (M)$ $- - \rightarrow$ if M_1 is already "naturalized"] appears; (3) following either (1) or (2) the constituents in BUF are returned to the now "empty" component or components (in from "top-most" to "bottom-most" in BUF order), thereby completing cycle 1.

Topicalization:	A martíni I (= SPKR) will have $\Rightarrow$ SPKR will have a martini
	(1) Since *I* is unnatural for $- - (M) - - \rightarrow$ slot, BUF *a martini* $\rightarrow$ *a martini* in BUF
	(2) Shift remaining constituents "leftward" $\rightarrow$ [SPKR / will have / ø]
	(3) Returning *a martini* from BUF to empty M_2 slot $\rightarrow$ [SPKR / will have / a martini]
Passivization:	Napóleon is admired by everyone $\Rightarrow$ Everyone admires Napoleon
	(1) Since *is admired by* is an unnaturally directed relation, BUF *Napoleon* $\rightarrow$ *Napoleon* in BUF
	(2) "Leftward" shift yields $\rightarrow$ [is admired by / everyone / ø]
	(3) Since *is admired by* is unnatural as M_1, BUF it $\rightarrow$ *is admired by* / *Napoleon* in BUF

(4) "Leftward" shift of *everyone* yields → [everyone / $\emptyset$ / $\emptyset$]

(5) On return of *is admired by* from BUF, given $^+$Directional coding (M_1) of *everyone,* OPR shifts it to *admires* ($^+$Directional Relation)

(6) Return of *Napoleon* from BUF → [everyone / admires / Napoleon]

[NOTE: here again assumption is made that, except for the Directional feature, the semantics of *is admired by* and *admires* are identical.]

Dative Movement: John gave the topless wáitress a sweater → John gave a sweater to the topless waitress

(1) Since *a sweater* following *the topless waitress* as an M_2 is unnatural, BUF *the topless waitress* → *the topless waitress* in BUF

(2) Shift *a sweater* "leftward" into the Relation as the embedded (M) → [John / gave a sweater (to) / $\emptyset$]

(3) Return of *the topless waitress* to empty M_2 → [John / gave a sweater to / the topless waitress]

[NOTE: this analysis, of course, assumes that SVOD is the natural bitransitive structure (see Lecture V)—and also that the dative-marker *to* is "empty" semantically.]

WH-Q Movement: Whát did John see? ⇒ John saw something [?]

(1) Since initial *what* is unnatural as M_1, BUF as its semantically equivalent NP → *something* in BUF, and insert [?] in tag-slot

(2) "Leftward" shift of remaining information → [did / John / see / $\emptyset$]

(3) Since *did* unnatural as M_1, BUF *did* → *did* / *something* in BUF top-to-bottom

(4) Shifting remainder "leftward" → [John / see / $\emptyset$ / $\emptyset$]

(5) Return of *did* from BUF and fusion with *see* in Relation as past-tense feature → [John / saw / $\emptyset$]

(6) Return of *something* from BUF → [John / saw / something] [?]

(C) continued: (4) if (a) the simplex is now naturally ordered, Listener comprehends, OPR/BUF processing terminates and the cognition is transferred to MEM, but if (b) OPR still detects cues for unnaturalness, another cycle is initiated according to the same rules as above.

Subject-Verb(aux) In-
version:
Ís John a thérapist? ⇒ John is a therapist [?]

(1) Since *is* is unnaturally coded for M_1, transfer *is* to BUF and insert Q-symbol in tag-slot → *is* in BUF and [?] in tag-slot

(2) "Leftward" shift of remaining constituents → [John / a therapist / ø]

(3) Since *a therapist* is miscoded for a Relation, transfer *John* to BUF → *John* and *is* in BUF, top-to-bottom

(4) "Leftward" shift of remainder → [a therapist / ø / ø]

(5) Return of *John* and then *is* from BUF → [a therapist / John / is]

(6) Since *John* is still unnatural in the Relation slot, *initiate Cycle 2* by BUFfing *a therapist* → *a therapist* in BUF

(7) "Leftward" shift of remainder yields → [John / is / ø]

(8) Return of *a therapist* from BUF → [John / is / a therapist] [?]

Neg AV Preposing:
Néver have I been to the White House ⇒ SPKR has never been to the White House

(1) Since *never* in M_1 is unnatural, transfer to BUF → *never* in BUF

(2) "Leftward" movement of remaining constituents → [have / SPKR / been to / the WH]

(3) Since *have,* now in M_1, is also unnatural, BUF *have* → *have* / *never* in BUF top-to-bottom

(4) "Leftward" shift of remainder → [SPKR / been to / the WH / ø / ø]

(5) Return of *have* and then *never* from BUF → [SPKR / been to / WH / have never]

(6) Since *have never* is dangling part of the Relation, *initiate Cycle 2* by BUFfing immediately prior *the White House* → *the WH* in BUF

(7) "Leftward" shift of *have never* (= has never) into the Relation → [SPKR / been to has never / ø]

(8) Return of *the White House* from BUF → [SPKR / never has been to / the White House]

[NOTE that, *for the Listener,* there is no problem posed by the "unnatural" *within-constituent* VP word-ordering, because all of the semantic information *is* in the Relation constituent—i.e., *been to has never = has never been to* semantically.]

(C) continued: (5) if, due to redundancy deletions (for efficiency in communicating), certain components of simplexes are left "empty" (ϕ), OPR checks the most basic Substantivity feature for the "non-empty" components, entering either [+ ϕ], if the "empty" component would *naturally* be a $^+$Substantive Entity, or [− ϕ], if it would be a $^-$Substantivity Relation, sending the coded ϕ to BUF, and after the cognition has been "naturalized" OPR inserts the most probable semantic information [code-strip(s)], (a) from MEM (prior comprehending), (b) from its own parallel perceptual cognizing, or (c) simply on the basis of sheer convergent, contextual probabilities based on information in "non-empty" components.

Agent Deletion:	The groundhog was run over (ϕ) $\Rightarrow$ A car ran over the groundhog

      (1) Since *was run over* signals an unnatural passive Relation (even if truncated), BUF *the groundhog* → *the groundhog* in BUF

      (2) "Leftward" shift yields unnatural M_1, so BUF *was run over* → *was run over* / *the groundhog* in BUF top-to-bottom

      (3) "Leftward" shift yields → [ϕ / − / −] and return from BUF → [ϕ / ran over / the groundhog] (note, reversing the Relation to $^+$Directionality)

      (4) Since checking Substantivity feature for "non-empty" components yields a $^-$(*ran over*) and a $^+$(*the groundhog*), OPR assigns $^+$Substantivity to ϕ

      (5) OPR of Listener inserts feature code-strip of the most probable "something" → [a car / ran over / the groundhog]

[NOTE: general assumption is that Listeners elaborate features of "dummies" representing SPKR redundancy deletions (sometime erroneously, of course!); this could easily be checked with Memory experiments, where subjects' "false" suppletions should reflect most probable insertions.]

F VIII-II (D) When use of the BUFFER is required for comprehending *complexes* [and assuming that the included simplexes are in, or have been returned to, natural order via (C) above]: (1) given cues that the first clause *in complexes conjoined by adverbials* is the naturally subsequent cognition (Cog$_2$), (a) the constituents of this clause are transferred to BUF (*"right-to-left"*), (b) the features of the conjoiner are transferred to the tag-slot, (c) the constituents of the naturally prior clause (Cog_1), as received from LEX, are accepted in OPR as Cog_1, and (d) the constituents of Cog_2 are returned from BUF to OPR.

Simple Sequence: Before Mary skinned the súckling píg, she sharpened her hunting knife $\Rightarrow$ Mary sharpened her hunting knife [and then] Mary skinned the suckling pig

    (1) Since *before* preposed is an unambiguous cue that clause$_1$ is naturally Cog_2, transfer constituents of clause$_1$ to BUF ("right-to-left") $\rightarrow$ *Mary / skinned / the suckling pig* in BUF top-to-bottom

    (2) As received from LEX, accept in Cog_1 slot of OPR the constituents of clause$_2$ $\rightarrow$ [Mary / sharpened / her hunting knife]

    (3) Insert semantic features for which *before* is a semantically equivalent adverbial in the tag-slot $\rightarrow$ [and then] in tag-slot

    (4) Return of naturally Cog_2 from BUF $\rightarrow$ [Mary / skinned / the suckling pig]

    (5) OPR $\rightarrow$ MEM: [Mary / sharpened / her hunting knife] [and then (in tag-slot in MEM)] [Mary / skinned / the suckling pig]

[NOTE: such OPR $\rightarrow$ MEM final transfers could have been indicated everywhere above.]

Sequential Cause: Grámpa broke his lég because he slipped on the ice $\Rightarrow$ Grampa slipped on the ice [and so then] Grampa broke his leg

    (1) Upon receiving unambiguous cue for unnatural ordering of clauses (centered *because*), OPR (a) inserts features for which *because* is the semantically equivalent adverbial [and so then] in the tag-slot and (b) transfers the constituents of clause$_1$ (naturally Cog_2) to BUF $\rightarrow$ *Grampa / broke / his leg* in BUF top-to-bottom

    (2) OPR accepts from LEX the constituents of clause$_2$, as natural Cog_1 $\rightarrow$ [Grampa / slipped on / the ice]

    (3) BUF returns naturally Cog_2 $\rightarrow$ [Grampa / broke / his leg]

    (4) OPR $\rightarrow$ MEM: [Grampa / slipped on / the ice] [and so then] [Grampa / broke / his leg]

[NOTE: for simplicity of exposition, we use the (expanded) *and* and *but* forms in the brackets [ ], but in the tag-slot the *semantics* of these would be, e.g., [$^+$Junction] for simple *and,* [$^-$Junction, $^+$Sequence] for *but then,* and so forth.]

(D) continued: (2) given cues for *embedding of a relative clause in a matrix clause* (cues are usually *that* or more specific relative pronouns), (a) the features of the noun of the matrix clause immediately prior to the relative PN are "copied" onto those of the PN (thus expanding it into a full nominal, but with a shift to Indefinite coding), (b) the constituents of this embedded clause (*always* the naturally prior cognition) become Cog_1, (c) the features for the implied cojoiner (here representing simple *and* or *but,* for congruent or incongruent cognitions respectively) are inserted in the tag-slot, and (d) the constituents of the remaining clause (now with M_1 coded emphatic Definite, *that!* or *this!*) now become Cog_2.

Relativized SNP: The man who came to dínner stole the sílverware
⇒ A man came to dinner [and] that! man stole the silverware
(1) Given the cue for relative clause (Cog_1) embedding, here *who,* (a) the features of the preceding NP, now coded $^-$Definite, are added to those of the REL PN, yielding *a man* as the M_1 of naturally Cog_1, and, (b) the remaining constituents of the embedded clause complete Cog_1 in OPR → [a man / came to / dinner]
(2) The remainder of naturally Cog_2 shifts "leftward" and, with an emphatic feature added to the $^+$Definiteness of M_1 → [that! man / stole / the silverware]
(3) Since the cognitions are congruent, OPR inserts features for $^+$Junction [and] in the tag-slot
(4) OPR → MEM: [a man / came to / dinner] [and] [that! man / stole / the silverware]

[NOTE: here no use of the BUFFER is required.]

Relativized ONP: The man who(m) John hít had a concússion ⇒ John hit a man [and] that! man had a concussion
(1) Given cue for unnatural REL CLAUSE embedding (here, *who(m)*), the features of the preceding NP (*the man*) are copied into the REL PN and coded [$^-$Definite] → [a man / John / hit] – which, itself being unnaturally

ordered, is immediately "naturalized" while further processing of the complex is held up:

(a) *John* in the Relation slot is unnatural, hence the preceding constituent, *a man,* is transferred to BUF → *a man* in BUF

(b) "Leftward" movement of remainder of Cog_1 → [John / hit / ϕ]

(c) Return of *a man* from BUF → [John / hit / a man] as Cog_1

(2) The remainder of naturally Cog_2 is accepted from LEX, with a shift to emphatic [+Definite] for M_1 → [that! man / had / a concussion]

(3) Since Cog_2 is congruent with Cog_1, OPR inserts [+Junction] (= and) in the tag-slot

(4) OPR → MEM: [John / hit / a man] [and] [that! man / had / a concussion]

[NOTE: since pronouns representing relativized ONPs are often deleted by speakers, here *the man John hit had a concussion* (see analysis of this sentence under F VIII-I, EXPRESSING), we would assume that the sequence—*the man / John / hit / had*—would itself be a sufficient cue in OPR for conjoining of two cognitions, with the relative PN deleted. The following is the suggested analysis.]

Meta-rule: Whenever the listener encounters two verbs in a row, two conjoining cogs are signaled, and features of the first NP in the sentence are copied into the second cog. For example,

The man John hit had a concussion

(1) Given the second verb *had* following *hit,* process as Cog 1, with shift to Indefinite NP, [a man / John / hit], holding second verb, *had*

(a) *John* is unnatural as a relation, so BUF *a man*

(b) Move *John hit* "leftward" as M_1 and Relation → [John / hit / ϕ]

(c) Return *a man* from BUF as M_2 → [John / hit / a man] as natural Cog_1

(2) Copy features of *a man* into the second clause with shift to emphatic Definite → [that! man / had / a concussion] as natural Cog_2

(3) Insert features for simple congruent conjoiner (*and*) in tag-slot

[NOTE: this sentence, with the PN *who(m)* deleted by the speaker, should be somewhat easier to process in comprehending, since the "copying" of features of the prior N onto the PN (*who(m)* → *a man*) is eliminated.]

(D) continued: (3) given cues that the naturally subsequent cognition (Cog_2) *has a "commentative" relation* to the necessarily prior "topical" cognition (Cog_1) *being commented on* (the cues are verbs like *think, seem, believe,* etc., optionally followed by *that* as an "empty" syntactic marker, signaling that a complex is involved), then (a) the "commentative" Cog_2 constituents (completed with a ϕ in M_1 or M_2 components, representing Cog_1) are transferred to BUF (right-to-left), (b) the naturally prior "topical" Cog_1 constituents shift "leftward", (c) the features of the implied conjoiner (again representing simple *and* or *but*) are placed in the tag-slot, and (d) the constituents of the commentative clause are returned from BUF to OPR, now as Cog_2 and with the ϕ in the M_2 component comprehended as "Cog_1".

Negating Commentative:

I dóubt that Mary is pregnant ⇒ Mary (be) pregnant [but] SPKR doubts (that Cog_1)

(1) Given cue for "comment" by SPKR (. . . *doubt that*), transfer naturally "commentative" Cog_2 to BUF → [SPKR / doubts (that) / Cog_1]

(2) "Leftward" shift of remainder in OPR yields naturally prior ("topical") Cog_1 → [Mary / (be) / pregnant]

(3) Return from BUF yields naturally subsequent "commentative" Cog_2 → [SPKR / doubts (that) / Cog_1]

(4) Since cognitions are incongruent, OPR inserts features for *but* [⁻Junction] in tag-slot

(5) OPR → MEM: [Mary / (be / pregnant] [but] [SPKR / doubts / Cog_1]

[NOTE: shift from definite *is* to indefinite (*be*) seems reasonable for listener.]

Oblique Commentative:

It is óbvious that Peter Pan is a fairy ⇒ Peter Pan (be) a fairy [and] (Cog_1) is obvious to SPKR

(1) Given the cue for "comment" by SPKR (. . . *obvious that*), transfer naturally Cog_2 to BUF → [(Cog_1) / is obvious to / SPKR] in BUF

(2) "Leftward" shift of remainder in OPR yields naturally prior ("topical") Cog_1 → [Peter Pan / (be) / a fairy]

(3) Return from BUF yields naturally subse-

quent "commentative" $Cog_2 \rightarrow$ [(Cog_1) / is obvious to / SPKR]

(4) Since these cognitions are congruent (for SPKR), OPR inserts features for *and* [$^+$Junction] in tag-slot

(5) OPR $\rightarrow$ MEM: [Peter Pan / (be) / a fairy] [and] [Cog_1 / is obvious to / SPKR]

Alter (by Ego) *Commentative:*

Mary was annóyed to find John in the bar $\Rightarrow$ Mary found in the bar John [and] (Cog_1) annoyed Mary

(1) Given cue for "comment" by SPKR (. . . *was annoyed to*), transfer naturally Cog_2 to BUF $\rightarrow$ [(Cog_1) / annoyed / Mary]

(2) "leftward" shift of remainder, with shift from *to find* to *Mary found,* yields naturally prior "topical" $Cog_1 \rightarrow$ [Mary / found / John / in the bar], and since this simplex is unnaturally ordered, naturalize it while holding naturally subsequent Cog_2 in BUF

   (a) since dangling *in the bar* is the cue for discontinuous VP, BUF immediately prior *John*

   (b) leftward movement with fusion of Relation features $\rightarrow$ [Mary / found in the bar / ϕ]

   (c) Return of *John* from BUF yields natural $Cog_1 \rightarrow$ [Mary / found in the bar / John]

(3) Return from BUF yields naturally subsequent "commentative" $Cog_2 \rightarrow$ [(Cog_1) / annoyed / Mary]

(4) Since these cognitions are congruent (for SPKR), OPR inserts features for *and* [$^+$Junction] in tag-slot

(5) OPR $\rightarrow$ MEM: [Mary / found in the bar / John] [and] [Cog_1 / annoyed / Mary] – according to SPKR, of course

[NOTE: here, again, applying *passivization test* to Cog_1, we indicate as the full VP *found in the bar;* both this additional simplex processing and the longer "holding" of naturally Cog_2 in BUF increase processing difficulty, of course.]

(Now try your psycholinguistic teeth on this fellow!)

Double-embedded Commentative: I regrét télling you that you are fíred $\Rightarrow$ I

(LSTNR) am fired (= Cog_1) [and] SPKR is telling me Cog_1 (= Cog_2) [and] SPKR regrets Cog_2 (= Cog_3)

(1) Given first cue for embedding (. . . *regret telling*), transfer naturally Cog_3 (as it turns out!) to BUF → [SPKR / regrets / (Cog_2)]

(2) "leftward" shift yields → [SPKR / is telling / me (that) / Cog_1], in which *telling me that* is the cue in OPR for further embedding and OPR transfers Cog_2 to BUF → [SPKR / is telling / me] *on top of* (because of "pushdown" nature of BUF) [SPKR / regrets / Cog_2]

(3) "Leftward" shift yields naturally Cog_1 (phew!) → [I (LSNR) / am / fired]

(4) Return, along with *congruence* indicator, of "topmost" Cog_2 from BUF → [and] [SPKR / is telling / me (Cog_1)]

(5) Return of "bottom-most" Cog_3, again along with *incongruence* signaling indicator, from BUF yields → [but] [SPKR / regrets / (Cog_2)]

(6) OPR → MEM: [I / am / fired] [and] [SPKR / is telling / me (Cog_1)] [but] [SPKR / regrets / (Cog_2)]

[AND NOW, let's see how SOV Kannada is much more efficient in this situation.]

nānu ninnannu   vajā mādiddēne   endu   tiḷisalu   viṣādisuttēne.

I   you-acc.   fire - do - past   that   to tell   regret - 1st sing.-masc.
                                                       have - 1st sing.-masc.

'I have fired you (and) I tell you that (and) I regret (it)'
(which is the equivalent of) I regret telling you that you are fired (in English)

(1) Process naturally Cog 1 (with routine substitutions), as [SPKR / me / has fired]

(2) Given cue for embedding (the complementizer, *endu*), insert a place-holding ϕ for M_1 and insert Cog 1 marker for M_2 of Cog_2 → [ϕ / Cog_1 / to tell]

(3) Given nonfinite status of the preceding verb, insert a place-holding ϕ for M_1 and insert Cog 2 as M_2 of Cog 3 → [ϕ / Cog 2 / regret].

(4) Given the first person masculine singular marking on the terminal verb, insert (the appropriate substitution of) *I* as M_1 of Cog

> 3 and Cog 2 → [SPKR / Cog 2 / regrets] and
> [SPKR / Cog 1 / to tell].

This comparison of theoretical processing difficulties *across languages* for the same type of *communication* (information transmission between Speaker and Listener)—*not*, of course, the same type of *transformation*—raises the most intriguing possibility of *cross-language comparative research* on production and comprehension of sentences. Just for example, would it be demonstrable that certain languages—or perhaps better, certain language types (SVO vs SOV, highly inflecting with relatively free constituent-ordering vs minimally inflecting with relatively constrained constituent-ordering, etc.)—display *generally greater or less* processing difficulty *or* would languages tend to average out in overall processing difficulty, yet display *uniquely different patterns* of processing difficulty which could be related to language typology? The "adumbrations" to which we now come—particularly the proposal for systematic research on processing difficulty—should offer some suggestions as to how to go about such research.

Adumbration on Unnatural Sentencing

Here we will first propose *a hierarchy of processing difficulty* for transforms of various types, as predicted from the postulates of this Abstract Performance Grammar. Then a proposal *for systematic experimental research* on processing times for comprehending transforms at various "levels" of difficulty in the hierarchy will be made in some detail—with several sets of illustrative comparisons across theoretical levels of difficulty given. Since our theory assigns a maximum difficulty for multiply commentative sentences, we will make an excursion into *the processing of multiply center-embedded sentences*—almost certainly the most complex cognizing task for human language users. Following a subsection on the relations (or lack thereof) between our APG theory of processing *in the production* of unnatural sentences by speakers and Victor Yngve's *"Depth Hypothesis"* (1960), we will finally bring to bear at least some of *the linguistic and psycholinguistic evidence* (necessarily briefly) on comprehension of unnaturally ordered sentences.

A Predicted Hierarchy of Processing Times for Comprehending Types of Transforms

An exploration of some neurophysiological speculations leads to our predicted hierarchy of *listener comprehension processing-times* for a wide variety of transforms. Right at this point, you may well be wondering why this sort of analysis was not attempted for *unnatural sentence productions by speakers* (under F VIII-I in Lecture VII). The answer is quite straightforward: Unlike sentence comprehension, where the *types* of transforms can be easily manipulated by the investigator, it is hard to see how the types of speaker-produced transforms could be controlled experimentally. How could one induce subjects "on demand" to produce specific types of disorderings? [It will be recalled how difficult it was, in my "Simply Describing" study (1971), to get speakers to use anything *other* than naturally ordered sentences.] Furthermore, since transforms reflect *salience dynamics* operating on the speaker, how could one possibly *create* such states in any systematic fashion? All of which, of course, does not imply that such research would be flatly impossible!

Some Neurophysiological Speculations about Increments in Processing Time (Δ PT)

We assume that each OPR $\rightarrow$ BUF and each BUF $\rightarrow$ OPR *constituent transfer* adds a constant increment and that each increase in *duration of storage* in BUF adds a variable increment to processing time (and hence difficulty). The reasoning here involves some generally accepted assumptions about the functioning of the Central Nervous System (CNS). What I am calling semantic feature-sets ($r_M = [m_1, m_2, \ldots m_n] = s_M$, or more informally, "code-strips") are assumed to be reverberating impulses among sets of neurons representing the *m* feature-components. These are what Donald Hebb (1958) aptly termed "cell-ensembles", representing in the CNS—the "where" not specified—the meanings of word forms or of whole constituents. Such reverberating cell-ensembles have the negatively accelerated property of decreasing in amplitude over short internals of time (hence, "fading of meaning")—*unless* discharged as a set in initiating neural activity elsewhere.

What I refer to as "transfer" from OPR to BUF is a case of discharge of activity at a locus A (OPR), eliminating neural reverberation there (i.e., "emptying" that locus), and excitation of corresponding activity at a locus B (BUF)—and also vice versa, of course. It follows, therefore, that the shorter the interval [t $(A-B)$] the greater will be the probability of excitation at B [p (B)], i.e., of transfer—and conversely, of course, the longer the storage time at B the less the B $\rightarrow$ A probability.

These neurological speculations lead to the following notions in this APG about OPR/BUF interactions: If t (A-B) is sufficiently short to "guarantee" transfer (which should be the usual case), then we can make the simplifying assumption (1) *that ΔPT (increment in processing time) will be roughly constant for each OPR $\rightarrow$ BUF and BUF $\rightarrow$ OPR transfer.* Another simplifying assumption is (2) *that ΔPT will be roughly constant per constituent regardless of its semantic complexity*—this following from the fact that semantic feature-sets are at least *near-simultaneous* "bundles". The combination of these two simplifying assumptions leads to the conclusion, (3) *that total ΔPT will equal 2 × N (constituents) transferred,* where the multiplication by 2 simply indicates the necessary OPR → BUF transfer and then the BUF → OPR return of each constituent. And, finally, the rapid "fading" in neural reverberation of the cell-ensembles representing constituent meanings leads to the assumption (4) *that ΔPT will be a variable increasing function of time in BUF storage which* (given the "push-down" nature of BUF) *is equivalent to the N of constituents requiring transfer in any one cycle.*

The Predicted Hierarchy of Processing Times

We are now in position to rather specifically predict a hierarchy of processing difficulties in comprehending—as functions of (a) *the number of OPR/BUF transfers in a single cycle,* (b) *the number of cycles required for processing any simplex sentence,* and (c) *the number and nature of simplex clauses conjoined into complex sentences.* We do *not* assume, by the way, that the same hierarchy as predicted here for comprehending (by listeners) would necessarily hold for expressing (by speakers).

In analyzing and comparing processing difficulties, we will move from relatively easy to relatively difficult types, first *within* SIMPLEX sentences and then *within* COMPLEX (conjoined) sentences. However, predicted processing difficulties also vary *across* these simplex vs complex categories. Therefore we will use *numbers in parentheses before each subtype*—from zero (naturally ordered simplexes) to twenty (unnaturally ordered, multiply commentative, complexes)—*to indicate the overall hierarchy of increments in processing time (Δ PT) predicted in APG theory, from least (0) to most (20).*

→

SIMPLEXES

Naturally Ordered

(0) Stative: *a squirrel is on the lawn; the bearded old men are sitting in the local bar*

(0) Action: *Pierre chased the squirrel; the bartender fetched his best wine*

[We see no theoretical reason for expecting any differences in processing times for naturally ordered stative vs action simplexes; nor would we expect constituent complexity (where no embedding is involved) to increase PT significantly—e.g., *the bearded old men vs a squirrel.*]

Unnaturally Ordered, Single Cycle

(1) Single $0 \rightleftharpoons B$ transfer: sentential examples already analyzed would be Topicalization, *A martíni I will have,* and Dative Movement, *John gave the topless wáitress a* sweater[1]

(2) Double $0 \rightleftharpoons B$ transfer: previously analyzed examples would be Passivization, *Napóleon is admired by everyone,* and WH-Q Movement, *Whát did John see?*

(8) Triple $0 \rightleftharpoons B$ transfer: we had trouble finding a transformation-type meeting this requirement, and no illustrative sentence was offered in the analyses earlier; however, more diligent recent search of the long list of English Transformations from which we worked—prepared originally by Georgia Green and Jerry Morgan for a course in syntax at the University of Illinois—yielded a contender, WH Question Movement, *Whén will John go to Chicago?* → *John will sometime go to Chicago* [?]

    (1) Given *when* in M_1 slot, insert [?] in tag-slot and transfer *when* to BUF, with shift to appropriate Indefinite NP → *sometime* in BUF top to bottom

    (2) Leftward movement yields → [will / John / go to / Chicago]

    (3) Since *will* in M_1 slot is unnatural, BUF it → *will / sometime* in BUF top-to-bottom

    (4) Leftward movement yields → [John / go to / Chicago / ø]

    (5) Return from BUF of *will* and *sometime* → [John / go to / Chicago / will sometime]

    (6) Given discontinuous Relation, *go to . . . will sometime,* BUF *Chicago* → *Chicago* in BUF

    (7) Leftward movement yields → [John / go to will sometime / ø]

    (8) Return of *Chicago* from BUF yields [John / will sometime go to / Chicago] [?] (note that here, as elsewhere, the ordering of semantic information within a single constituent is irrelevant for comprehending by the Listener—all of the necessary features of the Relation are there)

(Just prior to our "discovery" of *Whén will John go to Chicago?*, we tried out another "contender" here, *There–insertion—There is a cát on the windowsill;* application of our rules yielded a triple $0\rightleftharpoons B$ transfer, all right—*but the analysis required three cycles of OPR/BUF transfers!* Since, intuitively, Listener comprehension of *There is a cát on the windowsill* seems reasonably simple, we were led to the following general conclusion: Under close analysis, most superficially *simplex* cognitions requiring BUFfing of three (or more) constituents will prove to be *complexes* "in disguise"—that is, the *fusion* of two (or more) conjoined cognitions by the Speaker. Thus here we would have [a cat / is on / the windowsill] [and] [I (SPKR) / call your attention to / Cog_1].)

Unnaturally Ordered, Double Cycle

(6) Single $0 \rightleftharpoons B$ transfer in Cycle 2: Negative AV Preposing, *Néver have I been to the White House,* and Subject-Verb (aux) Inversion, *Is John a thérapist?*, provide examples.

---

[1] Analyses of most of these transform types were given earlier in this lecture.

[The reason we predict processing times here *only as a function of N OPR/BUF transfers in Cycle 2* is that any double-cycle operation should require more time than any single-cycle one—because initiation of another cycle *presumes* an extra Naturalness check (F VII) by the OPERATOR.]

(7) Double $0 \rightleftarrows B$ transfer in Cycle 2: We were unable to find any English example of this.

(9) Triple $0 \rightleftarrows B$ transfer in Cycle 2 (?): Here we were also unable to come up with any English example – if there *are* any!

COMPLEXES

Naturally Ordered

(3) Stative: The roses are in the vase and that is on the front porch

(3) Action: Puss scratched Fido and then Fido chased Puss

[Again, we see no reason why naturally ordered stative and action complexes should differ in processing time. *Naturally* ordered complexes—and even unnaturally ordered, with naturally ordered simplexes—are indicated as involving less processing time than the double-cycle simplexes above; this is because we assume that lack of BUFfing (for naturally ordered complexes), and even single-clause BUFfing (for unnaturally ordered complexes with natural simplexes), more than compensates for the difficulties of double-cycling—which is debatable, of course!]

Unnaturally Ordered, Conjoining via Adverbials

(4) With naturally ordered simplex clauses and the adverbial centered: *Fido chased Puss because Puss scratched Fido;* a sentential example already offered would be Sequential Cause, *Grámpa broke his lég because he slipped on the ice*

(5) With naturally ordered simplex clauses and adverbial preposed: *Before Fido chased Puss, Puss scratched Fido;* another earlier example, *Before Mary skinned the súckling píg she sharpened her hunting knife*

[We expect that, generally, unnaturally ordered complexes *with adverbials preposed* will be somewhat more difficult to process than those *with adverbials centered;* this is because in the adverbial-preposed condition insertion of the semantic equivalent of the adverbial in the tag-slot must be *delayed* until clause 1 has been transferred to BUF (compare analyses of the *Mary/pig* and *Grampa/leg* examples earlier in this lecture).]

(10) With simplex clause 2 unnaturally ordered: *Fido chased Puss because Fido was scratched by Puss;* although no sentential examples were given for this type, a modification produces *Before Mary skinned the súckling píg, her húnting knife she sharpened*

(15) With simplex clause 1 unnaturally ordered: *Puss was chased by Fido because Puss scratched Fido;* here we can easily generate *Before the súckling píg was skinned by Mary, she sharpened her hunting knife*

(The reason for the large increases in predicted processing times from unnaturally ordered complexes with *naturally* ordered simplexes [(4) and (5)] to those with *unnaturally* ordered simplexes [(10) and (15)], of course, is that—according to F VIII-II (B - 3)—" . . . if any of the clauses of complexes . . . have themselves, as simplexes, unnaturally ordered constituents, then rules (*governing naturalizing of simplexes*) are immediately applied, with further processing of the complex held up until the simplex is naturalized." So, in effect, we add to the processing of complexes the processing of simplexes. Unnatural constituent ordering, when in clause 1, is assumed to create much more difficulty (15) then when in clause 2 (10)—simply because "holding" clause 2 in LEX (with "fading" of its neural representation) is required in the clause 1 case but not in the clause 2 case.)

(18) With both simplex clauses unnaturally ordered: *Puss was chased by Fido because Fido was scratched by Puss;* again generating an example, *the súckling píg was skinned by Mary after her húnting knife she sharpened*

[This, of course, is simply "adding insult to injury"! Having "held" in LEX (with "fading") clause 2 while OPR is straightening out clause 1, now OPR itself has to "hold with fading" clause 1 (as Cog_1) while it struggles with "faded" unnatural clause 2 (Cog_2)—if the whole complex is to be comprehended.]

Unnaturally Ordered, Conjoining via Relative Clauses

(13) With SNP relativized: the sentential example analyzed above was *The man who came to dinner stole the silverware*

[Note that, although both clauses in the analysis are in natural order—*a man came to dinner* (and) *that! man stole the silverware*—(a) we have one discontinuous cognition (*the man . . . stole the silverware*) and (b) there is the rather complicated business of "copying" a preceding nominal onto a relative pronoun, along with a shift on the Definiteness feature (here, from *the man* onto *who = a man*). These are the reasons why this "simplest" of our *relative clause* types has much greater Δ PT than unnaturally ordered *adverbial* complexes [(4) and (5)] and even ones with an unnatural clause 2 [(10)].]

(17) With ONP relativized: our example here, using the simplifying "meta-rule" where the REL PN is deleted, was *The man John hit had a concússion*

[Here, although the "copying" complication is eliminated, the underlying Cog_1 must be unnatural [a man / John / hit] so we have an added single $0 \rightleftarrows B$ transfer simplex naturalizing process while the naturally Cog_2 [ø / had / a concussion] is held up – along with a "copying" of *a man* into the M_1 (ø) = *that! man.*]

(19) With a PP-phrase relativized: *The knífe with which John sliced the salami was very shárp* was our example of this type

[This relative clause type was by all odds the most complicated complex we analyzed; it involved not only "copying" of *the knife* onto *with + which* (= *with a knife*) but also generating an unnatural underlying Cog_1 [with a knife / John / sliced / the salami] which requires a double $0 \rightleftarrows B$ transfer to naturalize—hence the (19) difficulty level in the predicted hierarchy. Furthermore, it might be noted that in this case *both* underlying Cogs are discontinuous [John sliced . . . (with a knife) . . . the salami; the knife . . . was very sharp].]

Unnaturally Ordered, via Single Commentative Conjoining

(12) Negating commentative: our example here was *I doúbt* (that) *Mary is pregnant*

(Given the "comment" cue [*doubt* (that)], the naturally subsequent commentative clause [SPK / doubts (that) / Cog_1] is BUFfed and the naturally prior topical clause (being commented *on*) simply becomes Cog_1 via "leftward" movement, [Mary / (be) / pregnant], with return of the commentative clause from BUF completing the comprehending task.)

(14) Obliquely commentative: the example of this, previously analyzed, was *It is óbvious that Peter Pan is a fairy*

(There are two reasons for the increase in processing difficulty here: (1) the very "obliqueness" of the speaker comment itself (and there are many guises here, e.g., *it seems that . . . , there is reason to believe that . . . , could it be that . . . ?*, and so on ad infinitum) makes it more uncertain as a commentative; (2) here, as compared with *I doubt* (that), the representation of tacit Cog_1 shifts from the M_2 (ONP) slot forward to the M_1 (SNP) slot in the commentative Cog_2, thus from [SPKR / doubts (that) / Cog_1] to [Cog_1 / is / obvious (to SPKR)]—thus, a sort of passive.)

(16) Alter (by Ego) commentative: our example sentence here was *Mary was annóyed to find John in the bar*

[Note first that applying the Passivization test to Cog_1 justifies naturalizing this simplex (witness *John was found-in-the-bar by Mary* but **John-in-the-bar was found by Mary*). Note second that this Alter (by Ego) Commentative entails all of the Δ PTs of the Obliquely Commentative above (even further "obliqueness" itself, along with the Cog_1 representation as the M_1 of Cog_2), *plus* the additional Δ PT for naturalizing Cog_1—hence the increased overall processing difficulty.)

Unnaturally Ordered, via Multiple Commentative Conjoining

(20) Double commentative: our final sentential example above, *I regrét télling you that you are fired,* was a case in point

[We feel that this type of transform—with its triple-set of cognitions and hence two full cognitions (six constituents) being held in BUF—entails the most processing difficulty within our set of examples. There is not only the sheer N of constituents stored, but also the relatively long time through which (while "fading") BUFfing must be maintained.]

Redundancy-Deletion Suppletion

(Our single example of Listener comprehension of sentences from which information redundant for the Speaker has been deleted—*the groundhog was run over*—was given as a kind of "bridge" between Simplexes and Complexes. While this seems an appropriate location, since redundancy deletions can occur in either simplex or complex sentences, even casual consideration of a wide variety of examples indicated (a) that the comprehension difficulty varies with a number of factors, quite independently of the simplex/complex categorization, and (b) that these factors have little, if anything, to do with transformations *per se*.

(1) *The source of the suppletion by the Listener:* (a) events cognized in the parallel *perceptual channel* [e.g., SPKR: "fell off!"—LSNR: THE BALL (fell off) THE TEE]; (b) cognitions freshly stored in MEM from *immediately prior conversation* (e.g., ALTER: "I went to a play last night"—EGO: "How was it?"—ALTER: "A farce!"— EGO: (the play) *was a poorly acted comedy;* (c) *sheer probablistic suppletion* (e.g., our one example, SPKR: "The groundhog was run over"— LSNR: . . . *by a car*); (d) more extended *search of long-term* MEM (e.g., SPKR: "I gave THAT NOSY COP a lecture on the unalienable constitutional right to privacy!"—LSNR: searches MEM for *cop was nosy,* with unpredictable chances of success!

(2) *Number and nature of constituents deleted:* (a) although *single-constituent deletions* should be more easily suppleted than *double-constituent deletions,* other things equal, suppletion difficulty should also vary with the nature of the constituent: we suspect that -- (M) --> (VP) deletion would be most difficult (e.g., if given *John . . . Mary* "out of the blue" as a simplex) and that M_1 (SNP) deletion should be more difficult than M_2 (ONP) deletion (e.g., being given . . . *despises Mary* harder than being given *John despises . . .*), particularly in cases where MEM search is required (see earlier section on the memory in Lecture V); (b) however— perhaps paradoxically at first glance—it seems clear that *deletions in subsequently expressed clauses of conjoined complexes* (either single- or double-deletions) *are relatively much easier to supplete* [e.g., *the car ran off the road and ( ) hit a pole; the car ran into a fruit vender's cart and demolished* (it).]

A Proposal for Systematic Research on Comprehension Processing Times

Ideally, experimental testing of this predicted hierarchy would include comparing of processing times (latencies in sentence comprehension) of natural vs unnatural structures for all major types of sentences—simplexes and complexes, the latter by mode of conjoining (adverbial, relative clause, and commentative)—and determining if, in fact, the *differences* in Δ PT increase as predicted [via the parenthetical, (#)s in the hierarchy above]. However, since the sheer magnitude of such an experiment would be prohibitive, in practice *subsets* of types would probably be used for a start. Realizing fully well that "the best laid schemes o' Mice an' Men, gan aft agley", let us now nevertheless try to design the "ideal" experiment.

(1) Within each of the types of sentences (each as a "sub-experiment"

of the whole), the processing times of *natural* orderings of constituents and/or clauses for the given type would be compared with those for *unnatural* orderings, at all levels of predicted difficulty for that type (*see* illustrative sets in Table VIII.I below).

(2) For each difficulty level within the type, three sentential examples—two *acceptable* [Natural (N) vs Unnatural (UN) in ordering] and one *unnacceptable* [as a "foil", *see* (4) below]—would be devised and pretested. Four groups of native English-speaking subjects (A_1, B_1, A_2, and B_2) and two testing sessions (I and II, with at least a full-day interval between them) would be used. The following is the basic design (note: the foils would be randomly presented, in both natural and unnatural orderings, but their latencies would not be included in testing the primary predictions).[2]

		SESSIONS			
		I		II	
	A_1:	N_1	UN_2	UN_1	N_2
GROUPS	B_1:	N_2	UN_1	UN_2	N_1
	A_2:	UN_2	N_1	N_2	UN_1
	B_2:	UN_1	N_2	N_1	UN_2

Note the following with respect to this rather complex design:

(a) the A and B Groups in each set (sub_1 and sub_2) get different sequencing within sessions of Natural vs Unnatural versions of the two sentences at each level, and this sequencing shifts for each set from Session I to Session II, thus controlling for this order variable;

(b) within *each* of the four Groups, Session I vs Session II provides a *within-group* comparison of Natural vs Unnatural versions of the same sentences (thus, for Group A_1, N_1 vs UN_1 and UN_2 vs N_2, where the subscripts refer to the two acceptable sentences, and similarly for Group A_2, but with the sequential ordering of the N and UN versions within sessions reversed—whereby each subject serves as his own control;

(c) finally, *each* pair of Groups (A_1/B_1 and A_2/B_2) in *each* Session (I and II) provides a separate *between-group* comparison for the N vs UN sentences at each difficulty level [thus in Session I for A_1/B_1 we have N_1 (A) vs UN_1 (B) and N_2 (B) vs UN_2 (A)], and, since this same comparison for the same N and UN sentence-forms holds for each of the Group-pair/Session combinations, all four combinations can be combined into a single (much more powerful) significance test, in

---

[2] However, it would be most intriguing if, as we would expect, correct judgments of the "foils" displayed exactly the same predicted differences in processing times.

which all other major variables (sequencing within Sessions, Groups, and possible Session effects themselves) balance out.

(3) The test sentences would be presented on two-channel audiotape (since it is essential to include the critical shifts in stress, e.g., from *I will have a martíni* to *A martíni I will have*). The signal for starting a millisecond timer would coincide with the *terminal syllable* of the last word of each sentence (thus minimizing any slight length differences between Natural and Unnatural pairs in each test), this signal being inserted on the second channel of the tape, and this would be followed by a standard 4-sec. "silent" interval before a warning buzzer alerts the subject for the beginning of the next test sentence. The vocal reaction of the subject [see (4) below], activating a voice-key, would also be recorded on this second channel to facilitate the measurement of reaction latencies by the investigators. As must be obvious, four separate and different tapes must be made for each of the Groups of subjects in the design.

And this brings us to the most debatable aspect of this "ideal" experiment— just *what* judgmental "reaction" by the subject would best serve to index his processing time (by stopping the timer)? Obviously this couldn't be a "grammaticality" judgment ("yes" for test sentences, "no" for ungrammatical foils): (i) ordinary language users simply are not competent to make such judgments; (ii) some of our Unnatural sentencings are at least debatable as to grammaticality (e.g., again, *A martíni I will have*).

(a) We think the following should be the *general requirements* for selecting a reaction indicator of processing time: (i) neither the judgmental task nor the reaction should *distract* the subject from his normal sentence-processing, or in any other way *interfere* with processing; (ii) the reaction should require the *simplest possible vocalization* by the subject, and one initiated always by a voiced element ("yes" vs "no" would ideally suit these purposes); (iii) the judgmental task should require *full processing* of each sentence (test *or* foil) before the reaction can be made; (iv) the insertions of the "foils" (requiring, e.g., a "no" response) should be random, but averaging to ⅓ of the total sentences on the tape presentation.

(b) Among the "contenders" we have considered for the judgmental task are the following: (i) detecting semantic anomaly (e.g., *A martíni I will* HEAR, *the cat was chased by the* THOUGHT, *Before Mary róasted the turkey, she stuffed* US); (ii) deletion suppletion, with a buzzer masking an easily suppleted word or synonym (*The cat was* BZZZZ *by the dog, Before Mary róasted the turkey she* BZZZZ *it*); (iii) detecting "mind-boggling-ness" (*The tomcat was chased by the tiny mouse, Before Mary stúffed the turkey she roasted it*); (iv) correcting semantically anomalous words, again as near as possible to the ends of test sentences (e.g., *the cat was shased by the* THOUGHT–"dog"). In applying the criteria in (a) above for selecting a reaction indicator of processing time, however, only (i) here—*detecting semantic anomaly* (and saying simply "no" instead of "yes")—seemed to satisfy them reasonably well.[3] Therefore, in the illustrative materials which follow, only "foils" of this type are indicated.

Illustrative Test Materials for Simplexes and Complexes

Two illustrative sets of test materials are presented in Table VIII.1— for Simplexes and for Congruent Complexes Conjoined by Adverbials. Portions of the tapes for two paired Groups, A and B (either Sub_1s or Sub_2s), are given, in each set as shown *here* moving from *least* to *most* predicted Δ PT for Unnatural (UN) vs Natural (N) orderings (in an actual experiment, difficulty levels would vary, as would sentences, across the two Group-pairs). As indicated in this design diagram, half of the sentence test-pairs shift from (N) in Session I to (UN) in Session II for Group A and half in the other order; matched Group B has the reverse pattern of ordering of (N) and (UN). Again, the parenthetical (#)s indicate predicted PT levels, and at each level the (N) and (UN) sentences are of roughly equal length. Although lengths differ otherwise, e.g., from Simplexes to Complexes, this is irrelevant in our design since timing starts on the *last* syllable of sentences and it is *differences* in processing times that constitute the primary data. For Simplexes, Δ PT varies in terms of *number of* $O \rightleftarrows B$ *transfers* and *number of cycles;* for Complexes, it varies with the *centering vs preposing of adverbs* and with *added unnaturalness*—within *subsequent* clause 2, within *prior* clause 1, or both.

Center-Embedding: The Greatest Cognizing Complexity?

For the types of complexes we have just been considering in our predictive hierarchy of processing difficulty, we concluded with *Double Commentatives* as the most complicated. However, there is another type of complex that probably involves even greater processing difficulty—if such sentences can be comprehended at all! These are *Multiply Center-embedded Sentences*. These have been frequently discussed in the psycholinguistic literature (e.g., G. A. Miller, 1962; Bever, 1970), even though they are (for what will be obvious reasons) relatively infrequent

---

[3] Forster and Olbrei (1973), it may be recalled, used this type of "foil" in a study of processing times for simplex vs complex sentences, matched for length, e.g., *the wealthy child attended a private school* vs *the dress Pam wore looked ugly.*

Table VIII.1. Example Sets of Test Materials for Simplexes and
Adverbial Complexes

Session I	Session II

SIMPLEXES
Single O ⇌ B Transfer

A:[a] (O)[b] My poodle chased a big fat
squirrel (N)[c]
B: (1) A double martíni I will have
(UN)

(1) A big fat squírrel my poodle
chased (UN)
(O) I will have a double martini (N)

Foils: My poodle chased a big fat BUTTER; A double martíni I will WALK;
etc.

Double O ⇌ B Transfer

A: (2) George Wáshington is praised by
every statesman (UN)
B: (O) The home-plate umpire spied
something (N)

(O) Every statesman praises George
Washington (N)
(2) Whát did the home-plate umpire
spy? (UN)

Foils: The home-plate umpire spied HIMSELF; George Wáshington is
praised by every MINUTE; etc.

Double Cycle, Single O ⇌ B Transfer

A: (6) Néver have I been to the White
House (UN)
B: (O) Johnny Jones is now a thérapist?
(N)

(O) I have never been to the White
House (N)
(6) Ís Johnny Jones now a therapist?
(UN)

Foils: I have never been to the BLOODSTREAM; Ís Johnny Jones now a
FEBRUARY?; etc.

Triple O ⇌ B Transfer

A: (O) John will sometime go to visit
his aunt? (N)
B: (8) Whére did Columbus land in the
New World? (UN)

(8) Whén will John go to visit his
aunt? (UN)
(O) Columbus landed somewhere in
the New World? (N)

Foils: John will sometime go to visit his SMOKE?; Whére did Columbus
land in the New SQUARE? etc.

ADVERBIAL COMPLEXES
Adverb Centered

A: (3) Because Grampa fell on the ice
he broke his leg (N)
B: (4) Mary skinned the súckling píg
after she sharpened her hunting
knife (UN)

(4) Grámpa broke his lég because he
fell on the ice (UN)
(3) Mary sharpened her knife before
she skinned the suckling pig (N)

Foils: Because Grampa slipped on the ice, he broke his NAP; Mary skinned
the súckling píg after she sharpened her hunting LACE; etc.

Table VIII.I. (*continued*)

Session I	Session II

Adverb Preposed

A: (5) Before Aunt Grace róasted the turkey, she stuffed it (UN)   (3) After Aunt Grace stuffed the turkey, she roasted it (N)

B: (3) John drilled a hole in the coconut in order to drink its milk (N)   (5) In order to drink its mílk, John drilled a hole in the coconut (UN)

Foils: John drilled a hole in the coconut in order to drink its SHELL; Before Aunt Grace róasted the turkey, she stuffed US; etc.

With Clause 2 Also Unnaturally Ordered

A: (3) Because the tomcat scratched the bulldog, the bulldog chased the tomcat (N)   (10) The bulldog chased the tómcat because the bulldog was scratched by the tomcat (UN)

B: (10) Before he climbed the télephone pole, his spiked bóots the repairman put on (UN)   (3) After the repair man put on his spiked boots, he climbed the telephone pole (N)

Foils: Because the tomcat scratched the bulldog, the bulldog chased the MOONLIGHT; Before he climbed the télephone pole, his spiked bóots the repairman SWITCHED OFF; etc.

With Clause 1 Also Unnaturally Ordered

A: (15) The gardener his heavy woolen swéater took off, since the summer sun was hot (UN)   (3) Since the summer sun was hot, the gardener took off his heavy woolen sweater (N)

B: (3) After Senator Sam crowned her, Sally gave him a great big kiss (N)   (15) Senator Sam was given a great big kíss by Sally, after he crowned her (UN)

Foils: After Senator Sam crowned her, Sally gave him a great big MOON; The gardener his heavy woolen swéater took off, since the summer sun was LOOSE; etc.

With Both Clauses Also Unnaturally Ordered

A: (3) After the mechanic tuned up the motor, he gave a road test to the old car (N)   (18) The mechanic gave the old cár a road test after the motor had been tuned up (UN)

B: (18) Sailor Jim sold a línguist the parrot because only Pórtugese it spoke (UN)   (3) Because the parrot only spoke Portugese, Sailor Jim sold it to a linguist (N)

Foils: After the mechanic tuned up the motor, he gave the old car a BREAKFAST; Sailor Jim sold a línguist the parrot because only Pórtugese it ATE; etc.

[a]Group A_1 and B_1 (or A_2 and B_2)

[b]Predicted (#) processing difficulty level

[c]Natural (N) vs Unnatural (UN) ordering

in ordinary language use. It has been claimed, for example, that such sentences are the Waterloo for any Markovian (word-to-word transitional probability) model of sentence generation—to which claim I would also subscribe.

Take the following *grammatical* sentence (from Miller, 1962) as a particularly complex example: *the race that the car that the people whom the obviously not very well dressed man called sold won was held last summer.* Note first the extremely low transitional probability of the sequence of the VPs *called sold won was held* (the argument against the sufficiency of any strictly Markovian model); but note also that (a) center-embedded sentences are very rarely produced by ordinary speakers [only one instance by 26 (speakers) × 32 (demonstrations) = 832 sentencings in my Simply Describing study, Osgood, 1971] and (b) even college students have trouble comprehending doubly center-embedded sentences (as Miller, 1962, demonstrated experimentally).

It might be instructive to ask ourselves under just what conditions *of expressing,* and in what way, might an ordinary speaker produce Miller's "monster"—the phrase structure of which I reproduce here as Fig. VIII.1. We should keep in mind that one of a speaker's motives—his part of the Given-New Contract—is to keep a running estimate of his listener's (L below) available information (i.e., what's in *his* MEM as compared with the speaker's). Our earnest speaker begins to express his destination cog, *the race . . .* (L DOESN'T KNOW *what* RACE, SO BUF *. . . was held last summer!) that the car . . .* (L MUST KNOW *what* CAR, SO BUF *. . . won!) that the people . . .* (FOR L'S SAKE, *what* PEOPLE, SO BUF *. . . sold) whom the . . .* (L HAS NO IDEAS WHICH MAN I'M ABOUT TO MENTION, SO BUF *. . . man called!) obviously not very well dressed . . .* —and now our thoroughly harried speaker begins picking up the pieces stacked in "push-down" fashion in the BUFFER—*man/called/sold/won/was held last summer.* WHOOF! Our speaker's actual language behavior would probably be more like this: "the race that . . . the car that . . . (ah)..the people . . . whom the-obviously-not-very-well-dressed man called . . . (ah–er) . . . well, thóse people sold the car . . . (ah) . . . that-I-was-télling you! . . . won the ráce last summer . . . do you see?"

The processing difficulty *in comprehending* such sentences is not due simply to the number of OPR/BUF transfers (and therefore duration of storage), but also to the fact that in such center-embeddings the *NPs shift their grammatical functions* (i.e., their basic ±Directionality semantic codings in this APG) in the underlying cognitions (clauses)—thus here we have [the car . . . won the race] embedded with *the race* as ONP in [the race . . . was held last summer] with *the race* as SNP, and so on down into this sentence. It is also important to note that in such sentences *the more deeply embedded clauses must always be prior in cognizing—*

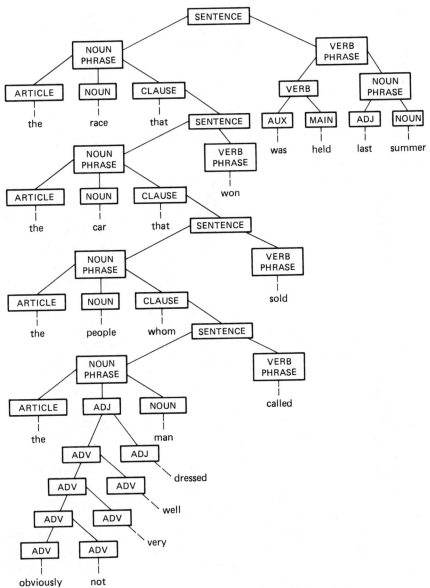

Fig. VIII.1. Syntactic structure of a self-embedded sentence

thus here (forgetting the deepest left-branching NP) we have [the man called some people] and [those people sold a car] and [that car won a race] and [that race was held last summer]. Note further the shift from relative indefiniteness to definiteness as each NP moves "up" the cog hierarchy (thus cognitively *a race* "upward" to *that race*); this reflects the fact that each embedding derives from a WH-clause which, in effect, more selectively characterizes the NP it modifies—thus *the race* is the race *which* the car won—and, as Fodor and Garrett (1967) have demonstrated, sentences like *the car which the man who the girl likes bought crashed* are at least easier than *the car the man the girl likes bought crashed!* The issues of concern here for APG_0 are the following.

(1) *Does the notion that embedded clauses must be prior in cognizing to those they embed fit the Naturalness Principle as applied to complexes?* Testing with simpler single-embeddings, this seems to be the case: for Source-Recipient Action Relations, *the ball the boy batted broke the window* expands naturally into [the boy batted a ball] *and then* [that ball broke the window], **the boy the ball broke batted the window* and **the boy the ball batted broke the window* being semantically impossible; for Figure-Ground Stative Relations, *the mat the cat is on is by the window* expands naturally into [the cat is on a mat] *and* [that mat is by the window], **the cat the mat is on is by the window* and **the cat the mat is by is on the window* being semantically impossible.

(2) *Do the postulated natures and transfer relations of OPR and BUF yield "naturalizing" of center-embedded sentences?* In the Action relation above, since *the ball* could be either SNP or ONP, the first cue for disorder is the second NP (*the boy*) appearing in the - - (M) -→ slot [*see* F VIII-II (C)]: transferring immediately prior *the ball* to BUF, with "leftward" shift of *the boy* and *batted* into M_1 and - - (M) -→, return of *the ball* yields natural Cog_1 [the boy / batted / the ball]; with insertion [and then] in the tag-slot as the conjoiner and reduplication of the immediately prior NP, *the ball,* as M_1, we get the natural Cog_2 [the ball / broke / the window]. In the Stative relation above, since *the mat* is similarly ambiguous as SNP (Figure) or ONP (Ground) status, the first cue for unnaturalness is *the cat:* again, shifting *the mat* to BUF, moving *the cat* and *is on* forward, and returning *the mat* from BUF, we get naturally ordered Cog_1 [the cat / is on / the mat]; again, inserting congruent [and] in the tag-slot and reduplicating immediately prior NP, *the mat* as M_1, we get the natural Cog_2 [the mat / is by / the window]. But now we have another problem.

(3) *How can the double function of a noun phrase* (ONP then SNP) *which appears only once in the surface structure be represented in this APG?* The answer suggested in (2) above is that the ONP of naturalized Cog_1, necessarily just prior to Cog_2 [ϕ / - - (M) -→ / M_2], is simply "copied" semantically as its M_1. In the Action relation, after the first cog is "naturalized" [holding up further LEX to OPR transfer—*see* F VIII-II (B (3)], only two constituents appear in the

second cog—leaving [the boy batted the ball] *and then* [φ / broke the window]; however, note that *the boy batted the ball and broke the window*—and even more . . . *which broke the window*—capture the full meaning of *the boy batted the ball and the ball broke the window.* The same holds for the Stative relation, where *the cat is on the mat which is by the window,* or even just . . . *by the window,* fully captures the meaning of the full 2-cog expression. In other words, if ordinary rules of redundancy deletion were applied to the full expression, we would get exactly what this APG predicts. In our analyses of sentential examples earlier, we followed a rule that was to the effect that when an NP is missing from one of two conjoined cognitions, the nearest NP *from the prior cognition* is repeated (inserted).

Yngve's "Depth Hypothesis" and the OPERATOR/BUFFER Interactions in this APG

I had assumed that Victor Yngve's "Depth Hypothesis" (*see* his "A Model and a Hypothesis for Language Structure", 1960) would prove to be rather closely related to my OPERATOR/BUFFER transfers as they function in the processing of various transforms—and, in fact, that it might predict a similar hierarchy of difficulty levels. However, the similarities seem to lie more in purpose than in theory. Both theories are concerned with a kind of "naturalness" principle in sentencing, with a notion of "depth" in the sense of how much must be stored and how long, and with predicting processing difficulty as a function of what each theory defines as sentential complexity—but the mechanisms and dynamics postulated in the two theories are quite different. Following a sketch (necessarily brief here) of Yngve's hypothesis and a comparison with this APG, I will summarize some relevant experimental evidence on comparative processing difficulties; finally, I ask myself how some of the methods used in such experiments might be applied to testing the predictions made in APG theory.

The Depth Hypothesis (essentially, that human short-term memory is sharply limited—BUFFER storage here) leads Yngve (1960) to the following picture of *language production* (quoting from his summary, p. 465): "Human speech is produced by a finite-state device and by an essentially left-to-right process. There exists a temporary or working memory that can contain about seven items. . . . The actual process of sentence production corresponds in our model to applying rules by successive expansion from the top down." It should be noted that each step in the top-to-bottom generation of a sentence in his model necessarily precedes initation of the left-to-right production process (see his pp. 445–447). He also explicitly states (p. 465) that his temporary memory, like our BUF, is a "push-down" affair—in his terms, "last item in, first item out."

Yngve goes on to claim (p. 465) " . . . that all languages have devices to limit depth, devices to circumvent this limitation, and that these devices represent much of the syntactic complexity of language . . [and further] . . that depth phenomena play an important role in language change." In this last connection, Yngve (1975) offers an intriguing paper titled "Depth and the Historical Change of the English Genitive"; here he relates his hypothesis to the shifts from roughly 900 to 1300 A.D.— from about 50% either *the handle of the door* or *the door's handle* (both greater depth), but *the door-handle* (less depth) only 1%—to over 80% *the door-handle*. Writing like a good behaviorist, Yngve (1960, p. 466) says: "Whenever speakers embark on grammatical sentences that exceed the depth limit, they become trapped and have to start over. If this becomes a frequent occurrence, speakers will try to avoid the constructions that got them into trouble"—i.e., the effects of negative reinforcement!

Now we may note some of the major differences between Yngve's Depth Hypothesis and the notion F VII and F VIII of this APG.

First, as far as language performance is concerned, Yngve's theory is clearly a *production* model, in which there is progressive, from "top-to-bottom", expansion of grammatical symbols (this being essentially like the Chomskyan TGG); the only way it can make predictions about *comprehension* is via "analysis-by-synthesis"—the problems with which are familiar.[4] This limitation on the Depth Hypothesis was noted by Bever[5] (1970, pp. 338–341), who suggests that many left-branching (high depth) structures may actually facilitate comprehension because of the way they "predict" later elements; this is elaborated in Fodor, Bever, and Garrett (1974, pp. 406 ff.). Our APG model involves *only* "left-to-right" processing—there is no "top-to-bottom" (or "bottom-to-top"), since hierarchical syntactic relations are, in effect, "translated" into linear semantic relations. Within the Representational Level, all processing involves transfers of and interactions among semantic-feature code-strips (between and within LEX, OPR, BUF, and MEM). The distinction between comprehension and production lies in the *direction* of information transmission by the LEXICON—*in comprehending, encoding percepts* into semantic feature sets and transferring this information "up" to the OPERATOR and, *in producing*, decoding constituent semantic feature sets

---

[4] Primarily, in theory, the inefficiency of a model which generates trees more-or-less ad libitum in search of a match to the structure of a received sentence and, empirically, the general failure of DTC (the Derivational Theory of Complexity).

[5] See Miller and Chomsley (1963, p. 475) for a much earlier expression of this same notion.

received from OPR "down" via LEX into *programs* for talking—and in the *details* of OPR/BUF interactions.

Second, Yngve's model (see particularly 1960, pp. 447 ff.) includes the following as "mechanisms": a *register,* which is the "top-to-bottom" expansion of grammatical symbols into lexical items (e.g., in his Fig. 2, S → NP → T → *the* → N → *man* . . . etc., vertically); a *temporary memory* which stores, also vertically, those "rightward" syntactic symbols which must be delayed in production (e.g., the VP of the S → NP + VP expansion above) while the "leftward" symbols at each level are fully expanded into lexical items; and an *output tape,* which transforms "top-to-bottom" into "left-to-right" (the last line in which for this example being S NP T *the* N *man* VP V *saw* NP T *the* N *boy*). This "left-to-right" string of lexical items presumably begins to be expressed as soon as terminal lexical items appear in the output tape. It is the *temporary memory,* of course, that is the analogue of my BUFFER; but note that the former is a storing of *grammatical symbols*—the maximum number of which at any level in the derivation being the index of the "depth"-value of the sentence (here, 2 units when we have both N and VP stored)—no semantics being involved whatsoever. It also turns out, however, that the "depth" computation (and hence predicted difficulty in production) is made on a *word-by-word* basis, whereas what is stored in the BUFFER of this APG is *whole constituents* (except for discontinuous ones)—and *as sets of semantic features* ("code-strips").

In the many phrasal and sentential examples of different "depth" structures for conveying the same information that Yngve (1960) offers, one is often struck by the minimal (if any) differences in comprehensibility. The first sentence below has a depth of eight (beyond the "magic number 7" tolerance level he suggests):

> if what going to a clearly not very adequately staffed school really means is little appreciated, we should be concerned

whereas the second has a depth of "two or three" (p. 462):

> we should be concerned if there is little appreciation of what it really means to go to a school that clearly isn't very adequately staffed

yet (for this reader) there seems to be little difference in difficulty. Similarly, compare this "deep" left-branching ("regressive", according to Yngve) sentence, *this is his mother's brother's son's daughter's hat,* with the relatively "shallow" *this hat belongs to the daughter of the son of the brother of his mother;* again there seems to be little difference in difficulty. But we are here dealing (necessarily) with listener *comprehension*—what about speaker *production,* to which Yngve's theory should directly apply? One thing I note in subvocalizing many of his examples is that the left-branching segments seem to come out in "bursts"—as if they were drawn as wholes from MEM (e.g., with the "burst" suggested by dashes, *when very-clearly-projected-pictures appeared, they applauded*) or were truncated embeddings, hence analyzable as complexes (compare depth-of-1, . . . *in their big new red house,* with depth-of-3 . . . *in their very-well-built house*). These might be two ways in which the present APG could handle some of these production phenomena.

There are also differences in processing difficulty predictable from this APG on the basis of Naturalness that either cannot be predicted from Yngve's Depth Hypothesis (apparently) or flatly conflict with it. As an example of conflicting predictions, witness that (p. 456) *he does it whenever they ask him* has a depth of 1 whereas *whenever they ask him, he does it* has a depth of 2—yet it is the latter which is in natural order for complexes. As another example, observe the ordinary passive: according to Yngve (1960, p. 457), active *the boy loves the girl* and passive *the girl is loved by the boy* have the *same* "depth" (2), but Naturalness clearly predicts more processing difficulty for the passive. An example of failure to predict what seems (his p. 456) to be an obvious difference is the following: although both models agree that the *regressive* sentence *because because because she wouldn't give him any candy, he called her names, she hit him, he cried* is intolerable, the Depth Hypothesis cannot predict *any* differences between *progressive* naturally ordered *she wouldn't give him any candy, so he called her names, so she hit him, so he cried* and unnaturally ordered *he cried because she hit him because he called her names because she wouldn't give him any candy*— the latter being more than a bit "mind-boggling" for me!

As far as the psycholinguistic experimental testing of the Yngve "Depth Hypothesis" is concerned, *confusion reigns!* Fodor, Bever, and Garrett (1974, pp. 268–270, 406–419) summarize much of the literature (adding a bit to the confusion here and there), and I will for the most part let the interested reader check the full references in this source. There are a number of studies in which sentence recall was measured, hence involving *comprehension* difficulty as a function of depth (usually mean depth for all words) rather than *production* difficulty, which is what Yngve's theory is all about. In any case, completely inconsistent results were obtained. In the best of these studies (in my opinion), Perfetti and Goodman, (1971) did manipulate *maximum* depth (d_{max}) and with extreme differences in same: In their Experiment I, recall of sentences with d_{max} = 7 (e.g., *when a clearly less than carefully concealed weapon was noticed by detectives, the man was arrested*) were compared with recall of informationally identical sentences with d_{max} = 3 (e.g., *the man was arrested when detectives noticed a weapon which clearly was less than carefully concealed*), and what was found was an exactly equal 50/50 split in correctness of recall (however, it is interesting that errors were significantly more frequent in the *first* halves of high-depth and in the *last* halves of low-depth sentences).

The earliest experiment (to the best of my knowledge) in which *production* difficulty was at least approached was a 1966 study by Neal Johnson. He had subjects learn "paired-associates" in which digits were paired with sentences varying in depth à la Yngve—the dependent variable being *latency in initiating a sentence,* given its digit. Although results generally confirmed the Yngve hypothesis, Fodor, Bever, and Garrett (p. 410) note that many of the sentences with higher depth (e.g., *the boy near me who stood . . .*) seemed much less acceptable in ordinary English than their lower-depth matches (*the boy who stood near me . . .*). Fodor, Bever, and Garrett (pp. 411–415)—quite correctly seeking some real *speaker production* data against which to test the Yngve hypothesis—report a reanalysis of data originally collected by Kenneth Forster with something other than this particular hypothesis in mind.[6]

Forster was interested in left-to-right processes in sentence production (in fact, this experiment was one of the earliest on sentence production per se). The basic method was to take fairly long sentences from various everyday sources, delete either their left (LD) or right (RD) halves [leaving the same number of blanks as words in the original sentences— e.g., (LD) —— —— —— —— —— —— —— —— *the woman in a state of great agitation* vs (RD) *on his return to the house he found* —— —— —— —— —— —— —— ——], and then have subjects simply complete the sentences in their own words. As would be expected—but still testifying to the importance of left-to-right processing principles (in both Yngve's model and in this APG)—Forster found RD sentences to be much easier to complete than LD sentences. In a later study, Forster (1968) demonstrated that as left-branching tendencies increase from English to German to Japanese to Turkish, the speakers of these languages display less and less of a difference between RD and LD—*but, even with Turkish, RD sentences are easier to complete than LD sentences,* a finding which is not inconsistent with the Yngve hypothesis or this APG.

Some Relevant Linguistic and Psycholinguistic Evidence

Very recently in linguistics there has been an explosion (almost literally!) of papers on Pragmatics and Functionalism—clearly, in my opinion, moving toward a performance theory (including perceptual, discourse,

---

[6] The original research was done by Forster as his doctoral thesis in 1964 under my direction and subsequently published in Forster (1966, 1967).

and social determinants)—along with correlated pressures toward fundamental changes in the Chomskyan TGG, e.g., the recent developments in Relational Grammar. In the early 1970s there were a few anticipations of this (e.g., Robin Lakoff's, 1972, paper titled "Language in Context"), but the "explosion" came around 1975.

Oriented particularly toward Pragmatics was Vol. 3 of the series titled *Syntax and Semantics*, edited by Peter Cole and Jerry Morgan and subtitled *Speech Acts* (1975); taking off from seminal papers by philosophers H. Paul Grice and John R. Searle, this volume included many papers particularly relevant to this APG.[7] Oriented particularly toward Functionalism (obviously) was a special 1975 volume by the Chicago Linguistic Society titled *Papers from the Parasession on Functionalism*, edited by Grossman, San, and Vance. This volume contains several papers of direct relevance to our present concern, salience principles and OPERATOR/ BUFFER functions in clefting, optional transformations, and the like. Also, oriented toward Relational Grammar, in 1977 we have Vol. 8 of the *Syntax and Semantics* series, subtitled *Grammatical Relations*, edited by Peter Cole and Jerrold Sadock, including many papers particularly relevant to *any* APG.

There is some experimental evidence—and much speculation—in the literature about the comparative processing difficulties of different types of simplex and complex structes. In his important 1970 paper, titled "The Cognitive Basis for Linguistic Structures", Bever describes a wide variety of such structures (see particularly pp. 313–341) and proposes several "perceptual strategies" that people develop for processing them. In a section titled "Sequences With Two Simultaneous Functions—Three's a Crowd" he deals with center-embeddings and related phenomena. One of the latter is the case where " . . . there is a phrase (indicated by 'Y') that is related to a previous phrase in the same way that it relates to a following phrase" (p. 340), e.g., modifying his example slightly:

They were tired of discussing *evaluating* producing toys.

Bever points out how much easier is the comprehension of a sentence with only two such phrases (i.e., no "y" having a dual function), *they were tired of discussing producing toys,*[8] or of a sentence in which the internal relations are varied, *they were tired of discussing thinking*

---

[7] Here I can only indicate these many linguistic sources of relevance to the developing APG; in the full version, of course, the individual papers will be treated in detail and related to the various functional notions. Also, much of this recent work is most relevant to what will be the later chapters of the expanded version, particularly planned chapters on *Efficiency vs Complexity in Speaker/Listener Interactions, Pragmatics of Language Use in Situational Contexts,* and *Relations to Other Linguistic and Psycholinguistic Models.*

[8] Note that the same applies to center-embeddings (*the boy the girl Pierre loves likes hates spaghetti* vs *the boy the girl like hates spaghetti*).

producing toys. Whether this poses a problem for an APG, or can be considered simply a case of semantics reducing an xyz to an xy structure (compare *they were tired of discussing language-producing toys*), I'm not at this point sure.

After reviewing empirical evidence on the *Derivational Theory of Complexity* (DTC) and concluding (p. 328) that "DTC is in trouble",[9] Fodor, Bever, and Garrett (1974) propose an alternative, "clausal analysis" theory (pp. 329–348) which turns out to be rather similar to this APG as so far presented. The major hypothesis is that " . . . an early process in sentence recognition involves grouping together items from the same sentoid" (simplex cognition in my terms), and they present considerable evidence ("click" location and other) that" . . . the boundaries between clauses have a unique and characteristic role in the perceptual (*conceptual*) organization of sentences" (p. 329). Referring to studies by Bever, Lackner, and Stolz, and Bever, Lackner, and Kirk (both 1969), Fodor, Bever, and Garrett (p. 336) say that "what was discovered . . . was that much of the variance is contributed by a tendency to displace clicks into surface boundaries which mark the ends of embedded sentences", i.e., whole-cog boundaries in APG terms, and they go on to note that this implies that conceptual processing involves grouping together ". . . surface material belonging to a common sentoid" and segmenting it ". . . from surface material belonging to other sentoids".

Pushing this notion still further, Tannenhaus and Carroll (1975), working with Bever, propose that a listener tries to "map clauses onto complete propositions" (cf full cogs here), and they outline a hierarchy of clause types which—in terms of (a) propositional incompleteness (number of functional relations missing) and (b) lack of surface markedness (of sentential material as being subordinate)—should make the listener's task increasingly difficult: easiest to process should be (I) *main clauses* (simplexes or the main clauses of complexes); next are (II) *complete embedded clauses* (e.g., relative clauses); next we have (III) *nominalizations* (e.g., gerundives like *John's refusing to eat . . .*); and most difficult (in this hierarchy) are (IV) *noun phrases,* with no residual verb (e.g., *John's annoying habits . . .*)—(III) and (IV) being conjoined complexes "in disguise"!

Interestingly, Fodor, Bever, and Garrett propose a processing analysis of center-embedded sentences (pp. 342–343)—without actually making any explicit distinction between analytic (OPERATOR) and storage (BUFFER) functions—that is quite similar to the OPR/BUF relations in this APG, as witness the following: "We assume, first, that there is only

---

[9] In an already-written Chap. 2 of my in-progress *Toward an Abstract Performance Grammar,* I reach exactly the same conclusion.

a limited amount of short-term memory available . . . and, second, that no constituent of a sentence can be dismissed from short-term memory until it has been assigned to a sentoid. . . . As the sentence is received, it is assigned to a short-term memory store where the fragments that constitute each of its sentoids are collected together [my OPR/BUF functions] . . . it is because each sentoid is dismissed from this store [to MEM in this APG] *en bloc* that the clause functions as a unit in speech perception.''

At a somewhat later point (pp. 344–345), in discussing the "canonical-sentoid" strategy, we find statements very similar to what I have discussed as the Naturalness Principle (in my APG, deriving from prelinguistic cognizing): this strategy is that ". . . whenever one encounters a surface sequence NP V (NP), assume that these items are, respectively, subject verb and object of a deep sentoid"—and, as they point out, this strategy can render very difficult sentences like *the horse raced past the barn fell* which are ridiculously simple once one realizes that it is *the horse (which was) raced past the barn fell!* Coming back to center-embedding, Schlesinger (1968) has shown that comprehension can be somewhat simplified if there is distinctive semantic selectivity between the nouns and verbs involved; compare, for example, *the boy the girl Pierre loves likes hates spaghetti* with *the boy the cat Pierre barked at scratched hates spaghetti.*

Considerable research on the processing of complexes by both adults and children is now available, and it is generally consistent with these predictions. In Lecture V I reported studies of clauses conjoined by *before* and *after* by Herb and Eve Clark (1968) with adults and by Eve Clark (1971) with children indicating that, in comprehension tasks, *naturally* ordered sentences were processed more easily than *unnaturally* ordered sentences. Worth noting again is the fact that, in both of these studies, there were no differences between *after* preposed (hence sub-ordinate-to-main clause ordering) and *before* centered (hence main-to-subordinate clause ordering)—consistent with the Naturalness Principle but not with the linguistic notion that main-clause-followed-by-subordinate-clause should be easier. Two doctoral theses completed at our Center for Comparative Psycholinguistics in 1973 (one by Rumjahn Hoosain and another by Gordana Opačić) were explicitly designed to test predictions from the Naturalness Principle.

Opačić used all of the semantic modes and syntactic orderings shown in Fig. V.3. For each test item subjects were first shown on slide 1 two clauses, one above the other vertically (top-to-bottom, either naturally or unnaturally ordered), then on a slide 2 a conjoiner that was either possible or impossible to use with the given pair of clauses, and then, if the subject had said "possible", he was to produce the whole complex sentence as he recalled it. Opačić recorded on a tape both the "comprehension-time" required to say "possible" after seeing the conjoiner (slide 2) and the sentence "production-time" from immediate memory. For all complexes where two clause orderings, *Natural* (N) or *Unnatural* (U), are possible, the following hierarchy of processing times was obtained: Natural given and Natural produced (NN) were the most rapidly processed; Unnatural given but *Natural* produced (UN) were only slightly slower in processing; Unnatural given and Unnatural produced (UU) were actually much harder to process (significantly more so than NN); most difficult (and relatively rare in occurrence) were Natural given but *Unnatural* produced (NU). This study has been replicated by Opačić with native Slovenian speakers in Yugoslavia, and the results were essentially the same.

Hoosain used a very different design, in which the processing of *triple-clause* complexes was measured as functions of both Naturalness *and* Congruence (*and* vs *but* types); thus, for an example, processing times for BECAUSE *rain flooded the golf course John got awfully wet* AND *he came down with a cold* (both Natural and Congruent) were compared with those for both *John got awfully wet* BECAUSE *rain flooded the golf course* AND *he came down with a cold* (Unnaturally ordered but Congruent) and BECAUSE *rain flooded the golf course John got awfully wet* BUT *he didn't come down with a cold* (Naturally ordered but Incongruent). The results confirmed both Naturalness and Congruence expectations. In two additional experiments Hoosain was able to show that Congruence predictions hold both for conjoined outline facial expressions (i.e., perceptual signs) and for the conjoining of outline faces with sentences (e.g., an ALERT SMILING FACE with *I passed the exam* vs *I flunked the exam*). These studies are reported in Hoosain (1974; 1977).

An Implication for Linguistics

At the core of this Abstract Performance Grammar is a Naturalness Principle of information ordering in sentences. Considerable research, some of it cross-linguistic in nature, has already shown that this principle predicts cognitive processing ease or difficulty quite effectively. What Sridhar and I have now added to this picture—Osgood and Sridhar (1979), "Unambiguous Signaling of Naturalness in Clause Ordering: A Language Universal?"—is the intriguing fact that, in both English and Kannada, the adverbial *form* or its *locus* (centered or preposed), or *both combined,* serve to *unambiguously* signal whether the temporal order of clauses is Natural or Unnatural. That such signaling appears to be unambiguous for five other, highly diversified, languages as well— Chinese, Hebrew, Japanese, Spanish, and Turkish—strongly suggests that such signaling of Naturalness in clause ordering may be *a language universal*.

However, the fact that it *is* Naturalness, *not* Grammaticalness, which is being unambiguously signaled would seem to raise problems for the science (or is it the art?) of linguistics. In a purely *syntactic* analysis either Natural or Unnatural clause orderings have equal status—both Natural *Mary stuffed the turkey before she roasted it* and Unnatural *Mary roasted the turkey after she stuffed it* are perfectly grammatical. And—to the best of our knowledge—there is nothing *ungrammatical* about !*John poisoned his mother-in-law because he was executed,* about !*although he wore his heavy sweater it was stifling hot,* or even about !*John drank its milk in order to drill a hold in the coconut*—despite the absolute "mind-boggling-ness" of these sentences.

It is important to note that, at least for English and Kannada, ordinary *speakers* are blissfully unaware that—by their salience-motivated placements of adverbials, either preposed or centered—they *are* signaling Naturalness or Unnaturalness of clause ordering unambiguously, and certainly ordinary *listeners* are equally unaware that such signaling is occurring. Yet the listener's comprehension is obviously being facilitated by the signaling, as indicated by experimental psycholinguistic data. Such blissful unawareness is, of course, characteristic of the kind of "knowing one's language" that TGG linguists describe as the *competence* of ordinary language-users. It would therefore seem necessary for linguistic theory to include the sort of "competence" we have described—unambiguous signaling of Naturalness—despite its development out of an abstract "performance" theory. The question, of course, is *how!* The broader implication is that the study of perception-based language universals of this sort may help bridge the gap between competence and performance theories, as well as contribute to the ambitious goals of *predictive* as well as *explanatory* adequacy sought by both theories.

Functional Notions F I to F VIII

Relating to the LEXICON

F I. When a percept which elicits no predictable pattern of behavior has repeated and reinforced paired with another percept which does (e.g., SIGHT OF COOKIE paired with EATING COOKIE), the former will become a sign of the latter as its significant, by virtue of becoming associated with a mediation process (r_M/s_M) that distinctively represents the behavior produced by the significant and therefore serves to mediate overt behaviors appropriate to ("taking account of") the significate (e.g., salivating and reaching for perceived COOKIE OBJECT).

F II. To the extent that differences in percepts are associated with reciprocally antagonistic differences in behavior, the central representations of these differences ($+r_{m_i}$ vs $-r_{m_i}$) in the LEXICON will become the bipolar semantic features which distinguish the significances of percepts (of first perceptual and later linguistic signs).

F III. (a) The greater the overall frequency with which mediator components ($\pm r_{m_i}$ = semantic features) have been elicited in the LEXICON by signs, the shorter will be the latencies of their evocation; (b) the more recent the prior elicitation of sets of related components (r_M "code-strips"), the more available will be such sets for re-elicitation; (c) massed repetition of related sets of mediator components will result in reduced availability.

Relating to the OPERATOR, Simplex Processing

F IV. (A) Postulation of three, primitive, perception-based distinctions yields a semantic characterization of the constituent structure of simplex cognitions: (1) *Substantivity,* distinguishing $+$Substantive Entities from

⁻Substantive Relations; (2) *Directionality,* distinguishing ⁺Salient (directionally prior) Figures and Sources from ⁻Salient (directionally subsequent) Grounds and Recipients; (3) *Stativity,* distinguishing ⁺Static (stable, spatial) Stative Relations from ⁻Static (unstable temporal) Action Relations.

F IV. (B) This semantic characterization implies that simplex prelinguistic cognitions will be naturally (1) *tripartite in structure,* thus $[M_1 -$ $- (M) - \rightarrow M_2]$ (where the Ms refer to meanings, the subscripts to Entities, and the dashed arrows to Relations), (2) *salience-ordered* (with M_1s representing Figures of states and Sources of actions and the M_2s the Grounds of states and the Recipients of actions), and (3), depending on the Relation, *of two basic types,*

(a) *Stative Cognitions* [FIGURE (M_1) – – (STATE) – $\rightarrow$ GROUND (M_2)] and
(b) *Action Cognitions* [SOURCE (M_1) – – (ACTION) – $\rightarrow$ RECIPIENT (M_2)],

both implying necessarily an underlying SVO structure for natural sentencing of simplexes.

Relating to LEXICON/OPERATOR Interactions

F V. (A) Whereas *the* LEXICON *functions on a "wordlike" unit basis, the* OPERATOR *functions on a "whole constituent" unit basis:* (A) IN COMPREHENDING, (1) LEX encodes *word-forms,* both free morphemes and morphemes bound in larger wordlike forms, into their feature codes as their percepts are received from the Sensory Integration Level, transmitting this semantic information-sequence to OPR; (2) *OPR,* utilizing language-specific cues that signal the boundaries of NP and VP constituents, *assigns this information-sequence "horizontally" to its* M_1, $- - (M) - \rightarrow$, *and* M_2 *components for simplexes* (regardless of the Naturalness of codings for SNP, VP, and ONP ordering—see F IV and F VII); (3) utilizing cues for the conjoining of simplexes into complexes, *OPR assigns the clauses of complexes "vertically" to its successive levels,* (again, regardless of the Naturalness of cog-ordering—*see* F VI).

F V. (B) IN EXPRESSING, (1) *OPR transmits to LEX semantic codestrips for whole constituents,* or parts of constituents having associated lexical word-forms, *with either natural or unnatural ordering of the constituents of simplexes or the clauses of complexes* (see F VIII for detailed rules here), LEX not processing each subsequently received constituent *until all features* of each prior constituent *have been decoded into "wording" programs* at the Motor Integration Level (and LEX is momentarily empty, "featureless"). (2) On receiving code-strips of semantic features for a given constituent from OPR, LEX (a) *extracts those subsets of semantic features for which word-forms are available in the language* (or, strictly speaking, in the speaker's idiolect) such that, taken together, the word-forms so extracted *exhaustively express the semantic content of the whole constituent,* and (b) outputs these feature-sets *to the Motor Integration Level,* in the order established by the speaker's experience of the language (i.e., constituent structure) in comprehending, where the related programs for expressing are activated successively.

Relating to the OPERATOR, Processing of Complexes

F VI: (A) In both comprehending and expressing complexes (conjoined clauses in sentencing), the natural order of processing is that which corresponds to the order in which the states or events (referred to in the clauses) *are typically cognized in prelinguistic experience;* (B) complexes MUST be so ordered if they are to be comprehended, but they MAY be disordered in expressing (to satisfy efficiency and salience needs of the speaker—*see* F VIII); (C) all reordering, for both comprehending and expressing, *involves temporary transfers of whole clauses between* OPERATOR *and* BUFFER, and hence increased processing difficulty (*see* F VIII); (D) *congruent cognitions* are conjoined by ANDs (and their adverbial semantic equivalents) and *incongruent cognitions* are conjoined by BUTs (and their adverbial semantic equivalents), with the features of the conjoiner being entered in the tag-slot for Cog_1.

Relating to OPERATOR/BUFFER Interactions

F VII. Utilizing both cues for Naturalness derived from prelinguistic perceptual cognizing and language-specific cues for acceptability/gram-maticality derived from early linguistic experience (*see* F IV–VI), the OPERATOR *scans semantic information received from the* LEXICON, and assigned ("left-to-right") to its M_1, – – (M) – $\rightarrow$ and M_2 components (*see* F V), *for compatability with the rules it has developed.*

(A) Within each component, OPR scans features *in the order of their criticality* in determining adaptive behaviors to the states and actions being comprehended: (1) *affective features* (Evaluation, Potency, and Activity) prior to denotative features, by virtue of their primitive survival value; (2) *for denotative information characterizing entities* (later NPs), *substantive* (identifying) features prior to modulating (adjectival modifying, etc.) features; and, (3) *for denotative information characterizing relations* (later VPs) similarly, *nature-specifying* (identifying) features prior to modulating (adverbial, tense modifying, etc.) features.

(B) *In comprehending simplexes,* OPR (1) checks component code-strips for Naturalness within and Compatibility between constituents of the codings on basic Substantivity, Directionality, and Stativity features (see F IV), (2) the code-strips for constituents that are unnaturally disordered are transferred cyclically to the BUFFER, being stores in "push-down" fashion, and then, (3) as "leftward" movement of the remaining information within the simplex occur [*see* F VIII–II (C) below for details], the temporarily stored constituent information is returned to the cog components left open.

(C) *Whole cognitions having Incompatible codings* are either processed and sent to the MEMORY *as acceptable "metaphors"* or rejected *as semantically anomalous,* dependent upon the degrees of featural incongruity (*see* functional notions relating to fine, cross-constituent, congruity dynamics at end of Lecture VI).

(D) *In comprehending complexes,* subsequent to processing of Cog_1 (naturally prior clause linguistically) according to (B) and (C) above, given the cue for *Unnatural clause ordering* (combined form and locus of conjoiner—*see* F VI), (1) the prior clause$_1$ is transferred constituent-by-constituent to BUF in the reverse order of that received (i.e., "right-to-left"), (2) the naturally prior cognition but subsequent clause$_2$ becomes Cog_1 (in effect, is "moved up" in OPR), and (3) the BUFfed constituents for the naturally subsequent cognition are returned to OPR, now as Cog_2 [*see* F VIII–II (D) for details].

F VIII–I EXPRESSING: (A) For the Speaker, the ordering *in the* OPERATOR of constituents within simplexes and of simplex clauses within complexes *is always natural;* when constituents are expressed *in natural order,* the ordering of word forms *within* constituents always conforms to the surface rules of the particular language and always exhaust the semantic information in each constituent (see F–V).

(B) Salience dynamics operating on the Speaker may produce *displacements* of constituents (or parts thereof) of simplexes and whole clauses of complexes from their natural order, leaving semantically "empty" (ϕ) or reduced components: (1) if, *for simplexes,* the displacement via overt expression (movement "leftward" for earlier expression) or via transfer to the BUFFER (movement "rightward" for later expression) leaves the remaining constituents (or parts thereof) *in natural order* for expression, the remainder of the cognition is simply expressed, and no (further) use of BUF is required; (2) if, *for simplexes,* the displacement of constituents (or parts thereof) leaves the remainder *in an order unnatural for expression,* then (further) use of BUF is required (see C below); (3) *for complexes,* displacement of a naturally subsequent clause for earlier expression *always* requires BUFfing of the naturally prior clause or clauses (transferred to BUF from right-to-left by constituents).

(C) When use of the BUFFER is required for expressing *simplexes* [B (2) above]: (1) if the salience-motivated constituent (or part thereof) *is shifted to utterance initial (or terminal) position,* (a) it is expressed (or transferred to BUF), leaving a constituent-holding ϕ, (b) unnaturally coded constituents (or parts) are transferred to BUF (left-to-right), (c) remaining constituents (or parts), if any, are expressed, and (d) code-strips from BUF are expressed as they are returned to OPR; (2) if the salience-motivated constituent (or part thereof) *is shifted to a non-initial (or non-terminal) utterance position,* (a) the constituents (or parts) cognitively *prior to* ("leftward" of) that position are expressed, (b) those *subsequent to* ("rightward" of) that position are transferred to BUF (left-to-right), (c) the salience-motivated constituent (or part) is expressed, and (d) code-strips remaining in BUF are expressed as they are returned to OPR.

(D) When use of the BUFFER is required for processing *complexes* [B (3) above]: (1) if the naturally subsequent cognition (Cog_2) in complexes *conjoined by adverbials* is more salient to the Speaker, (a) the naturally prior cognition (Cog_1) is transferred to BUF (right-to-left), (b) Cog_2 is expressed, either preceded or followed by expression of the conjoiner (coded in the tag-slot) depending on Naturalness signaling requirements, and (c) Cog_1 is expressed as its constituents are returned from BUF to OPR; (2) if the naturally subsequent cognition (Cog_2), *embedding as a relative clause* a naturally prior cognition (Cog_1), is more salient to the Speaker, (a) the naturally prior Cog_1 is transferred to BUF (again, right-to-left), (b) the naturally subsequent Cog_2 (now remaining in OPR) is expressed up to and including the NP which Cog_1 will further characterize, (c) Cog_1 is expressed, initiated by the semantically appropriate relative PN replacing that NP,[1] followed by the remaining constituents in BUF, and (d) the remainder of Cog_2 (if any) is expressed; (3) if the naturally subsequent cognition (Cog_2) *has a "commentative" relation* to the necessarily prior "topical" cognition (Cog_1) being commented on, but is more salient to the Speaker, then (a) the "Topical" Cog_1 is transferred to BUF (again, right-to left), (b) the "commentative" Cog_2 is expressed (with its redundant embedded Cog_1 component deleted (ϕ) in anticipatory fashion), followed optionally by a semantically "empty"

---

[1] If the relativized NP is part of a prepositional phrase, then the preposition must accompany the relative PN.

syntactic marker (like *that*), and (c) "topical" Cog_1 is expressed as its constituents are returned from BUF to OPR.

F VIII–II COMPREHENDING: (A) For the Listener, in order to comprehend simplex and complex sentences, the OPERATOR *must* have the constituents of simplexes and the clauses of complexes *in their cognitively natural order:* (1) if the sentences received from a Speaker *are already in natural order* (*see* F IV, VI) then no use of the BUFFER is required; (2) if, due to salience dynamics operating on the Speaker, either the constituents of simplexes or the clauses of complexes *are in unnatural order,* as determined by OPR checks (*see* F VII), interactions between OPR and BUF must be initiated to restore natural ordering; (3) if, following its OPR/BUF interaction rules (see below), no natural ordering can be obtained, there is no transfer to MEM and the Listener typically displays the behavioral signs of comprehension failure.

(B) Assuming that (a) salience dynamics have caused the Speaker to produce an unnaturally ordered sentence and (b) the Listener's OPERATOR has detected cues for the disordering: (1) if, *within simplexes,* following the rules for constituent transfers to the BUFFER (*see* C below), *a single* $OPR \rightarrow BUF \rightarrow OPR$ *cycle* yields a natural ordering, Listener comprehends, OPR/BUF processing terminates and the cognition is transferred to MEM; (2) if a single cycle still yields unnatural ordering, *a second* $OPR \rightarrow BUF \rightarrow OPR$ *cycle is initiated* (following the same rules), and if it yields natural ordering, Listener comprehends, OPR/BUF processing terminates and the cognition is transferred to MEM; (3) given cues for unnatural ordering of *the clauses of complexes,* (a) the naturally prior cognition *always* becomes Cog_1 in OPR, and then the naturally subsequent Cog_2 is completed, either via "leftward" shift of constituents into the components "emptied" by the "upward" shift of Cog_1 or via transfers to BUF (*see* D below), and (b), if any of the clauses of complexes in the processing via (a) above have themselves, as simplexes, unnaturally ordered constituents, then rules governing (1) and (2) above are *immediately* applied, with further processing of the complex held up until the simplex is "naturalized".

(C) When use of the BUFFER is required for comprehending *simplexes* [B (1) and B (2) above]: (1) if the constituent in which unnaturalness is detected *is itself initial* (i.e., in the M_1 component), (a) it is transferred from OPR to BUF, (b) remaining constituents move "leftward", and (c) such OPR/BUF transfers continue (with "push-down" storage in BUF) until a constituent natural in M_1 appears; (2) if the constituent in which unnaturalness is detected *is noninitial* [i.e., in the $- - (M) - \rightarrow$, the M_2 or in information subsequent to a completed cognition], (a) the single constituent *immediately prior to* ("leftward" of) that providing the unnaturalness cue is transferred from OPR to BUF, (b) remaining constituents move "leftward", and (c) such OPR/BUF transfers continue until a constituent natural in M_1 [or in $- - (M) - \rightarrow$ if M_1 is already "naturalized"] appears; (3) following either (1) or (2) the constituents in BUF are returned to the now "empty" component on components (in from "top-most" to "bottom-most" in BUF order), thereby completing cycle 1; (4) if (a) the simplex is now naturally ordered, Listener comprehends, OPR/BUF processing terminates, and the cognition is transferred to MEM, but if (b) OPR still detects cues for unnaturalness, another cycle is initiated according to the same rules above; (5) if, due to Speaker redundancy deletions (for efficiency in communicating), certain components of simplexes are left "empty" (ϕ), OPR checks the most basic Substantivity feature for the "nonempty" components, entering either $[+\phi]$, if the "empty' component would *naturally* be a $^+$Substantive Entity, or $[-\phi]$, if it would be a $^-$Substantivity Relation, sending the coded ϕ to BUF, and after the cognition has been "naturalized" OPR inserts the most probable semantic information [code-strip(s)], (a) from MEM (prior comprehending), (b) from its own parallel perceptual cognizing, or (c) simply on the basis of sheer convergent, contextual probabilities based on information in the "nonempty" components.

(D) When use of the BUFFER is required for comprehending *complexes* [and assuming that the included simplexes are, or have been returned to, natural order via (C) above]: (1) given cues that the first clause *in complexes conjoined by adverbials*[2] is the naturally subsequent cognition (Cog_2), (a) the constituents of this clause are transferred to BUF ("*right-to-left*"), (b) the features of the conjoiner are transferred to the tag-slot, (c) the constituents of the naturally prior clause (Cog_1), as received from LEX are accepted in OPR as Cog_1, and (d) the constituents of Cog_2 are returned from BUF to OPR; (2) given cues for *embedding of a relative clause in a matrix clause* (cues are usually *that* or more specific relative pronouns), (a) the features of the noun of the matrix clause immediately prior to the relative PN are "copied" onto those of the PN (thus expanding it into a full nominal, but with a shift to Indefinite coding), (b) the constituents of this embedded clause (*always* the naturally prior cognition) become Cog_1, (c) the features for the implied conjoiner (here representing simple *and* or *but,* for congruent or incongruent cognitions, respectively) are inserted in the tag-slot, and (d) the constituents of the remaining clause (now with M_1 coded emphatic Definite, *that!* or this!) now become Cog_2; (3) given cues that the naturally subsequent cognition (Cog_2) *has a "commentative" relation* to the necessarily prior "topical"

---

[2] Basic *and* and *but* conjoiners *always* must be centered between clauses.

cognition (Cog_1) *being commented on* (the cues are verbs like *think, seem, believe*, etc., optionally followed by *that* as an "empty" syntactic marker, signaling that a complex is involved), then (a) the "commentative" Cog_2 constituents (completed with a ϕ in M_1 or M_2 components, representing Cog_1) are transferred to BUF (right-to-left), (b) the naturally prior "topical" Cog_1 constituents shift "leftward", (c) the features of the implied conjoiner (again representing simple *and* or *but*) are placed in the tag-slot, and (d) the constituents of the commentative clause are returned from BUF to OPR, now as Cog_2 and with the ϕ in the M_2 component comprehended as "Cog_1".

Structural Notions S I to S XIII

Here the notions relating to the four "mechanisms"—LEXICON, OPERA-TOR, BUFFER and MEMORY—are ordered from most gross to most fine.

S I: The LEXICON is a semantic encoding and decoding mechanism, transforming analogically coded percepts (perceptual and linguistic signs) into digitally coded significances (meanings) in comprehending and transforming the same digitally coded information, now intentions, into analogically coded programs for behaving (linguistically or otherwise) in expressing.

S II: The OPERATOR is a tripartite mechanism that gives structure to functionally related sets of semantic outputs from the LEXICON or from the MEMORY and within which the dynamic interactions among such sets occur.

S III: The BUFFER is a temporary information-holding mechanism, receiving from OPR constituent code-strips that are prior in ordering to that which is "natural" and transferring these code-strips back to OPR as the displaced constituents are moved forward ("leftward") into "natural" order.

S IV: The MEMORY is a mechanism for long-term storage of semantic information inputted from the OPERATOR; it is organized both in terms of the tripartite structure of the OPERATOR and the feature-ordering structure of the LEXICON.

S V: The near-simultaneous sets ("code-strips") of semantic features, elicited "upward" in the LEXICON by the signs of entities (later NPs) and relations (later VPs) in comprehending or by transfer from the OPERATOR "downward" in expressing are the semantic representations of the components of perceptual cognitions and (later) the constituents of linguistic cognitions.

S VI: Single perceived events or states (later, linguistic clauses or "sentoids") are represented in the OPERATOR as simple cognitions (simplexes) having tripartite form, the three components being the complete semantic representations of a pair of entities (later, subject and object NPs), M_1 and M_2, and the signed and directed action or stative relation (later, VPs), — (M) → , between them.

S VII: All complex cognitions, involving multiple but related perceived actions or states (later, conjoined clauses in sentencing), are analyzable into concatenations (complexes) of simple cognitions, represented in parallel ("vertically", as shown in Fig. IV.3) in the three components of the OPERATOR; semantically, all complexes are representable as conjunctions of congruent simple cognitions (linguistically *and* and its elaborations) or disjunctions of incongruent simple cognitions (linguistically *but* and its elaboration).

S VIII: The BUFFER is structured ("vertically") as a "push-down" storage for constituents of simplexes that are displaced from "natural" order, or for the constituents of whole cognitions that are "unnaturally" ordered in conjoined complexes.

S IX: The MEMORY is structured "horizontally" in terms of the semantic representations of the "topics of processed cognitions (M_1s), each with its associated "commentary", the feature representations of the relations [— (M) → 's] and related (M_2s) of the same cognitions.

S X: Semantic features (r_m/s_m mediator components) are bipolar in nature and, in the general case, are continuously variable in intensity between zero (neutrality, absence of a feature from a code-strip, r_M/s_M) and some maximal value of one or the other of the poles.

S XI: In the general case, semantic features have polarities that are nonarbitrarily signed, Positive and Negative, cognitively.

S XII: In the LEXICON semantic features are ordered "left-to-right" (and "scanned") according to the overall frequency with which they differentiate the meanings of signs, both perceptual and linguistic; since all cognizing operates on "code-strips" outputted from the LEXICON, feature-processing order will be constant for LEX, BUF, and the components of OPR and MEM.

S XIII: The MEMORY is organized "vertically" by topics (M_1s) from maximum Positiveness on the ordered semantic features (+ + + . . +) to maximum Negativeness (. . . −) and "horizontally" within topics (M_1s) from most to least frequently differential features in usage.

References

Abelson, R.P., Rosenberg, M.J. (1958): Symbolic psycho-logic: A model of attitudinal cognition. Behav. Sci. **3**, 1–13

Anderson, J.R., Bower, G.H. (1973): *Human Associative Memory* (Winston, Washington, D.C.)

Anderson, R.C., Ortony, A. (1975): On putting apples into bottles: A problem of polysemy. Cognit. Psychol. **7**, 167–180

Austin, J.L. (1962): *How to Do Things with Words* (Harvard University Press, Cambridge, MA)

Bates, E. (1976, *in press*): "Pragmatics and Sociolinguistics in Child Language", in *Normal and Deficient Child Language,* ed. by D.M. Morehead, (University Park Press, University Park, MD)

Berlin, B., Kay, P. (1969): *Basic Color Terms: Their Universality and Evolution* (University of California Press, Berkeley, CA)

Berlyne, D. (1966): Mediating responses: A note on Fodor's criticisms. J. Verb. Learn. Verb. Behav. **5**, 408–411

Bever, T.G. (1968): "Associations to Stimulus-Response Theories of Language", in *Verbal Behavior and General Behavior Theory,* ed. by T.R. Dixon, D.L. Horton (Prentice-Hall, Englewood Cliffs, NJ)

Bever, T.G. (1970): "The Cognitive Basis for Linguistic Structures", in *Cognition and the Development of Language,* ed. by J.R. Hayes (Wiley, New York)

Bever, T.G., Fodor, J.A., Garrett, M. (1968): "A Formal Limitation on Associationism", in *Verbal Behavior and General Behavior Theory,* ed. by T.R. Dixon, D.L. Horton (Prentice Hall, Englewood Cliffs, NJ)

Bever, T.G., Lackner, J.R., Kirk, R. (1969): The underlying structures of sentences are the primary units of immediate speech processing. Percept. Psychophys. **5**, 225–231

Bever, T.G., Lackner, J.R., Stolz, W. (1969): Transitional probability is not a general mechanism for the segmentation of speech. J. Exp. Psychol. **79**, 387–394

Blansitt, E.L. (1973): "Bitransitive Clauses", in *Working Papers on Language Universals,* Vol.13 (Stanford University)

Bloom, L.M. (1970): *Language Development: Form and Function in Emerging Grammars* (M.I.T. Press, Cambridge, MA)

Bloomfield, L. (1914): *An Introduction to the Study of Language* (Henry Holt, New York)

Bloomfield, L. (1933): *Language* (Holt, New York)

Blumenthal, A.L. (1970): *Language and Psychology* (Wiley, New York)

Bock, J. (1975): "Given-New and Salience: The Effects of Two Sentence Production Principles on Syntactic Structure"; Doctoral Dissertation, University of Illinois at Champaign-Urbana

Boucher, J., Osgood, C.E. (1969): The Pollyanna hypothesis. J. Verb. Learn. Verb. Behav. **8**, 1–8

Bower, T.G.R. (1974): *Development in Infancy* (W.H. Freeman, San Francisco, CA)

Bransford, J.D. Barclay, J.R., Franks, J.J. (1972): Sentence memory: A constructive versus interpretive approach. Cognit. Psychol. **3**, 193–209

Bronowski, J., Bellugi, U. (1970): Language, name and concept. Science **168**, 669–673

Brown, J.F., Voth, A.C. (1937): The path of seen movement as a function of the vector-field. Am. J. Psychol. **49**, 543–563

Brown, R.W. (1958): *Words and Things* (The Free Press, Glencoe, IL)

Brown, R.W. (1970): *Psycholinguistics: Selected Papers* (Free Press, New York)

Brown, R.W. (1973): *A First Language: the Early Stages* (Harvard University Press, Cambridge MA)

Bühler, K. (1934): *Sprachtheorie* (G. Fischer, Jena)

Campbell, D.T. (1966): "Ostensive Instances and Entitativity in Language Learning and Linguistic Relativism". Paper presented at The Center for Advanced Study in the Behavioral Sciences, Palo Alto, CA

Carroll, J.B. (1971): Measurement properties of subjective magnitude estimates of word frequency. J. Verb. Learn. Verb. Behav. *10*, 722–729

Carroll, J.M., Tannenhaus, M.K. (1975): "Functional Clauses are the Primary Units of Sentence Segmentation", Psycholinguistics Program, Columbia University (mimeo)

Chao, Y.R. (1968): *A Reference Grammar of Spoken Chinese* (University of California Press, Berkeley, Los Angeles)

Chomsky, N. (1957): *Syntactic Structures* (Mouton, 's-Gravenhage, Holland)

Chomsky, N. (1959): B.F. Skinner (1957): Verbal behavior (a review). Language **35**, 26–58

Chomsky, N. (1965): *Aspects of the Theory of Syntax* (M.I.T. Press, Cambridge, MA)

Chomsky, N. (1968): *Language and Mind* (Harcourt, Brace, and World, New York)

Chomsky, N., Miller, G.A. (1963): "Introduction to the Formal Analysis of Natural Languages, in *Handbook of Mathematical Psychology,* ed. by R.D. Luce, R.R. Bush, E. Galanter (Wiley, New York and London)

Clark, E.V. (1971): On the acquisition of the meaning of *before* and *after.* J. Verb. Learn. Verb. Behav. **10**, 266–275

Clark, E.V. (1972): On the child's acquisition of antonyms in two semantic fields. J. Verb. Learn. Verb. Behav. **11**, 750–758

Clark, H.H. (1970): "Comprehending Comparatives", in *Advances in Psycholinguistics*, ed. by G.B. Flores d'Arcais, W.J.M. Levelt, (North-Holland Publ., Amsterdam)

Clark, H.H. (1970): "The Primitive Nature of Children's Relational Concepts", in *Cognition and the Development of Language,* ed. by J.R. Hayes (Wiley, New York) pp. 269–278

Clark, H.H. (1973): The language-as-fixed-effect fallacy: A critique of language statistics in psychological research. J. Verb. Learn. Verb. Behav. **12**, 335–359

Clark, H.H. (1974): The power of positive speaking. Psychol. Today **9**, 103–111

Clark, H.H., Clark, E.V. (1968): Semantic distinctions and memory for complex sentences. Quart. J. Exp. Psychol. **20**, 129–138

Clark, H.H., Haviland, S.E. (1977): "Comprehension and the Given-New Contract", in *Discourse Processes: Advances in Research and Theory*, Vol.1, ed. by R.O. Freedle (Ablex, Norwood, NJ)

Cole, P., Morgan, J.L. (eds.) (1975): *Syntax and Semantics, Volume 3: Speech Acts* (Academic Press, New York)

Cole, P., Sadock, J. (eds.) (1977): *Syntax and Semantics, Volume 8: Grammatical Relations* (Academic Press, New York)

Cooper, W.E., Ross, J.R. (1975): "World Order", in *Papers from the Parasession on Functionalism*, ed. by R.E. Grossman, L.J. San, T.J. Vance (Chicago Linguistic Society)

Cuceloǧlu, D. (1967): "A Cross-Cultural Study of Communication via Facial Expression"; Doctoral Dissertation, University of Illinois at Urbana-Champaign

Diebold, A.R., Jr. (1965): "A Survey of Psycholinguistic Research, 1954–1964", in *Psycholinguistics: A Survey of Theory and Research Problems* (Reissue) (University of Indiana Press, Bloomington, IN)

DiVesta, F. (1966): A developmental study of the semantic structure of children. J. Verb. Learn. Verb. Behav. **5**, 249–259

Ertel, S. (1977): "Where Do the Subjects of Sentences Come From?", in *Sentence Production: Developments in Research and Theory*, ed. by S. Rosenberg (Erlbaum, Hillsdale, NJ)

Esper, E.A. (1968): *Mentalism and Objectivism in Linguistics* (American Elsevier, New York)

Festinger, L. (1957): *A Theory of Cognitive Dissonance* (Rowe, Peterson, Evanston, IL)

Fillmore, C.J. (1977): "The Case for Case Reopened", in *Syntax and Semantics, Volume 8: Grammatical Relations*, ed. by P. Cole, J. Sadock (Academic Press, New York)

Fodor, J.A. (1965): Could meaning be an r_m? J. Verb. Learn. Verb. Behav. **4**, 73–81

Fodor, J.A. (1966): More about mediators: A Reply to Berlyne and Osgood. J. Verb. Learn. Verb. Behav. **5**, 412–415

Fodor, J.A. Bever, T.G., Garrett, M.F. (1974): *The Psychology of Language* (McGraw-Hill, New York)

Fodor, J.A., Garrett, M. (1967): Some syntactic determinants of sentential complexity. Percept. Psychophys. **2**, 289–296

Forster, K.I. (1966): Left to right processes in the construction of sentences. J. Verb. Learn. Verb. Behav. **5**, 285–291

Forster, K.I. (1967): Sentence completion latencies as a function of constituent structure. J. Verb. Learn. Verb. Behav. **6**, 878–883

Forster, K.I. (1968): Sentence completion in left- and right-branching languages. J. Verb. Learn. Verb. Behav. **7**, 296–299

Forster, K.I., Olbrei, I. (1973): Semantic heuristics and syntactic analysis. Cognition **2**, *319–347*

French, P.L. (1977): Non-verbal measurement of affect: the Graphic Differential. *Journal of Psycholinguistic Research*, **6**, 337–347.

Garder, R.A., Gardner, B.T. (1969): Teaching sign language to a chimpanzee. Science **165**, 664–672

Garrett, M., Fodor, J. (1968): "Psychological Theories and Linguistic Constructs'', in *Verbal Behavior and General Behavior Theory,* ed. by T.R. Dixon, D.L. Horton (Prentice-Hall, Englewood Cliffs, NJ)

Greenberg, J.H. (1957): *Essays in Linguistics* (University of Chicago Press, Chicago)

Greenberg, J.H. (1963): "Some Universals of Grammar with Particular Reference to the Order of Meaningful Elements", in *Universals of Language,* ed. by J.H. Greenberg (M.I.T. Press, Cambridge, MA)

Greenberg, J.H. (1966): "Language Universals", in *Current Trends in Linguistics: III. Theoretical Foundation,* ed. by T.A. Sebeok (Mouton, The Hague)

Grice, H.P. (1975): "Logic and Conversation", in *Syntax and Semantics, Volume 3: Speech Acts,* ed. by P. Cole, J.L. Morgan, (Academic Press, New York)

Grossman, R.E., San, L.J., Vance, T.J. (eds.) (1975): *Papers from the Parasession on Functionalism* (Chicago Linguistic Society)

Halliday, M.A.K. (1967, 1968): Notes on transitivity and theme in English. J. Ling. **3,** 37–81; **4,** 179–215

Hamilton, H.W., Deese, J. (1971): Does linguistic marking have a psychological correlate? J. Verb. Learn. Verb. Behav. **10,** 707–714

Hastorf, A.H., Osgood, C.E., Ono, H. (1966): The semantics of facial expressions and the prediction of the meanings of stereoscopically fused facial expressions. Scand. J. Psychol. **7,** 179–188

Hayes, K.J., Hayes, C. (1951): The intellectual development of a home-raised chimpanzee. Proc. Am. Philos. Soc. **95,** 105–109

Hebb, D.O. (1958): *A Textbook of Psychology* (W.B. Saunders, Philadelphia)

Heider, F. (1958): *The Psychology of Interpersonal Relations* (Wiley, New York)

Hoosain, R. (1973a): "Cognitive Processing Load as a Function of Embedding in Conjoined Cognitions"; Doctoral Dissertation, University of Illinois

Hoosain, R. (1973b): The processing of negation. J. Verb. Learn. Verb. Behav. **12,** 618–626

Hoosain, R. (1974): The processing and remembering of congruent and incongruent sentences. J. Psycholinguist. Res. **3,** 319–331

Hoosain, R. (1977): The processing of negative or incongruent perceptual and combined perceptual/linguistic stimuli. Br. J. Psychol. **68,** 245–252

Hull, C.L. (1930): Knowledge and purpose as habit mechanism. Psychol. Rev. **37,** 511–525

Hull, C.L. (1943): *Principles of Behavior: An Introduction to Behavior Theory* (Appleton-Century-Crofts, New York)

Jakobson, R., Fant, C.G., Halle, M. (1963): *Preliminaries to Speech Analysis* (M.I.T. Press, Cambridge, MA)

Johnson, N.F. (1966): On the relationship between sentence and structure and the latency in generating the sentence, J. Verb. Learn. Verb. Behav. **5,** 375–380

Karwoski, T.F. Odbert, H.S., Osgood, C.E. (1942): Studies in synesthetic thinking, II: The roles of form in visual responses to music. J. Gen. Psychol. **26,** 199–222

Kellogg, W.N., Kellogg, L.A. (1933): *The Ape and the Child* (McGraw-Hill, New York)

Key, M.R. (1974): "The Relationship of Verbal and Nonverbal Communication", in *Proceedings of the Eleventh International Congress of Linguistics,* August 28–September 2, 1972, ed. by L. Heilmann (Società editrice il Mulino Bologna)

Klima, E.S. (1964): "Negation in English", in *The Structure of Language,* ed. by J.A. Fodor, J.J. Katz (Prentice-Hall, Englewood Cliffs, NJ)

Kuhn, T.S. (1962): *The Structure of Scientific Revolutions* (University of Chicago Press, Chicago, IL)

Lakoff, R. (1971): "If's, and's and but's About Conjunctions", in *Studies in*

Linguistic Semantics, ed. by C.J. Fillmore, D.T. Langendoen (Holt, Rinehart, and Winston, New York)

Lakoff, R. (1972): Language in context. Language **48**, 907–927

Lashley, K.S. (1951): "The Problem of Serial Order in Behavior", in *Cerebral Mechanisms in Behavior: The Hixon Symposium,* ed. by L.A. Jeffress (Wiley, New York)

Lawrence, D.H. (1949): Acquired distinctiveness of cues: I. Transfer between discriminations on the basis of familiarity with the stimulus. J. Exp. Psychol. **39**, 770–784

Lawrence, D.H. (1950): Acquired distinctiveness of cues: II. Selective associations in a constant stimulus situation. J. Exp. Psychol. **40**, 175–188

MacCorquodale, K. (1970): On Chomsky's review of Skinner's *Verbal Behavior.* J. Exp. Anal. Behav. **13**, 83–99

Maclay, H., Osgood, C.E. (1959): Hesitation phenomena in spontaneous English speech. Word **15**, 19–44

Maclay, H. (1971): "Overview (to the Linguistics Section)", in *Semantics: An Interdisciplinary Reader in Philosophy, Linguistics, and Psychology,* ed. by D.D. Steinberg, L.A. Jakobovits (Cambridge University Press, London)

Maclay, H. (1973): "Linguistics and Psycholinguistics", in *Issues in Linguistics: Papers in Honor of Henry and Renée Kahane,* ed. by B. Kachru, et al. (University of Illinois Press, Urbana, IL)

McNeill, D. (1970): *The Acquisition of Language* (Harper, New York)

McWhinney, B. (1977): Starting points. Language **53**, 152–168

Meyer, D.E. (1973): Correlated operations in searching stored semantic categories. J. Exp. Psychol. **99**, 124–133

Miles, W.R. (1931): Movement interpretation of the silhouette of a revolving fan. Am. J. Psychol. **43**, 392–405

Miller, G.A. (1962): Some psychological studies of grammar. Am. Psychol. **17**, 748–762

Miller, G.A., Chomsky, N. (1963): "Finitary Models of Language Users", in *Handbook of Mathematical Psychology,* ed. by R.D. Luce, R.R. Bush, E. Galanter (Wiley, New York)

Miller, G.A., Galanter, E., Pribram, K.H. (1960): *Plans and the Structure of Behavior* (Holt-Dryden, New York)

Moeser, S.D., Bregman, A.S. (1972): The role of reference in the acquisition of a miniature artificial language. J. Verb. Learn. Verb. Behav. **11**, 759–769

Moeser, S.D., Olson, A.J. (1974): The role of reference in children's acquisition of a miniature artificial language. J. Exp. Child Psychol. **17**, 204–218

Morgan, J.L. (1975): "Some Interactions of Syntax and Pragmatics", in *Syntax and Semantics,* ed. by P. Cole, J.L. Morgan (Academic Press, New York)

Ono, H., Hastorf, A.H., Osgood, C.E. (1966): Binocular rivalry as a function of incongruity in meaning. Scand. J. Psychol. **7**, 225–233

Opačić, G. (1973): Natural order in cognizing and clause ordering in the sentencing of conjoined expressions. Ph.D. dissertation, University of Illinois, Urbana, IL

Osgood, C.E. (1953): *Method and Theory in Experimental Psychology* (Oxford University Press, New York)

Osgood, C.E. (1956): Behavior theory and the social sciences. Behav. Sci. **1**, 167–185

Osgood, C.E. (1957): "A Behavioristic Analysis of Perception and Meaning as Cognitive Phenomena", in *Contemporary Approaches to Cognition,* ed. by. J.S. Bruner (Harvard University Press, Cambridge, MA)

Osgood, C.E. (1957): "Motivational Dynamics of Language Behavior", in

Nebraska Symposium on Motivation, ed. by M.R. Jones (University of Nebraska Press, Lincoln, NB)

Osgood, C.E. (1958): A question of sufficiency. Review of B.F. Skinner, *Verbal Behavior.* Contemp. Psychol. **3,** 209–212

Osgood, C.E. (1960a): The cross-cultural generality of visual-verbal synesthetic tendencies. Behav. Sci. **5,** 146–169

Osgood, C.E. (1960b): Cognitive dynamics in the conduct of human affairs. Publ. Opin. Q. **24,** 341–365

Osgood, C.E. (1963): On understanding and creating sentences. Amer. Psych., *18,* 735–751

Osgood, C.E. (1964): Semantic differential technique in the comparative study of cultures. Amer. Anthro. *66* (No. 3, Part 2), 171–200, Special Publication, ed. by A.K. Romeny & R.G. D'Andrade

Osgood, C.E. (1966a): Dimensionality of the semantic space for communication via facial expressions. Scand. J. Psychol. **7,** 1–30

Osgood, C.E. (1966b): Meaning cannot be an r_m? J. Verb. Learn. Verb. Behav. **5,** 402–407

Osgood, C.E. (1970): "Interpersonal Verbs and Interpersonal Behavior", in *Studies in Thought and Language,* ed. by J.L. Cowan (University of Arizona Press, Tucson)

Osgood, C.E. (1971): "Where Do Sentences Come From?", in *Semantics: An Interdisciplinary Reader in Philosophy, Linguistics and Psychology,* ed. by D. Steinberg, L. Jakobovits (Cambridge University Press, London)

Osgood, C.E. (1975): A dinosaur caper: Psycholinguistics past, present, and future. Ann. N.Y. Acad. Sci. **263,** 16–26

Osgood, C.E. (1979): "What is a Language?", in *Psycholinguistic Research: Past, Present and Future,* ed. by D. Aaronson, R. Rieber (Erlbaum, Hillsdale, NJ)

Osgood, C.E. (in preparation): *Toward an Abstract Performance Grammar,* Springer Series in Language and Communication (Springer, Berlin, Heidelberg, New York)

Osgood, C.E., Bock, J.K. (1977): "Salience and Sentencing: Some Production Principles", in *Sentence Production: Developments in Research and Theory,* ed. by S. Rosenberg (Erlbaum, Hillsdale, NJ)

Osgood, C.E. Hoosain, R. (1974): Salience of the word as a unit in the perception of language. Percept. Psychophys. **15,** 168–192

Osgood, C.E., Hoosain, R. (in preparation): Pollyanna II: It is easier to 'simply get the meaning' of affectively positive than of affectively negative words

Osgood, C.E., May, W.H., Miron, M.S. (1975): *Cross-Cultural Universals of Affective Meaning* (University of Illinois Press, Urbana, IL)

Osgood, C.E., Richards, M.M. (1973): From Yang and Yin to *and* or *but.* Language **49,** 380–412

Osgood, C.E., Sebeok, T.A. (eds.) (1954): *Psycholinguistics: A Survey of Theory and Research Problems.* Indiana University Publications in Anthropology and Linguistics, Memoir 10 (Waverly Press, Baltimore, MD). Supplement to J. Abnorm. Soc. Psychol. **49,** No. 4, Part 2

Osgood, C.E., Sridhar, S.N. (1979): Unambiguous signaling of naturalness of clause-ordering: a language universal? (submitted to Language)

Osgood, C.E., Suci, G.J., Tannenbaum, P.H. (1957): *The Measurement of Meaning* (University of Illinois Press, Urbana, IL)

Osgood, C.E., Tanz, C. (1977): "Will the Real Direct Object in Bitransitive

Sentences Please Stand Up?'', in *Linguistic Studies in Honor of Joseph Greenberg*, ed. by A. Juilland (Anma Libri, Saratoga, CA)

Osgood, C.E., Zehler, A. (1980): Acquisition of bitransitive sentences. J. Child Lang. (in press)

Palermo, D.S. (1971): Is a scientific revolution taking place in psychology? Sci. Stud. **1,** *135–155*

Perfetti, C.A., Goodman, D. (1971): Memory for sentences and noun phrases of extreme depth. Q. J. Exp. Psychol. **23,** 22–33

Postal, P.M. (1974): *On Raising: One Rule of English Grammar and Its Theoretical Implications* (M.I.T. Press, Cambridge, MA)

Premack, D. (1971): Language in chimpanzee. Science **172,** 808–822

Pylyshyn, Z.W. (1973): The role of competence theories in cognitive psychology. J. Psycholing Res. **2,** 21–50

Ransom, E. (1977): "A Constraint on the Advancement and Demotion of NP's"; University of Illinois (Linguistics Department), unpublished manuscript

Richards, M.M. (1977): Ordering preference for congruent and incongruent English adjectives in attributive and predicative contexts. J. Verb. Learn. Verb. Behav. **16,** 489–503

Sachs, J.S. (1967): Recognition memory for syntactic and semantic aspects of connected discourse. Percept. Psychophys. **2,** 437–442

Sapir, E. (1911): Noun incorporation in American languages. Am. Anthropol. **13,** 250–282

Saporta, S. (ed.) (1961): *Psycholinguistics: A Book of Readings* (Holt, Rinehard and Winston, New York)

Schacter, P. (1973): Focus and relativization. Language **49,** 19–46

Schlesinger, I.M. (1968): *Sentence Structure and the Reading Process* (Mouton, The Hague)

Schlosberg, H. (1954): Three dimensions of emotion. Psychol. Rev. **61,** 81–88

Searle, J.R. (1969): *Speech Acts* (Cambridge University Press, New York and London)

Sedlak, P.A.S. (1975): "Direct/Indirect Object Word Order: A Cross-Linguistic Analysis", in *Working Papers on Language Universals*, No. 18, pp.117–164 (Stanford University)

Sheinkopf, S. (1970): "A Comparative Study of the Affective Judgments Made by Anomic Aphasics and Normals on a Nonverbal Task", Doctoral Dissertation, Boston University

Skinner, B.F. (1957): *Verbal Behavior* (Appleton-Century-Crofts, New York)

Smith, E.E., Shoben, E.J., Rips, L.J. (1974): Structure and process in semantic memory: a feature model for semantic decisions. Psychol. Rev. **81,** 214–241

Suppes, P. (1969): Stimulus-response theory of automata and TOTE hierarchies. Psychol. Rev. **76,** 511–514

Tannenhaus, M.K., Carroll, J.M. (1975): "The Clausal Processing Hierarchy . . . and Nouniness", in *Papers from the Parasession on Functionalism*, ed. by R.E. Grossman, L.J. San, T.J. Vance (Chicago Linguistic Society, Chicago, IL)

Thorndike, E.L. (1943): The origin of language. Science **98,** 1–6

Tolman, E.C. (1938): Determiners of behavior at a choice-point. Psychol. Rev. **45,** 1–41

Tolman, E.C. (1948): Cognitive maps in rats and men. Psychol. Rev. **55,** 189–208

Von Frisch, K. (1974): Decoding the language of the bee. Science **185,** 663–668

Watt, W.C. (1970): "On Two Hypotheses Concerning Psycholinguistics", in

Cognition and the Development of Language, ed. by J.R. Hayes (Wiley, New York)

Weisberg, R.W. (1971): On sentence storage: the influence of syntactic versus semantic factors on intra-sentence word association. J. Verb. Learn. Verb. Behav. **10**, 631–644

Wilhelm, R. (1967): *The I Ching or Book of Changes.* Rendered into English by C.F. Baynes (Bollinger Series, 19) (Princeton University Press, Princeton, NJ)

Yngve, V.H. (1960): A model and an hypothesis for language structure. Proc. Am. Philos. Soc. **104**, 444–466

Yngve, V.H. (1975): Depth and the historical change of the English genitive. J. Engl. Ling. **9**, 47–57

Zipf, G.K. (1949): *Human Behavior and the Principle of Least Effort* (Addison-Wesley, Cambridge, MA)

Author Index

Subject Index